DISCARD

J 910 ZEM
3908302854125
Zeman, Ann
Everything to know
about geography homework
P9-BYR-457

EVERYTHING YOU NEED TO KNOW ABOUT GEOGRAPHY HOMEWORK

Anne Zeman and Kate Kelly

An Irving Place Press Book

SCHOLASTIC REFERENCE

New York Toronto London Auckland Sydney

FRASER VALLEY REGIONAL LIBRARY

Cover design, Charles Kreloff; Cover illustration, James Steinberg
Interior design, Bennett Gewirtz and Catherine Bontempo, Gewirtz Graphics, Inc.;
Interior illustration, Moffit Cecil

For their assistance in the preparation of this manuscript, we gratefully acknowledge Betty Holmes, Director of UFT's Dial-A-Teacher; Dr. Joseph P. Stoltman; Judy Bock; Dr. Mark Monmonier; Bill Johnson, and Sean McCollum. Dial-A-Teacher is a collaborative program of the United Federation of Teachers and the New York City Board of Education.

Illustrations copyright © 1997 by Scholastic, Inc.

Copyright © 1997 by Scholastic Inc.
All rights reserved. Published by Scholastic Inc., 555 Broadway, New York, NY 10012.

No part of this publication may be reproduced, or stored in a retrieval system, or transmitted in any form or by any means, electronic, mechanical, photocopying, recording, or otherwise, without written permission of the publisher. For information regarding permission, write to Scholastic Inc., 555 Broadway, New York, NY 10012.

Library of Congress Cataloging-in-Publication Data

Zeman, Anne,
Everything you need to know about geography homework/ Anne Zeman and Kate Kelly.
p. cm. — (Scholastic homework reference series)
Includes index.

ISBN 0-590-34172-3

1. Geography—Juvenile literature. I. Kate Kelly. II Title. III. Series.
G133.Z46 1997
910—dc20 96-31171
CIP

12 11 10 9 0 1/0

Printed in the U.S.A. 09
First Scholastic printing, February 1997

CONTENTS

Introduction vii

Part 1. The Meaning of Geography

Geography Defined 2

What Is Geography?
The Five Themes of Geography
Geography and You
The Geography of Geography
Galactic Address
Geographical Thinking
The First Geographers
Thales: The First True Geographer?

Part 2. Representing the Earth: Globes, Projections, and Maps

1. Globes 8

Looking at Earth
Inventing the Globe
Lines of Longitude and Latitude
The Two North Poles
Geographers in Ancient Greece
The Geographic Grid
Light on Earth
The 24-Hour Globe: Time Zones

2. Maps 16

What Is a Map?
Map Projections
Some Common Map Projections
How Projections Are Made
Natural Features
Human-made Features
The First Maps
Three Basic Kinds of Maps
Charts
Maps for Special Uses
Altered States: Cartograms
Written References: Geographical Dictionaries and Almanacs
Parts of a Map
Understanding and Comparing Maps
Three Steps to Comparing Maps

Part 3. Land, Water, and Air: The Physical World

1. The Land 30

How the Earth Was Formed
Plate Tectonics
Tectonic Events That Shape the Land
Volcanoes
The Ring of Fire
Landforms
Erosion and Weathering
Glaciers

2. The Water 37

Oceans
The Briny Deep
Natural Events Under Water
Tides
Rivers
The World's Longest Rivers
Seas, Gulfs, and Bays
Lakes

3. The Air: Atmosphere, Weather, and Climate 43

The Atmosphere
Weather and Climate
Weather Fronts
Water Heaters: Land and Ocean Temperatures
Hurricanes, Tornadoes, Typhoons, and Cyclones
Water in the Air
Insulation: Clouds and Climate
Winds at Sea

Part 4. Plants and Animals

1. The Natural Regions of the World 50

Land Biomes

2. The Biomes 51

Tropical Rain Forests
Tropical Grasslands
Mediterranean Regions
Temperate Forests
Cool Forests
Cool Grasslands
Deserts
Tundra
Polar Regions
Mountains Biomes

Part 5. People on Land and Water

1. Location and Place 57

What Are Location and Place?

2. Counting People: Population 58

Population
Population Data
Population Pictures: Profiles and Pyramids
Population Density and Distribution
Urban vs. Rural
World Birthrates: 1910–1990

3. Culture 65

What Is Culture?
The Cultural Mosaic
Culture Basics
Language
Beliefs and Traditions: Religions, Customs, and Arts and Crafts
Greetings! Manners, Meanings, and Cultural Differences
Culture Crafts
Home, Sweet Home: The Architecture of Houses
Food! Glorious Food!
Political Systems
What Is Government?

4. How People Live 75

The Hunter-Gatherers
Subsistence Farmers
Industry and Technology
Agriculture
Old MacDonald Had a Farm
World Agriculture
Mining
Which Mine Is Mine? Different Types of Mining
Forestry
Fishing and Fisheries
Manufacturing
A Brief History of Manufacturing
Measuring Economies
The Geography of Production

5. Migration, from Exploration to Settlement 85

An Overview of Migration
Conquest and Empire
Can't Get There from Here: Transportation
Why Move?

Appendix

1. Glossary of Geographical Terms 88

2. Atlas 100

3. The World in Focus 112

4. The U.S. in Focus 122

Index 127

INTRODUCTION

It's homework time—but you have questions. Just how did your teacher ask you to do the assignment? You need help, but your parents are busy, and you can't reach your classmate on the phone. Where can you go for help?

What Questions Does This Book Answer?

In *Everything You Need to Know About Geography Homework*, you will find a wealth of information, including the answers to ten of the most commonly asked geography homework questions.*

1. Why do particular regions have different climates and what kind of climates are there? The world's climate regions, or biomes, are described on pages 50–56.
2. How do clouds affect climate? The effect of clouds on climate is explained on page 49.
3. Why do we have seasons? Seasons are described on page 14.
4. Where can I find descriptions of U.S. states, including nicknames, state name origins, populations, and capital cities? "The U.S. in Focus," found on pages 120–124, provides this type of information and more.
5. How can latitude and longitude be used to locate major cities and other features on the earth? How to use the geographic grid, which is formed by lines of latitude and longitude, is explained on page 12.
6. What are the different parts on a standard map, including scale, compass, index, legends, and dates? The parts of a standard map are illustrated and defined on pages 27–28.
7. What are the longest rivers in the world? The longest rivers in the world are listed and located on a map on pages 40–41.
8. What are the names of the layers of the earth? A diagram describing the layers of the earth is found on page 30.
9. Where can the border countries of the United States be found? All the countries of the world and the states of the United States are shown in maps illustrated in the Atlas, pages 100–111.
10. What are continents, how many are there, and what are they called? Continents are defined and identified on page 31.

* According to Dial-A-Teacher

What Is the Scholastic Homework Reference Series?

The Scholastic Homework Reference Series is a set of unique reference resources written especially to answer the homework questions of fourth, fifth, and sixth graders. The series provides ready information to answer commonly asked homework questions in a variety of subjects. Here you'll find facts, charts, definitions, and explanations, complete with examples and illustrations that will supplement schoolwork colorfully, clearly—and comprehensively.

A Note to Parents

The information for the Scholastic Homework Reference Series was gathered from current textbooks, national curricula, and the invaluable assistance of the UFT Dial-A-Teacher staff. Dial-A-Teacher, a collaborative program of the United Federation of Teachers and the New York City Board of Education, is a telephone service available to elementary school students in New York City. Telephone lines are open during the school term from 4:00 to 7:00 p.m., Monday to Thursday, at 212-777-3380. Because of Dial-A-Teacher's success in New York City, similar organizations have been established in other communities across the country. Check to see if there's a telephone homework service in your area.

It's important to support your children's efforts to do homework. Welcome their questions and see that they are equipped with a well-lighted desk or table, pencils, paper, and any other books or equipment—such as rulers, calculators, reference or textbooks, and so on—that they may need. You might also set aside a special time each day for doing homework, a time when you're available to answer questions that may arise. But don't do your children's homework for them. Remember, homework should create a bond between school and home. It is meant to enhance on a daily basis the lessons taught at school, and to promote good work and study habits. Although it is gratifying to have your children present flawless homework papers, the flawlessness should be a result of your children's explorations and efforts—not your own.

The Scholastic Homework Reference Series is designed to help your children complete their homework on their own to the best of their abilities. If they're stuck, you can use these books with them to find answers to troubling homework problems. And, remember, when the work is done—praise your children for a job well done.

EVERYTHING YOU NEED TO KNOW ABOUT GEOGRAPHY HOMEWORK

THE MEANING OF GEOGRAPHY

Geography Defined

A **geographer** *is a person who studies geography. A professional geographer is a person who studies or teaches geography for a living or who uses geography in his or her job. For example, people who make road atlases or people who decide where new toy stores should be built may be geographers.*

What Is Geography?

Geography is the study of the world, how it works, and how people use and change the world as they live in it. The word ***geography*** comes from the Greek words ***geo***, meaning "earth," and ***graph***, meaning "writing."

Geography explores many important questions about where and how we live, including:

1. **What is the earth like?**
2. **Where are things located on the earth?**
3. **Who lives where on the earth?**
4. **Why is one place different from another?**
5. **How do people and places influence one another?**

The Five Themes of Geography

Geographical thinking centers around five basic ideas, or themes.

1 PLACE
When a geographer says "place," he or she is talking about physical and human characteristics. Physical characteristics are the shape of the landforms and bodies of water, climate, soil, and plant and animal life. Human characteristics include how many people live somewhere and how close together they live, social traits, cultural traditions, and political institutions.

2 LOCATION
When a geographer says "location," he or she is talking about the importance of where one thing is in relation to another. When you study location, you study how physical characteristics (such as harbors, rivers, fertile plains, and mountainous terrain) affect human settlement and the way places are used.

3 HUMAN AND ENVIRONMENTAL INTERACTION
When a geographer talks about human and environmental interaction, he or she is talking about the changes people have made in their environment and the changes they continue to make.

4 HUMAN MOVEMENT
A geographer who studies human movement follows the routes people take when they move from one place to another and tries to explain why these movements are necessary. He or she also studies the effect of human movement on the areas where people move and settle.

5 REGIONS
A geographer thinking about regions looks at what makes one area different from another. To do that, he or she studies physical and human characteristics to see where they change.

Social traits *describe the things people do and say, and how they behave in a group. Social traits are influenced by* population *(see pp. 58-64) and* culture *(see pp. 65-74).*

Geography and You

You don't need textbooks or classroom teaching to begin learning and using geography. In fact, you use geography every day—probably without realizing it.

Mental Maps and Sketches

Mental maps are maps you picture in your mind.

Close your eyes and imagine the inside of your bedroom. Where is the bed? How do you get from the bed to the bedroom door? Once you're at the door, which way do you go to get to the kitchen? How about from the kitchen to the front door? From your home to your school, playground, park, or grocery store?

If you are able to picture places in relation to one another, you are creating mental maps. Mental maps can be of any place, large or small. You will use mental maps all your life to help you understand where you are compared to other parts of your world.

A rough drawing of a mental map is a ***map sketch***. If you draw your mental map on paper or on your computer, for example, you will have made a map sketch.

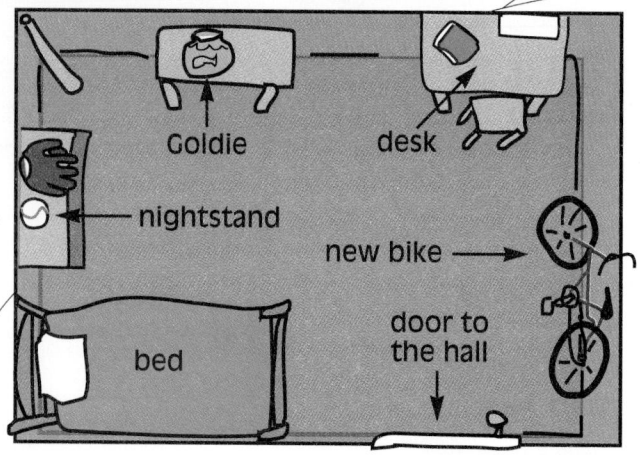

Our first mental maps are usually of our homes.

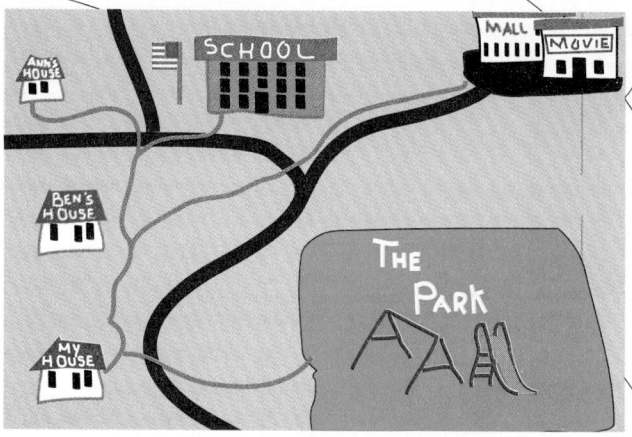

As we grow older, we create new maps to include neighborhoods and parks.

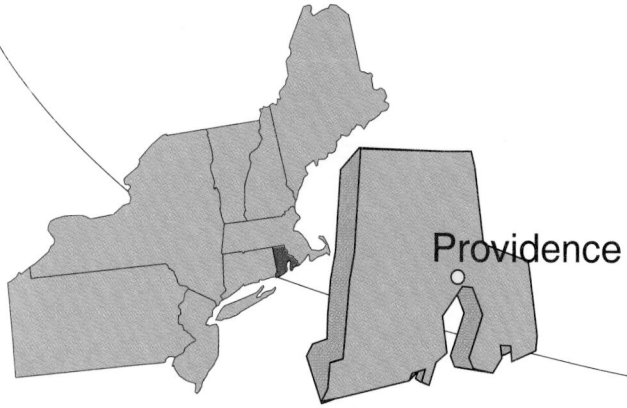

With more knowledge of the world, we are able to locate ourselves in larger areas. For example, we can think of our town within our state, our state within our country, our country within the world.

With still more knowledge, we can picture the earth in the solar system, the solar system in the galaxy, and the galaxy in the universe.

The Geography of Geography

Geography is about the "where" of things, so it's an important part of many subjects, including biology, weather sciences, history, and geology. Today, geographers usually study the geography important to one branch of learning. Among the many subfields of geography are:

1. **Agricultural geography, the study of farming in different parts of the world.**
2. **Biogeography, the study of plants and animals in different geographic locations and climates.**
3. **Cartography, the science of making maps.**
4. **Climatology, the study of world climates.**
5. **Cultural geography, the study of people and their ways of life in different parts of the world.**
6. **Geomorphology, the study and measurement of landforms on the earth's surface and under water.**
7. **Historical geography, the study of how geography affected historical events.**
8. **Industrial and marketing geography, the study of locations for businesses and factories and how particular locations can benefit or hurt them.**
9. **Meteorology, the study of daily weather, including air temperature, precipitation (rainfall, snowfall, etc.), and winds.**
10. **Political geography, the study of nations and states, including their natural habitats, cities and farms, and populations.**
11. **Resource geography, the study of the location of natural resources and the conservation of those resources to meet human needs.**
12. **Urban geography, the study of how cities develop and how they work.**

GALACTIC ADDRESS

U. R. Here
555 Nutley Avenue
Mapton, Massachusetts

U.S.A.
North America
Northern and Western Hemispheres
Earth
Solar System
Milky Way Galaxy
Universe

A good first step toward making a mental map of yourself within the universe is to write your galactic address.

Geographical Thinking

Picture yourself in Antarctica. What do you see? What are you wearing?

Now picture yourself near the equator. Now what do you see? Are you wearing a parka and snow pants?

You probably already know many geographical words and phrases that produce clear mental pictures. When you think "cold," for example, do you think "north," "south," "east," or "west?" If you live in North America, which direction makes you think "hot?" What do you picture when you think "mountain," "valley," "city," or "swamp?"

Geographical thinking is the ability to think about places and their characteristics. If Antarctica makes you think of a cold place or the equator of a hot one, you are thinking geographically.

Geographical thinking helps you select the appropriate clothes for climate and weather conditions, among other things.

The First Geographers

The first geographers were people who, like you, made mental maps and thought about things geographically. However, they didn't stop there. They traveled around, remembered what they saw, and reported their experiences so other people could learn from them.

Early humans who followed animal migrations in order to hunt food might be considered the first geographers. So, too, might those people who left their homelands to explore unknown areas and, later, returned to tell of their discoveries.

Thales: The First True Geographer?

Thales (c. 640 B.C.–550 B.C.) was a man who lived on the shores of the Aegean Sea in Greece more than 2,500 years ago. He established methods for observing places. Thales traveled widely. He journeyed to markets far from his home to trade goods. Along the way, he wrote down all the new things he saw and learned. He also described a way to measure the distances and directions that set one place apart from another. His method was much like the systems of miles and kilometers we use to measure distances today. His information helped later geographers make accurate globes and maps (see p. 12). Because Thales was so careful about his observations, many scholars consider him one of the first true geographers.

The ancient Greeks were the first people to make a specific list of things to observe about places, such as the distance from other places or landmarks, the number of people at the place, the number of buildings, the source of water, etc. Because of their attention to detail and careful descriptions, they are considered the first real geographers. The Greeks were also the first people to develop the theory that the earth is round, a theory proved to be true hundreds of years later.

Representing the Earth: Globes, Projections, and Maps

1 Globes

Looking at Earth

A map of the solar system shows the earth in relation to the sun and the other planets.

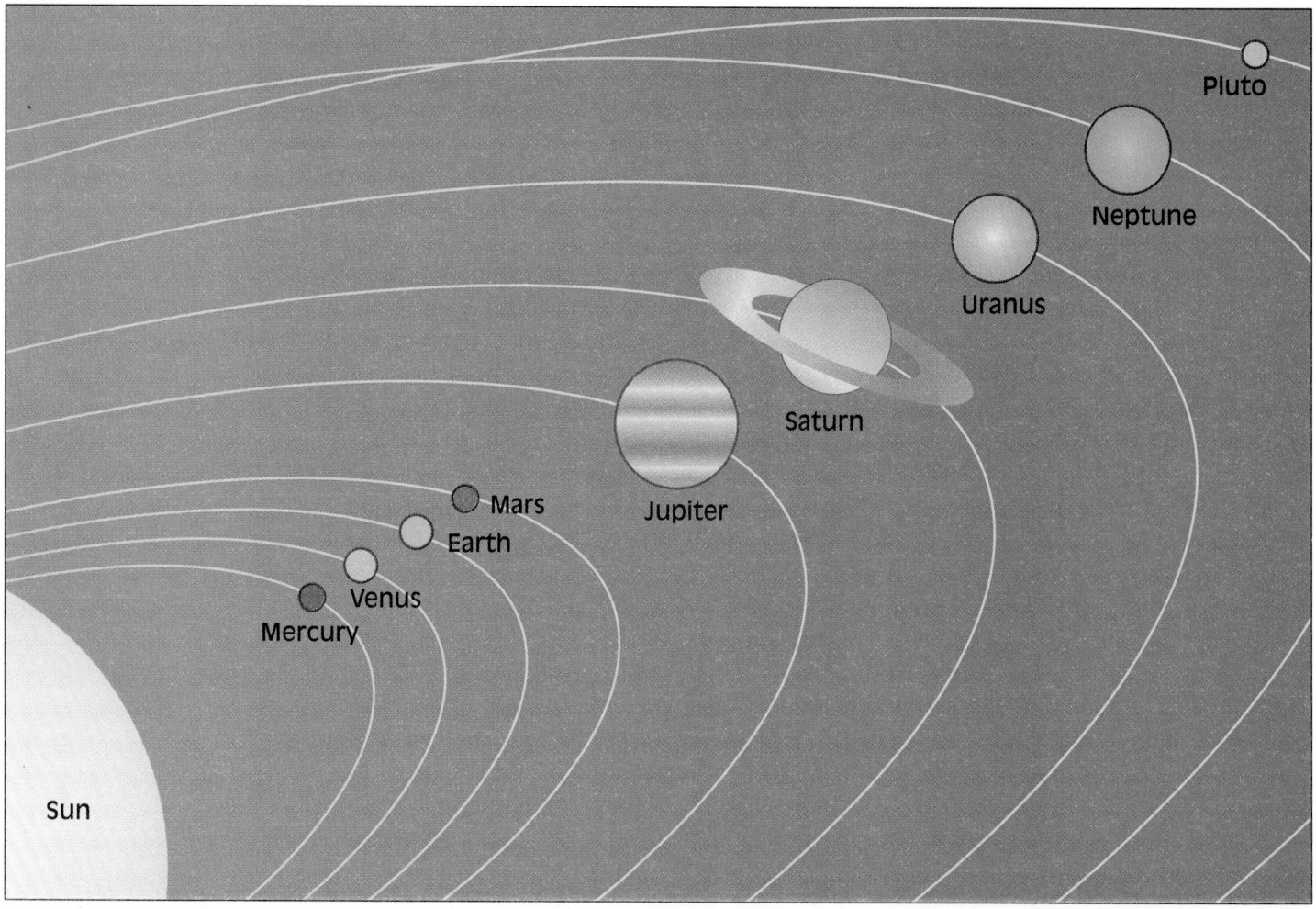

The solar system

Like the other planets, the earth is shaped like a sphere. From outer space, it looks like a disk covered by clouds.

Photograph of the earth from outer space shows water and land formations, as well as cloud cover.

But a photograph can show only half the earth—or one ***hemisphere*** (see p. 10). To show the whole earth, we use a ***globe***, or a sphere-shaped model of the earth. Although it doesn't show all the cloud formations and wind patterns in the atmosphere, it does show the land and water formations on the earth's surface. Globes also help us understand natural events, among them day and night and the seasons.

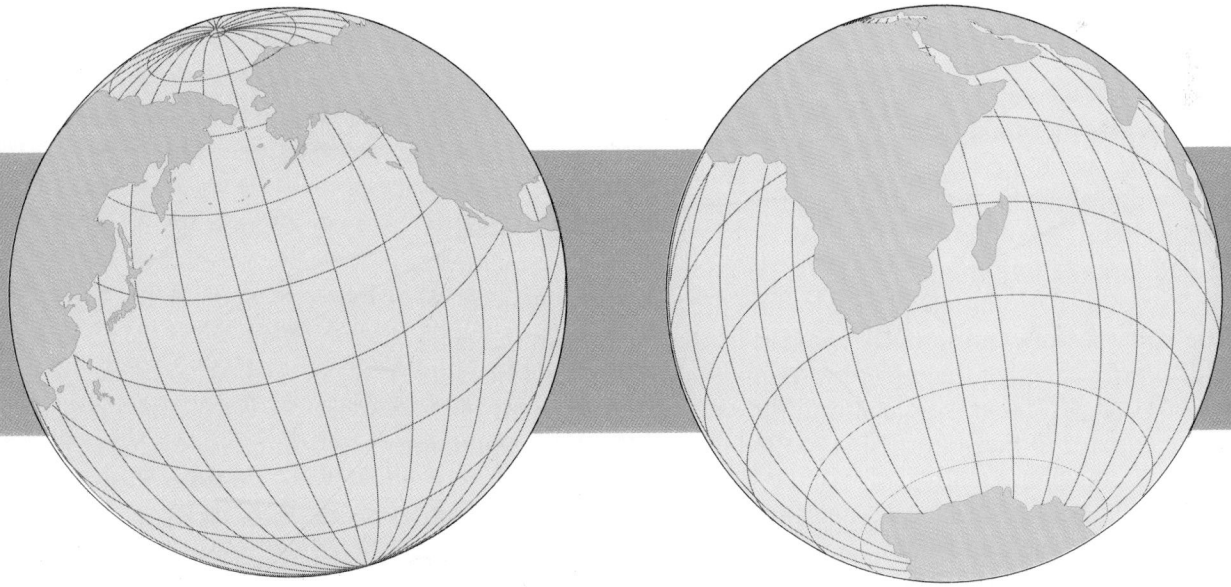

Globes show the water and land formations on the earth's surface.

Inventing the Globe

You can tell by photographs taken from space that the earth is round. But, if you look out a window at school or home, the surface of the earth appears mainly flat.

Yet more than 2,000 years before photography from space was possible, the ancient Greek geographers relied on observation and mathematics to figure out the shape and size of the earth. They made the first globes to show what the earth is like.

Lines of Longitude and Latitude

The ancient Greeks also used their globes to think about the location of places on the earth. They divided the globe into 360 segments, called ***degrees***. They used vertical lines called ***longitude*** to mark off the 360 parts. Lines of longitude, also called ***meridians***, are still used today to locate places on the earth, and to measure the distances between places. They can be seen on most globes.

The ***prime meridian***, or 0 degrees (0°) longitude, was agreed upon in 1884. It passes through the site of the Royal Naval Observatory in Greenwich, England. Distance is measured east and west of this line. Longitude lines east of the prime meridian are numbered 1° through 179°. This is the ***eastern hemisphere.*** Longitude lines west of the prime meridian are also numbered 1° through 179°. This is the ***western hemisphere***. The 180° line, reached by traveling east or west from the prime meridian, is exactly halfway around the earth from the prime meridian. Much of this line of longitude is used also as the ***international date line*** (see p. 15).

The ancient Greeks also drew lines to divide the earth horizontally. These lines are called ***lines of latitude*** or ***parallels***. Latitude is measured from the ***equator***, or 0 degrees (0°) latitude. Latitude lines are numbered from 0° to 90° from the equator to the north pole. The part of the earth from the equator to the north pole is called the ***northern hemisphere***. Latitude lines are also numbered 0° to 90° from the equator to the south pole. The part of the earth from the equator to the south pole is called the ***southern hemisphere***.

The northern hemisphere is divided into the tropics and temperate zone at the Tropic of Cancer, a line of latitude that runs parallel to the equator at 23°30′ north latitude. The temperate zone runs from 23°30′ to the Arctic Circle, a line of latitude located at 66°30′ north latitude. In the southern hemisphere, the Tropic of Capricorn, located at 23°30′ south latitude, divides the tropics from the southern temperate zone. The temperate zone ends at the Antarctic Circle, or 66°30′ south latitude.

Lines of ***latitude*** run parallel to each other; that means they never meet.

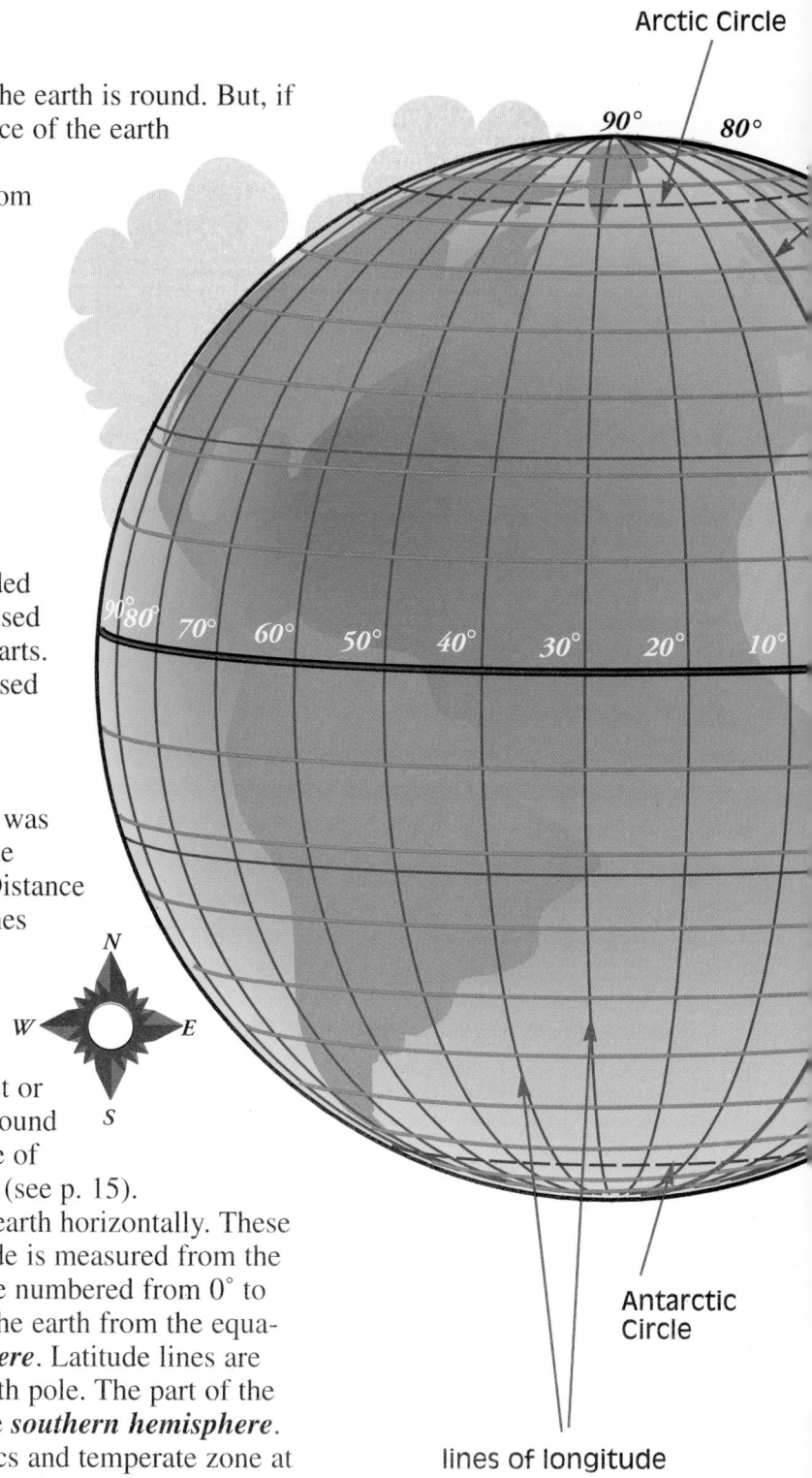

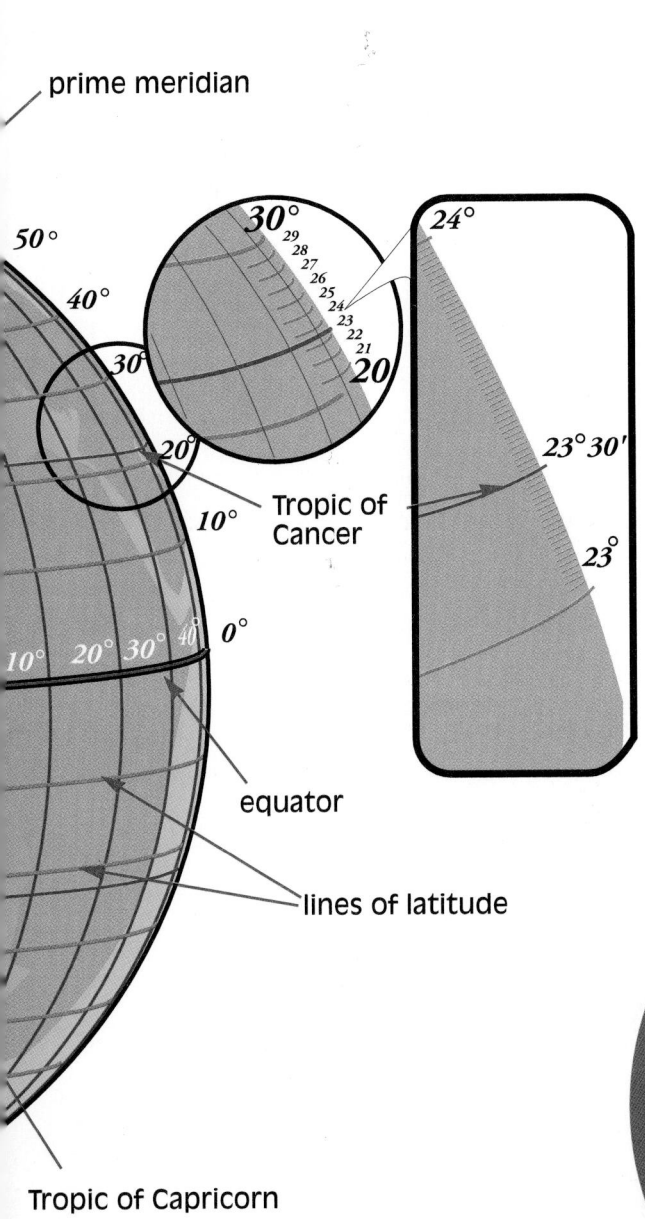

The Two North Poles

The spot where the lines of longitude meet at the northernmost point of the globe is called the north pole. It is also called ***true north***, or ***geographic north***.

There is another north pole, called ***magnetic north***. The magnetic north pole is not located in quite the same place as the geographical north pole, although they are very close. The difference between the location of the true north and magnetic north poles is shown on most globes.

You can find the magnetic north pole with a compass. A compass is made of a magnetized needle held up so that it turns freely. Because the earth itself is a huge magnet, no matter what direction you're going, the compass needle always points to magnetic north.

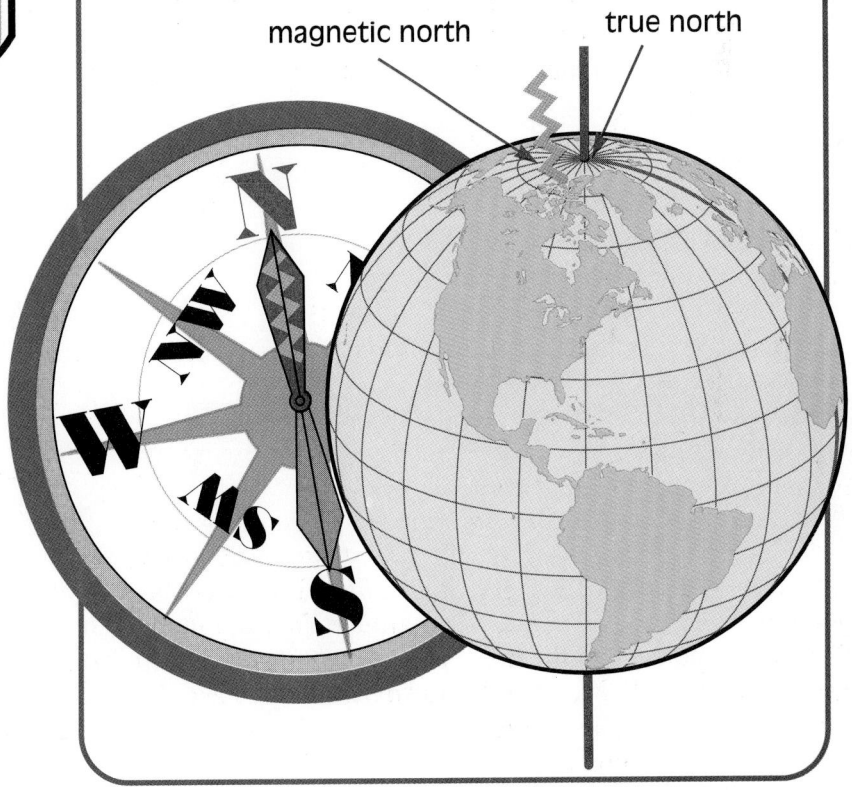

Degrees of longitude and latitude are divided into measures called minutes, and marked by the symbol ´. Like minutes in an hour, there are 60 minutes (60´) in a degree of longitude or latitude. Minutes are divided into seconds, and marked by the symbol´´. There are 60 seconds in each minute of latitude or longitude.

Geographers in Ancient Greece

Greek geographers established the science of making highly accurate globes. The globes are based on some of the most important discoveries made by early Greek geographers.

Eratosthenes of Cyrene (c. 280–200 B.C.) used math and his knowledge of round objects (spheres), to measure the circumference of the earth. His measurement was close to the measurement used by scientists today (24,902 miles; 40,075 kilometers).

Hipparchus (born c. 150 B.C.) refined measurements for ***latitude*** and developed measures for ***longitude*** (see p. 10). He was the first to divide the equator into 360 degrees. Hipparchus also divided the world as he knew it into climatic zones (see p. 50) and drew the first known map of the night sky.

Strabo (60 B.C.-A.D. 25) described his travels through Europe, North Africa, and western Asia in a work called ***Geographia***. Written as 17 books, ***Geographia*** describes in detail the world as the Greeks of his time knew it.

Claudius Ptolemy (2nd century A.D.) wrote an eight-volume book, also called ***Geographia***. In it, he described in terms of longitude and latitude (see p. 10) all the places in the world that were known to the Greeks of this time.

The Geographic Grid

Lines of latitude and longitude form a ***geographic grid***.

The geographic grid makes it possible to identify points on the earth and record their exact locations north or south of the equator and east or west of the prime meridian.

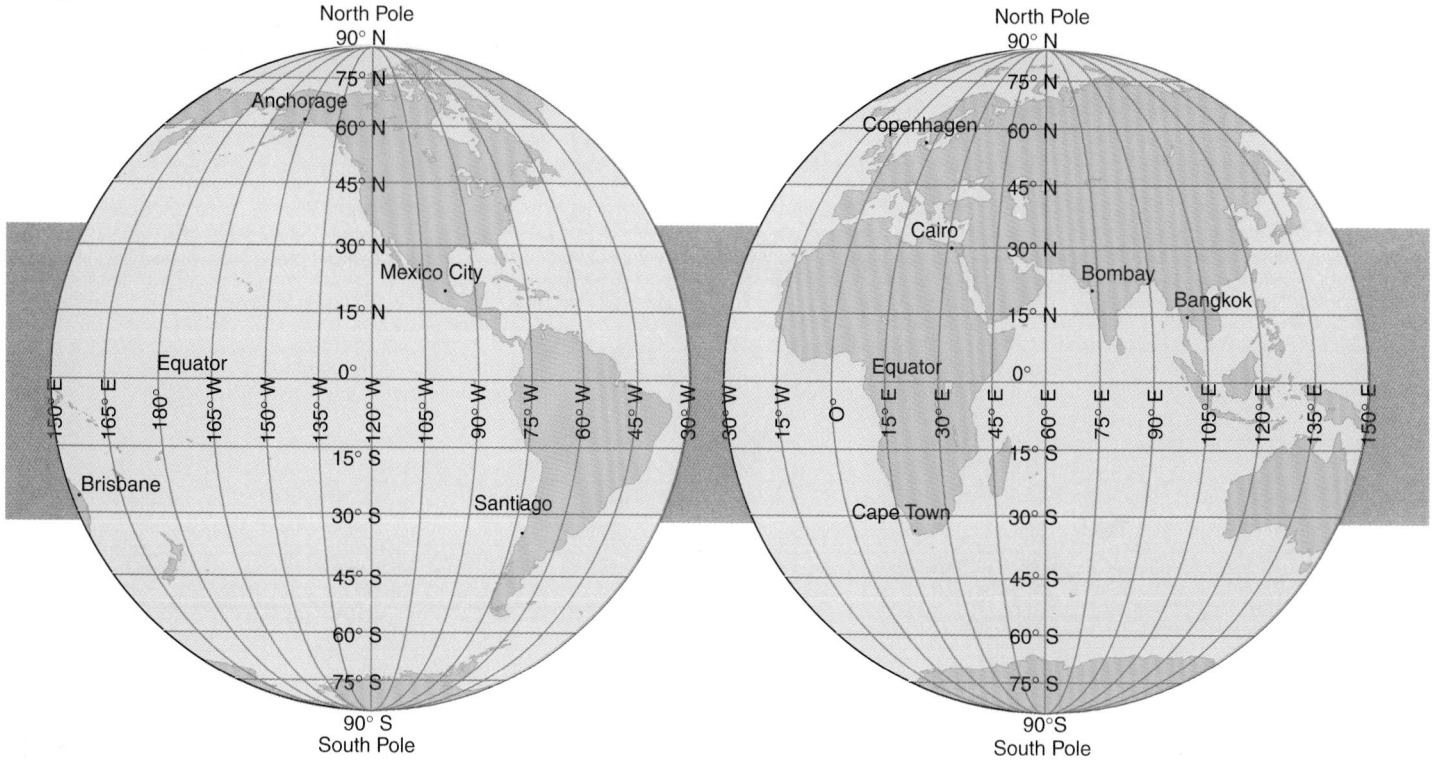

Using coordinates, or points of latitude and longitude, you can locate the places on the earth's surface, including Anchorage, Alaska (61° north latitude, 150° west longitude), Bangkok, Thailand (14° north latitude, 100° east longitude), Bombay, India (19° north latitude, 73° east longitude), Brisbane, Australia (27° south latitude, 153° east longitude), Cairo, Egypt (30° north latitude, 31° east longitude), Capetown, South Africa (34° south latitude, 18° east longitude), Copenhagen, Denmark, (56° north latitude, 12° east longitude), Mexico City, Mexico (19° north latitude, 99° west longitude), and Santiago, Chile (33° south latitude, 71° west longitude).

Light on Earth

Light on earth is a result of our planet's position in relation to the sun and moon. Our position in space results in such events as day and night, the seasons, solstices, eclipses, and tides.

Day and Night

A globe and a lightbulb illustrate how day changes into night. Only half the surface of the globe is covered in light at any time.

As the globe rotates on its axis, the part of the surface that is lighted changes.

Just like the globe in the example, the earth rotates on an axis. As a particular place on the earth rotates out of the sunlight, night falls. As that place rotates back into the light, day dawns.

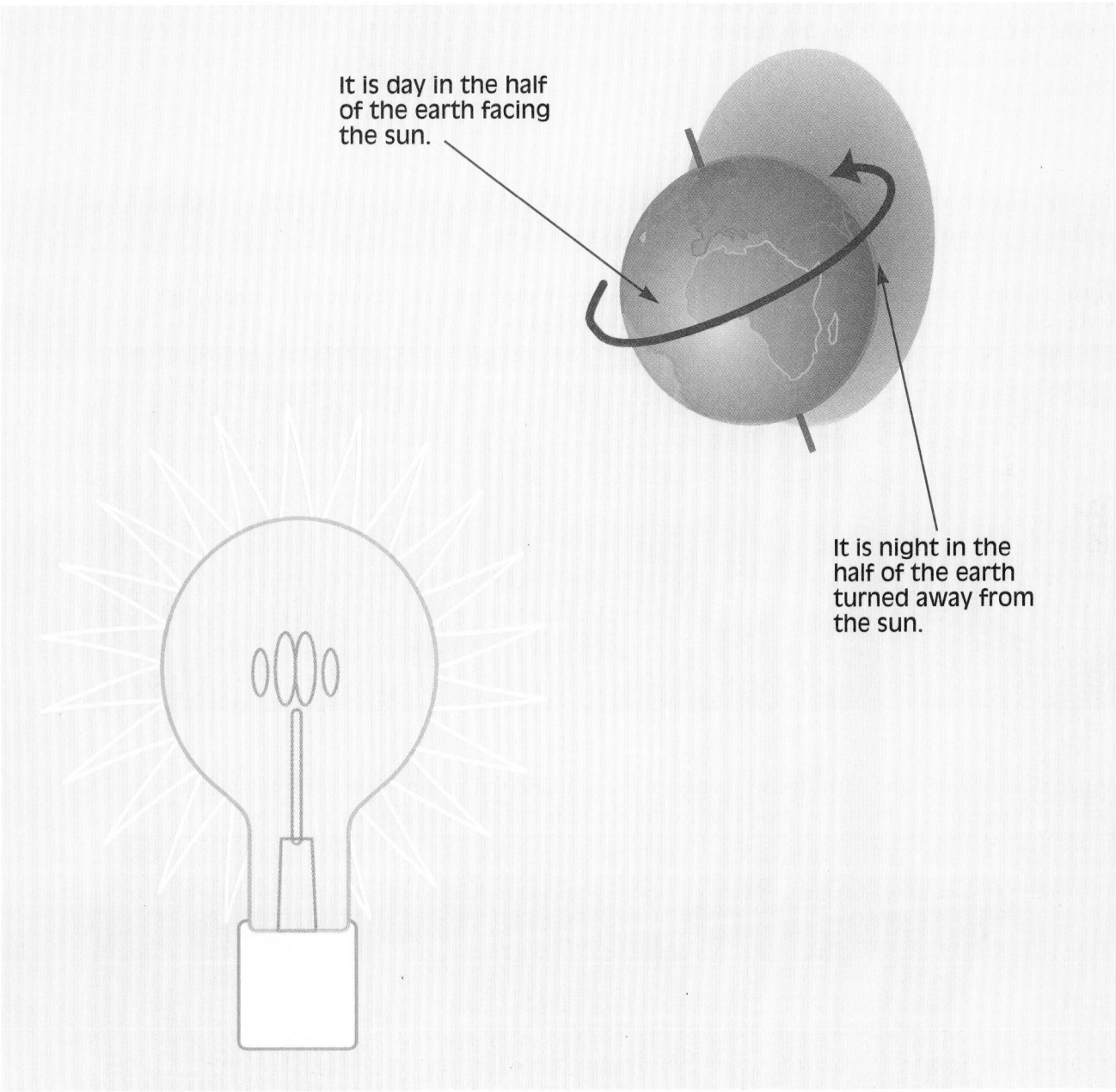

A lightbulb shining on a globe shows how the earth is lit by the sun. Half of the surface is covered by light, the other half is in shadow. As the earth rotates on its axis, every point on the earth moves from the light, or **day**, to shadow, **night**, and back again.

The Seasons

A globe and a lightbulb can also illustrate how the seasons change. Earth not only rotates on its axis, it also orbits the sun. The angle of the axis is tilted in relation to its orbit. When the earth is positioned so that the northern hemisphere is tipped toward the sun, it is summer there and winter in the southern hemisphere.

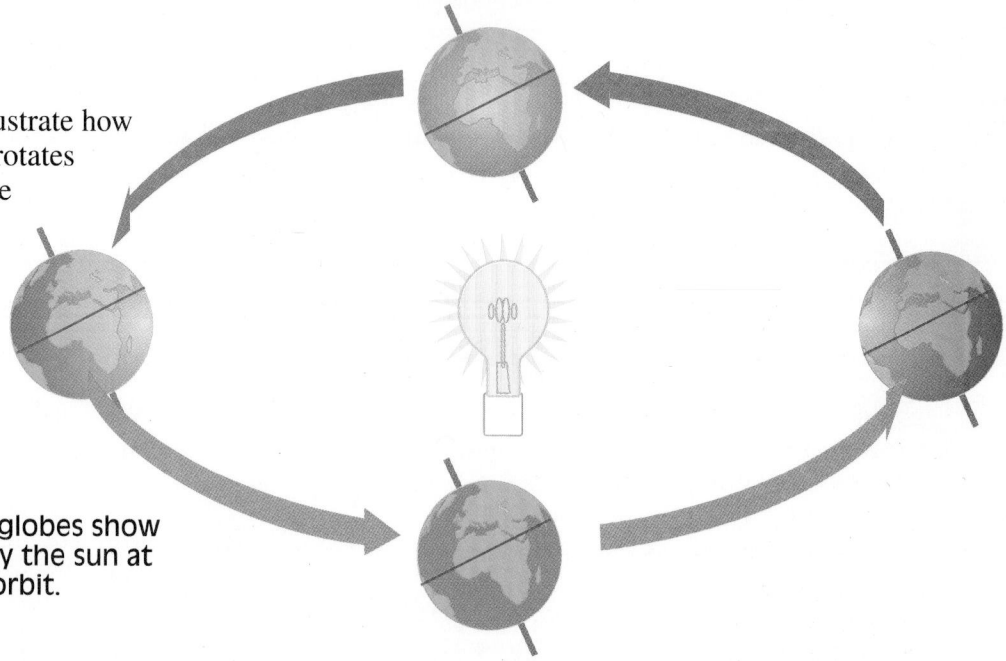

A lightbulb and four globes show how the earth is lit by the sun at various points in its orbit.

Eclipses

Occasionally the light from the sun or the sunlight reflected off the moon is kept from hitting the earth, or ***eclipsed***, by the position of the earth and moon in relation to the sun.

A ***solar eclipse*** occurs when the moon passes between the earth and the sun. People standing in the shadow see the moon pass in front of the sun, blotting out its light.

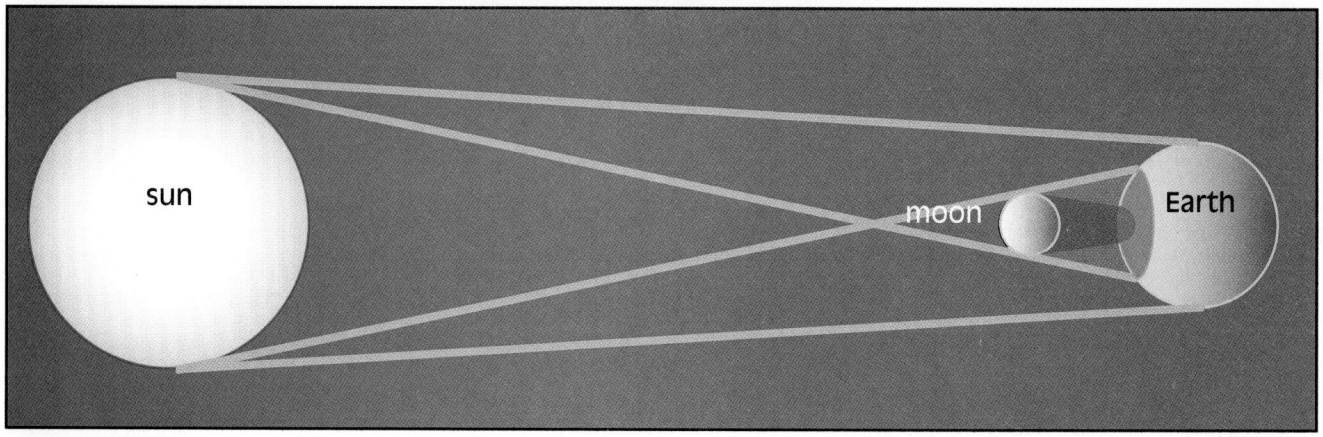

solar eclipse

A ***lunar eclipse*** occurs when the earth passes between the sun and the moon. People on the side of the earth facing the moon see the moon pass from sunlight into the shadow cast by the earth.

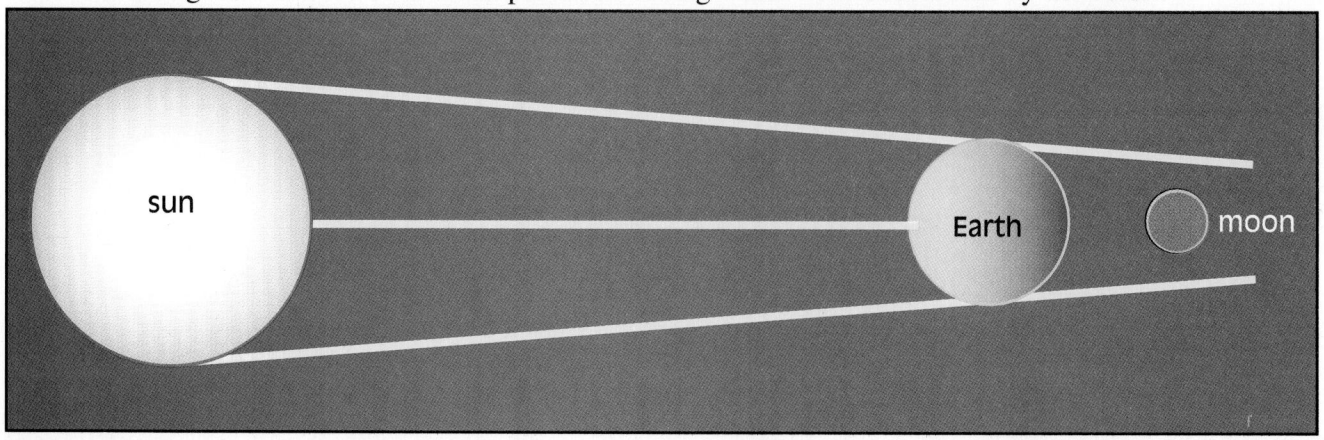

lunar eclipse

The 24 Hour Globe:

Time Zones

In addition to lines of longitude and latitude, the globe is marked off into 24 ***time zones***. The time zones run in the same direction as the lines of longitude, and begin at 0 degrees (0°), or the ***prime meridian***. The time zone that lines up roughly along 180° longitude follows the ***international date line***. Places to the east of this line are a calendar day behind places to the west. If you fly from west to east over the international date line on Saturday, you fly into Friday. You gain one day on your trip.

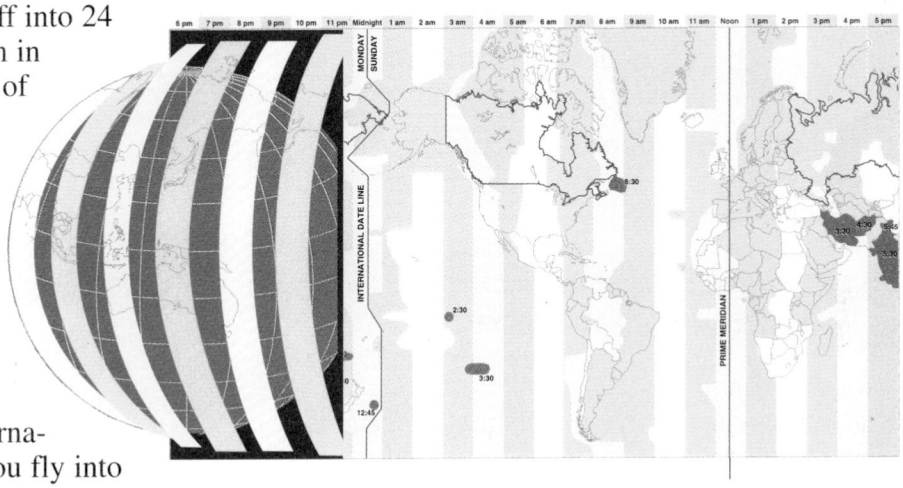

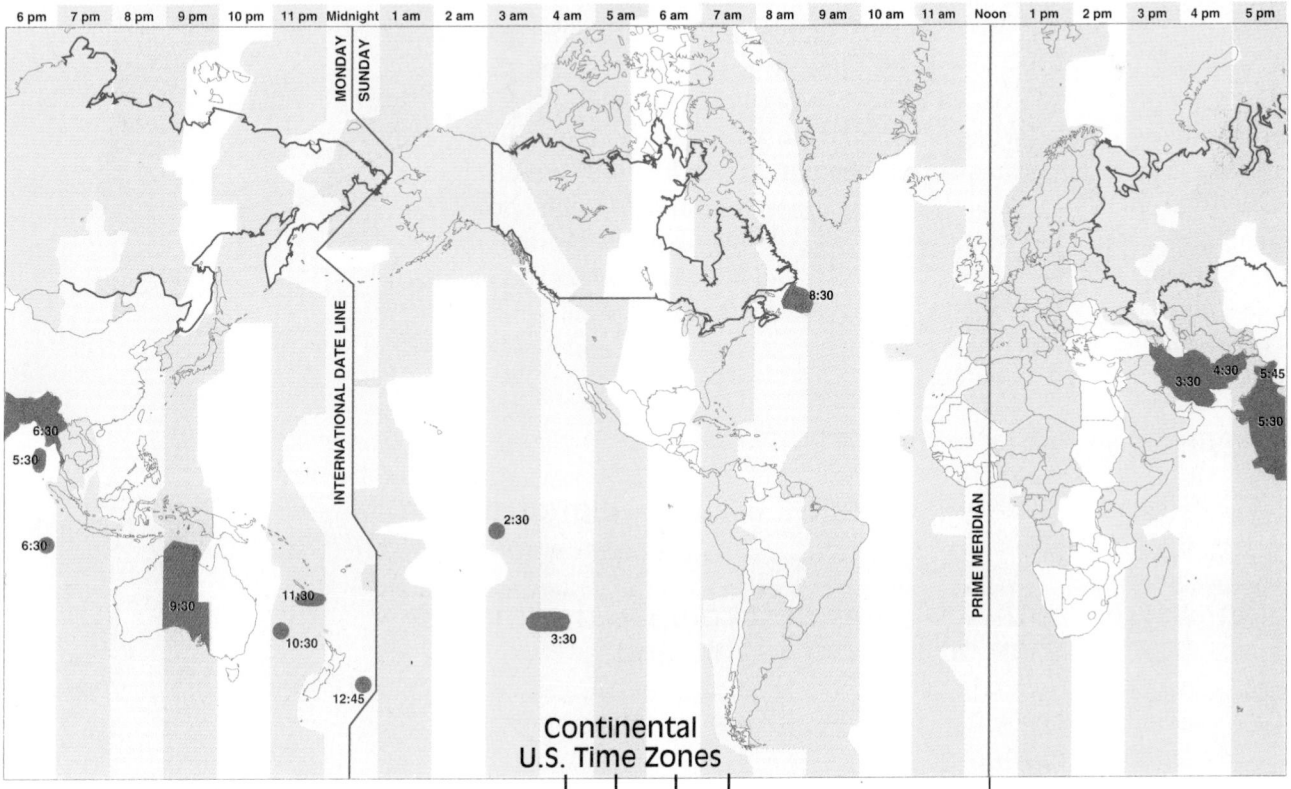

2 Maps

What Is a Map?

A ***map*** is a picture of a place on a flat surface. Most maps show a place drawn from above.

Different types of maps show different types of information, such as natural features, where humans live, historical and modern political boundaries, centers of industry, and variations in climate and weather.

Map Projections

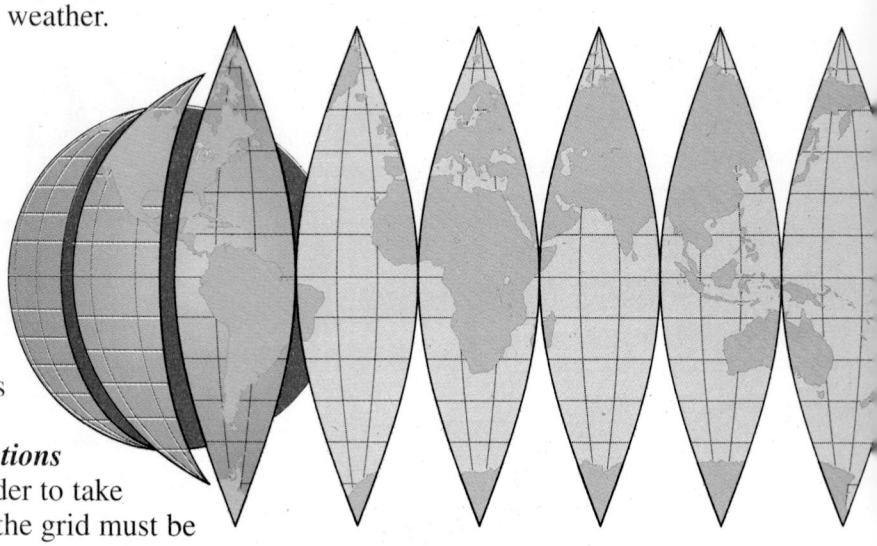

Imagine peeling the surface off a globe and laying it down flat. It would form a map with a very unusual shape.

Globes accurately show sizes, locations, and distances on the earth because the earth, like a globe, is roughly a sphere. Because they are flat, maps do not show the round earth exactly as it is shown on a globe.

In order to make maps, mapmakers use ***projections*** based on the geographical grid (see p. 12). In order to take the grid from a globe and open it flat on a map, the grid must be changed somewhat. These changes affect the accuracy of maps.

Standard map projections are created to represent the geographic grid as accurately as possible on flat surfaces. In inventing projections, mapmakers have four major concerns: area, direction, distance, and shape.

When mapmakers make projections, they must decide which elements need to be most accurate on their maps. If a map is going to be used to measure the distance between places, a mapmaker will choose a projection that shows the size of land and water areas as accurately as possible to scale. If a mapmaker needs to show direction and the shape of the land and water areas, he or she will choose a projection that depicts those features most accurately.

Mapmakers' Concerns

area	The size of land and water areas in relationship to each other.
direction	North, south, east, and west compared with their true location on the geographic grid.
distance	The distance on a map relative to the earth's surface, called scale.
shape	The shape of land and water areas compared with their shape on the earth or a globe.

Some Common Map Projections

Conic	Used for mapping a large piece of the earth's surface, it shows accurate distance, direction, and shape for the limited area mapped.	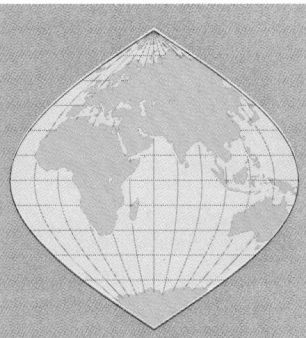
Interrupted	Shows accurate area and shape. Oceans have (equal area) open, pie-shaped interruptions to adjust for distance.	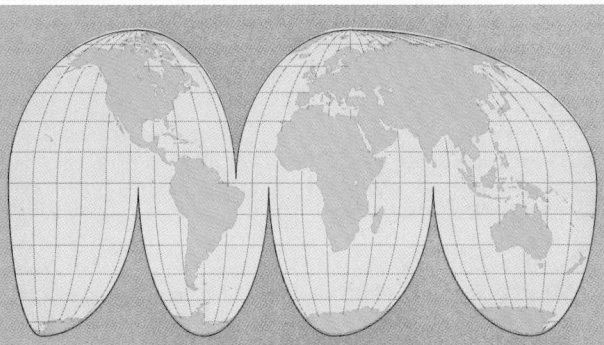
Mercator (cylindrical)	Shows accurate direction, but land and water areas are greatly distorted toward the north and south poles.	
Polar (azimuthal)	Used for mapping hemispheres instead of the whole earth; shows accurate distance and direction, but shape and size become more and more distorted toward the edges.	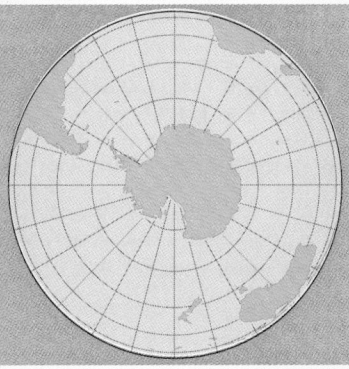
Robinson (oval)	Shows accurately the shape and size of continents, but the water areas are expanded to fill the extra space.	

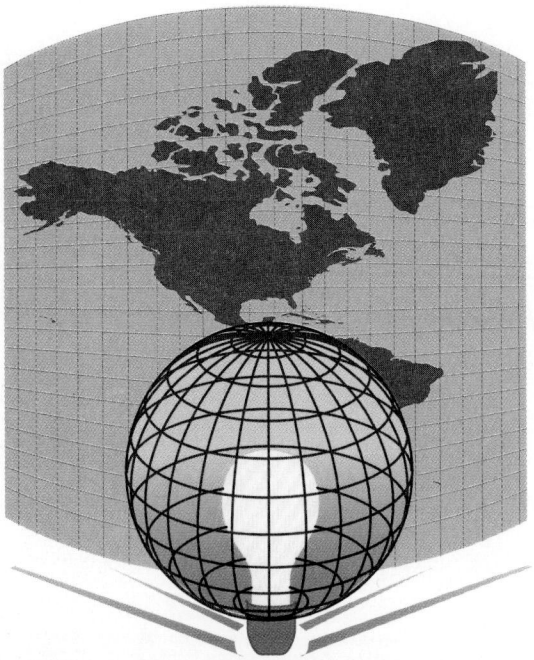

How Projections Are Made

Put a projector light inside a globe. The spaces formed by the geographic grid when ***projected*** from the globe onto a flat screen will change as the projector light is moved. While the location of a city is likely to fall in the same place on the globe and its projection, the sizes and shapes of countries and continents will change as the distances away from the center of the projected image change. Areas on the edges of the map appear stretched as they are flattened in the projection.

When cartographers make maps, they use mathematical calculations to project the geographic grid (see p. 12) onto paper.

Natural Features

Natural features are features on the earth's surface that were not made by humans. These features include nonliving things (rocks, minerals, soil, water, and atmosphere) as well as living things (plants and animals).

Cartography *is the art of making maps or charts. People who draw maps are called* **cartographers.** *The words come from the Latin* **carta,** *meaning "map," and the Greek* **graph,** *meaning "writing."*

Physical Features

Earth's nonliving, or ***physical***, features include mountains, plains, rivers, lakes, and oceans. The earth's physical features are constantly changing. A number of forces, such as erosion and weathering, gradually wear down the earth's surface. Other forces, such as fire, earthquakes, and volcanoes, make almost instant changes (see pp. 32-33).

Atmospheric Features

The earth's nonliving features also include ***atmospheric*** conditions, or climate and weather. Climate is the usual weather in a place over a long time period. It, along with physical features, determines which plants and animals can live in a particular place (see pp. 43-49).

Living Features

Earth's living features are its plants and animals, including humans. Different plants and animals thrive in different natural regions, or ***biomes*** (see pp. 50-56). Biomes are large environments that share the same general temperature and annual rainfall.

Human-made Features

Human-made features are features on the earth's surface created by human beings—for example, buildings, monuments, parks, roads, fields, and landfills.

The First Maps

No one knows for certain who made the first maps or what those maps looked like. But we know that humans have been making maps for thousands of years. Scratched into sand, painted on animal skins, carved into wood, or drawn on rock walls, maps helped people avoid danger, find good hunting grounds, and locate clean water. The ancient Egyptians even supplied maps to tax collectors to help them along their routes.

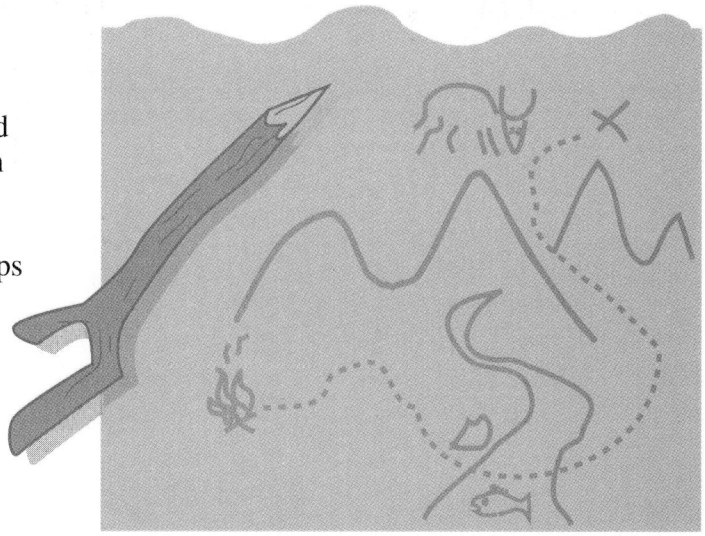

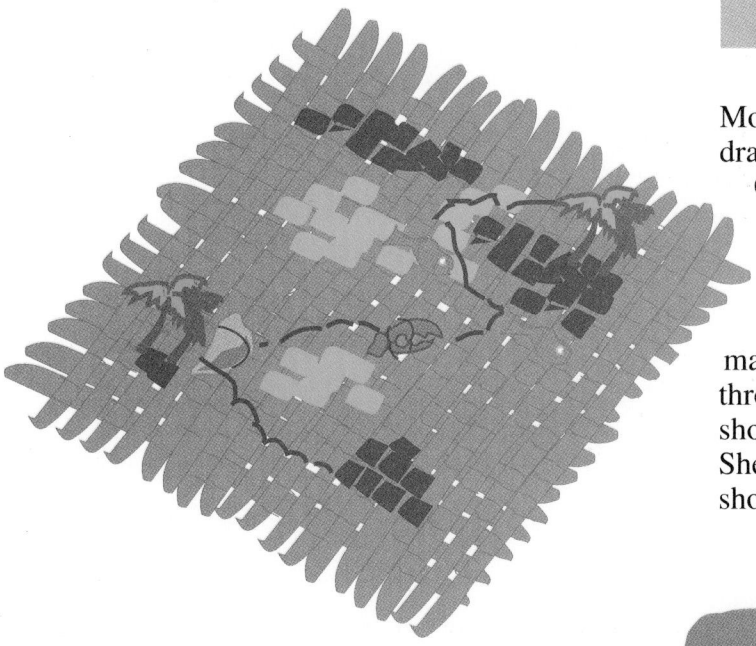

More than 2,000 years ago, Europeans were drawing maps to help them navigate at sea. Called ***charts***, these maps of waterways were drawn on skins and stones, carved in wood, or engraved into clay—in much the same way as land maps were made. Polynesian islanders in the Pacific Ocean made charts out of palm leaves woven through reeds. The pattern of the weaving showed ocean currents and wave directions. Shells were attached to the reed charts to show where islands were located.

The oldest maps that exist today were made in the ancient Middle Eastern civilization of Babylon. These maps are more than 4,000 years old, and are etched into large clay tablets.

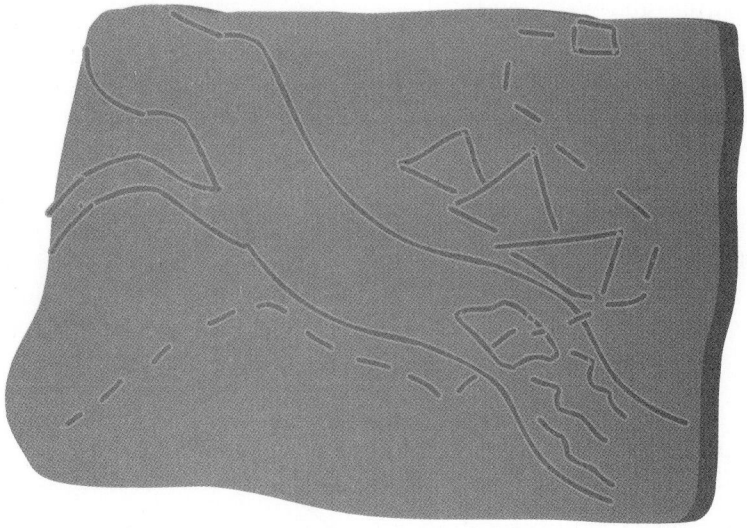

Three Basic Kinds of Maps

Geopolitical Maps *show political and physical features on one map. (See p. 28 for an example of a geopolitical map.)*

Political Maps

Political maps show how humans have divided up the earth's surface. They show borders between countries, the locations of cities and towns, building sites, neighborhoods, settlement plans, roadways, and other human-made features.

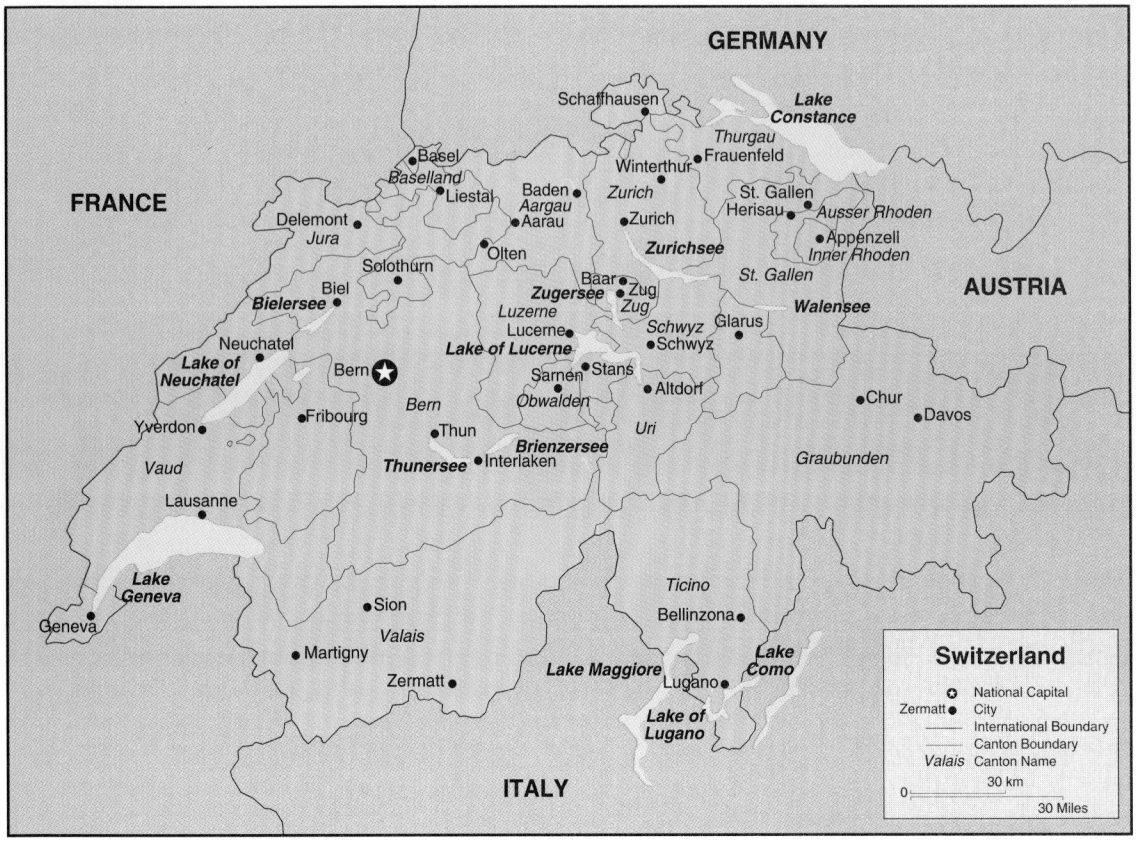

This political map of Switzerland shows the countries it borders, as well as its cantons (states) and major cities.

Physical Maps

Physical maps show the land formations and water on Earth's surface. Physical maps show mountains, valleys, plains, oceans, rivers, and lakes. They can also show locations of natural plant life, water currents, and wind patterns.

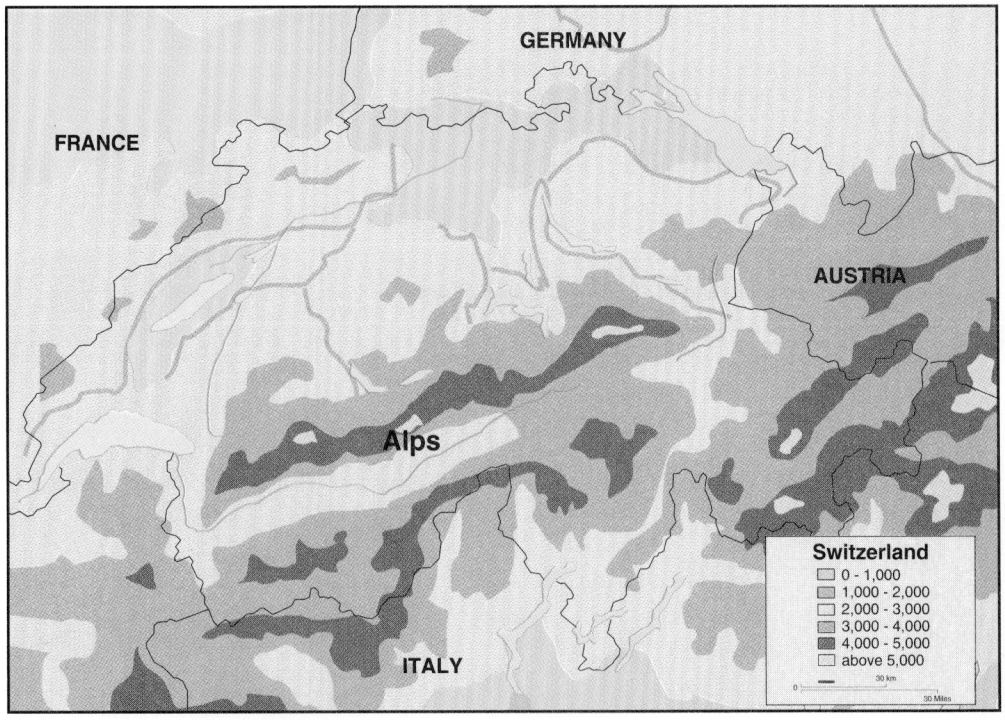

This physical map of Switzerland shows variations in the elevation of the land, as well as the location of major rivers.

Cultural Maps

Cultural maps show patterns of ethnic groups, religious practices, languages spoken, customs, educational levels, and recreational choices.

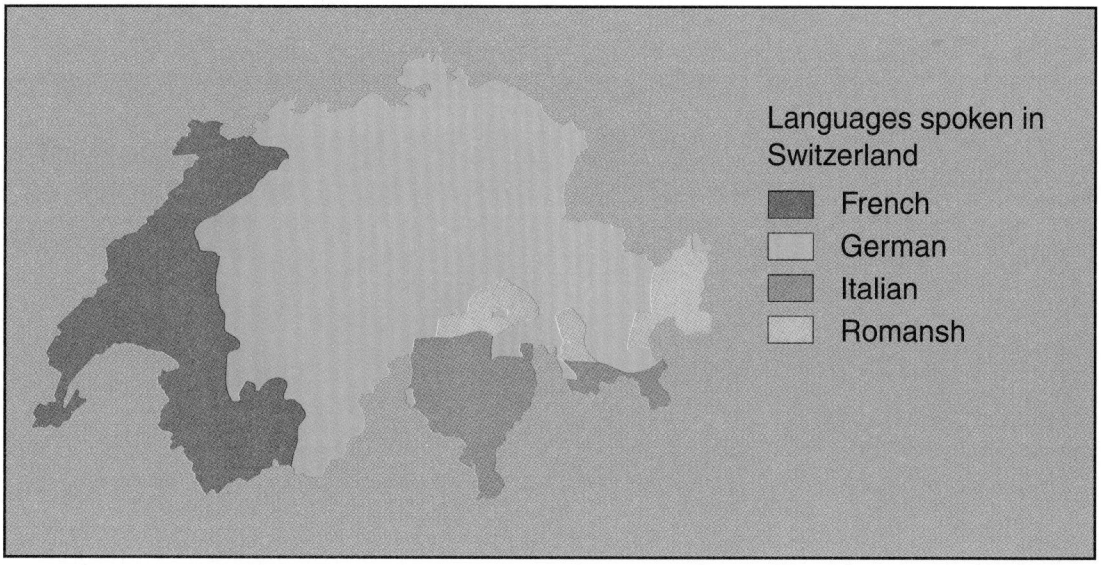

This cultural map of Switzerland shows where different languages are spoken within the country.

Charts

Charts are maps of bodies of water. Sailors use them to navigate in open ocean waters as well as on lakes and in shallow bays, inlets, and rivers. Charts show water depths, currents, and physical features found below the surface of the water. They also locate ports and places to anchor safely, as well as buoys, lighthouses, and other aids to seafarers.

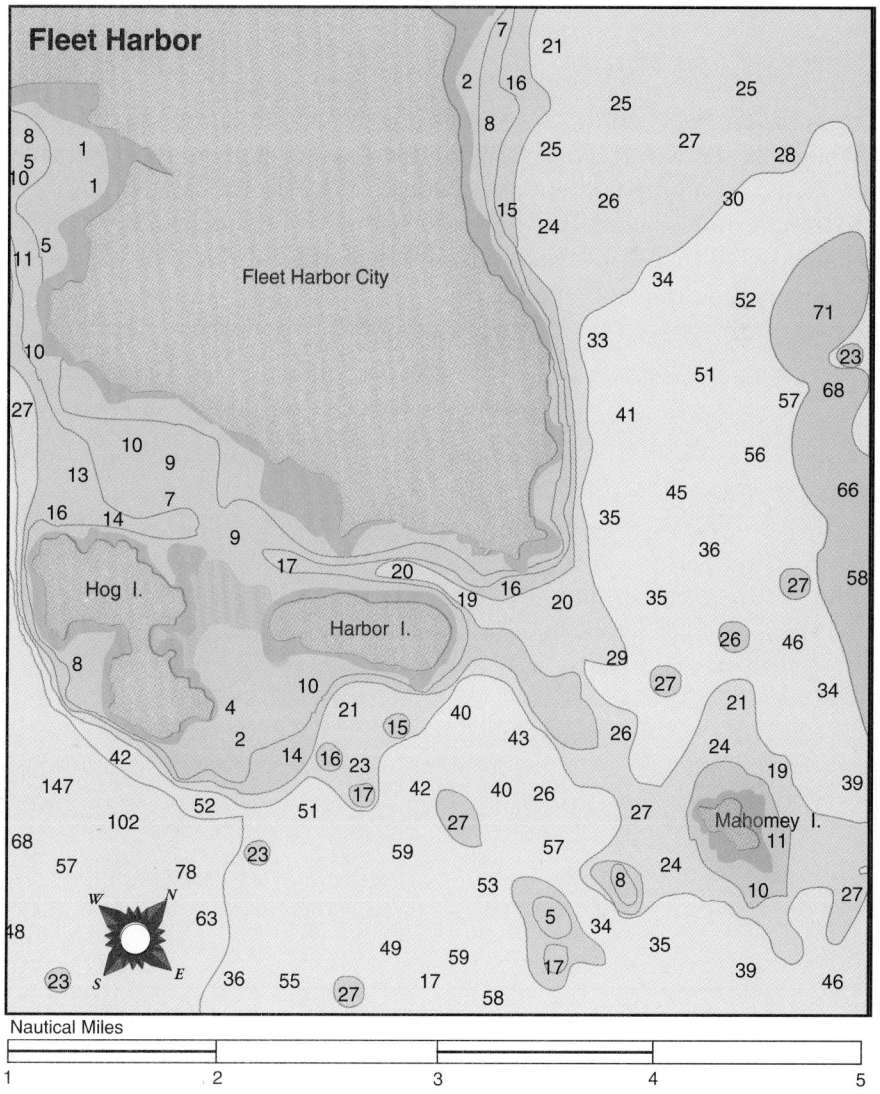

The depth of water is shown in feet on this sample chart.

Maps for Special Uses

Relative Location Maps

Relative location maps show the position of a place in relation to its surroundings. For example, such a map might show where a specific place is located in relation to the rest of the world.

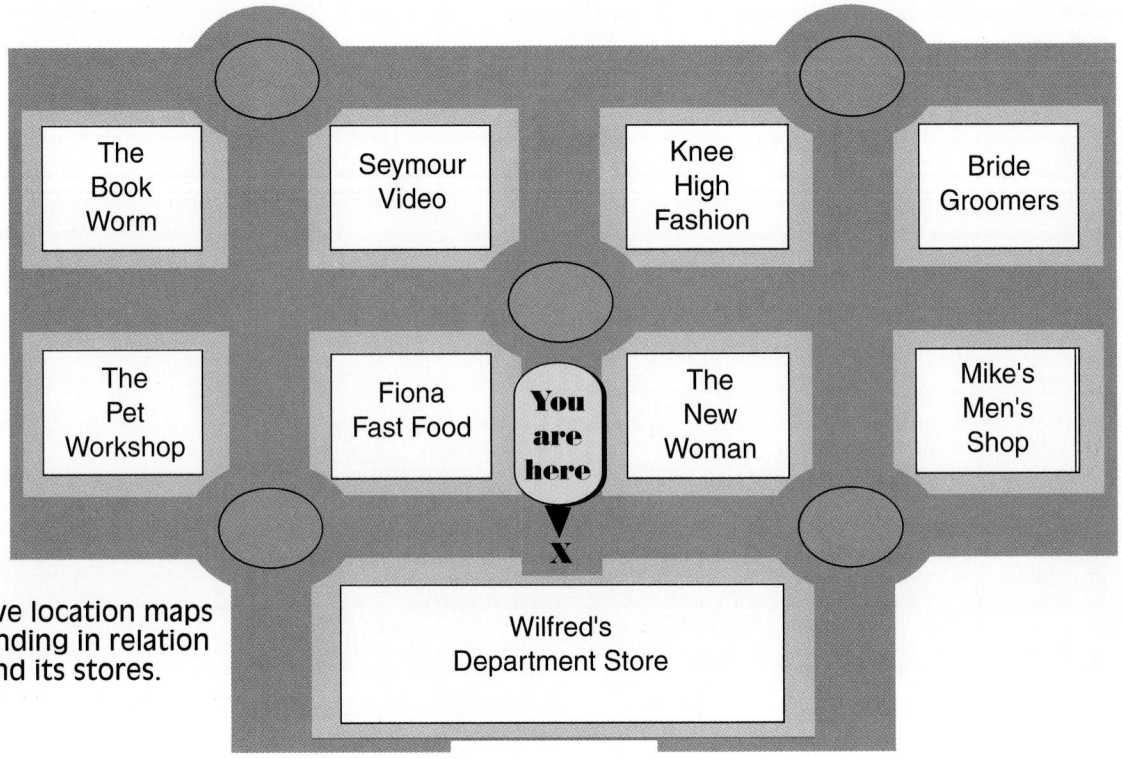

In shopping malls, relative location maps show where you are standing in relation to the rest of the mall and its stores.

Distribution Maps

Distribution maps show how things are spread out across an area or throughout the world. For example, distribution maps may show where sheep are raised on all the continents or where oil wells are located in Oklahoma. Distribution maps can also show where rain forests and timber mills are located, what kinds of rocks make up the earth's surface, or where bookstores are located in your home town.

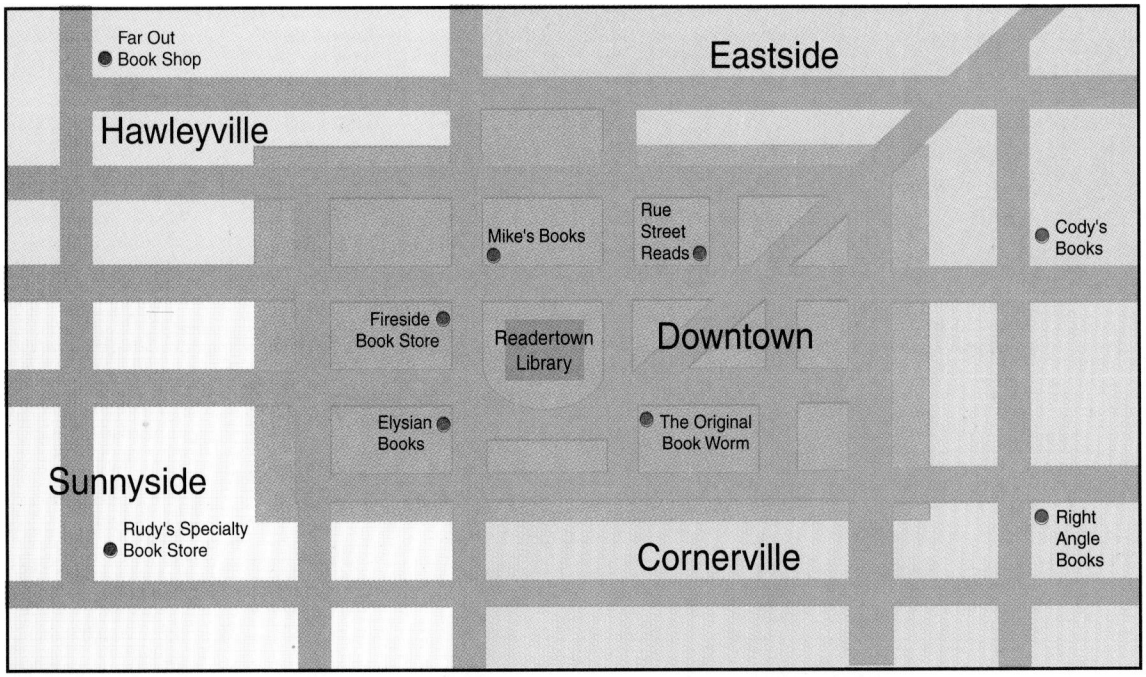

This distribution map shows the location of bookstores in Readertown, USA. According to the map, most bookstores are downtown, and the rest of Readertown's bookstores are evenly distributed in the residential neighborhoods.

Topographic Maps

Topographic maps show physical features, and are often drawn showing ***contours***, or lines that show differences in elevations. Any topographic map drawn to show contours may also be called a contour map.

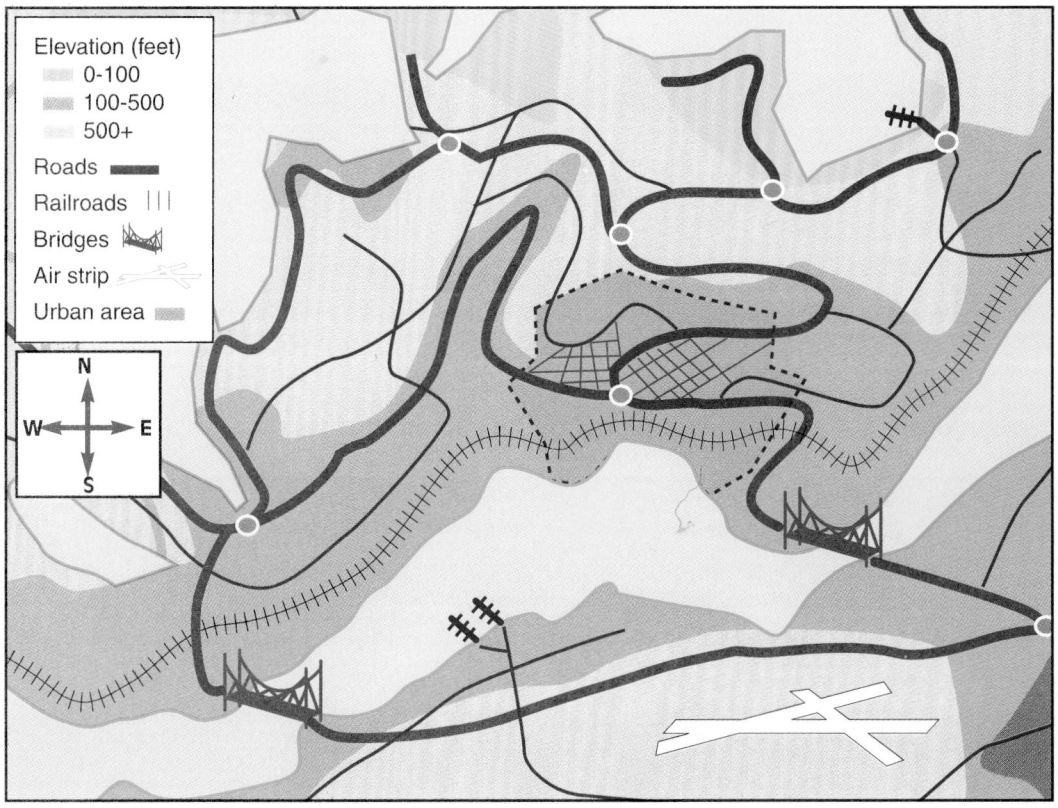

This section of a topographic map shows color-keyed contours, as well as a variety of physical features: rivers, roads, railroad tracks, bridges, and an air strip.

Climate and Weather Maps

Climate and weather maps show how and where climatic and weather conditions occur across a region or throughout the world.

Weather map illustrating a fall day in the United States

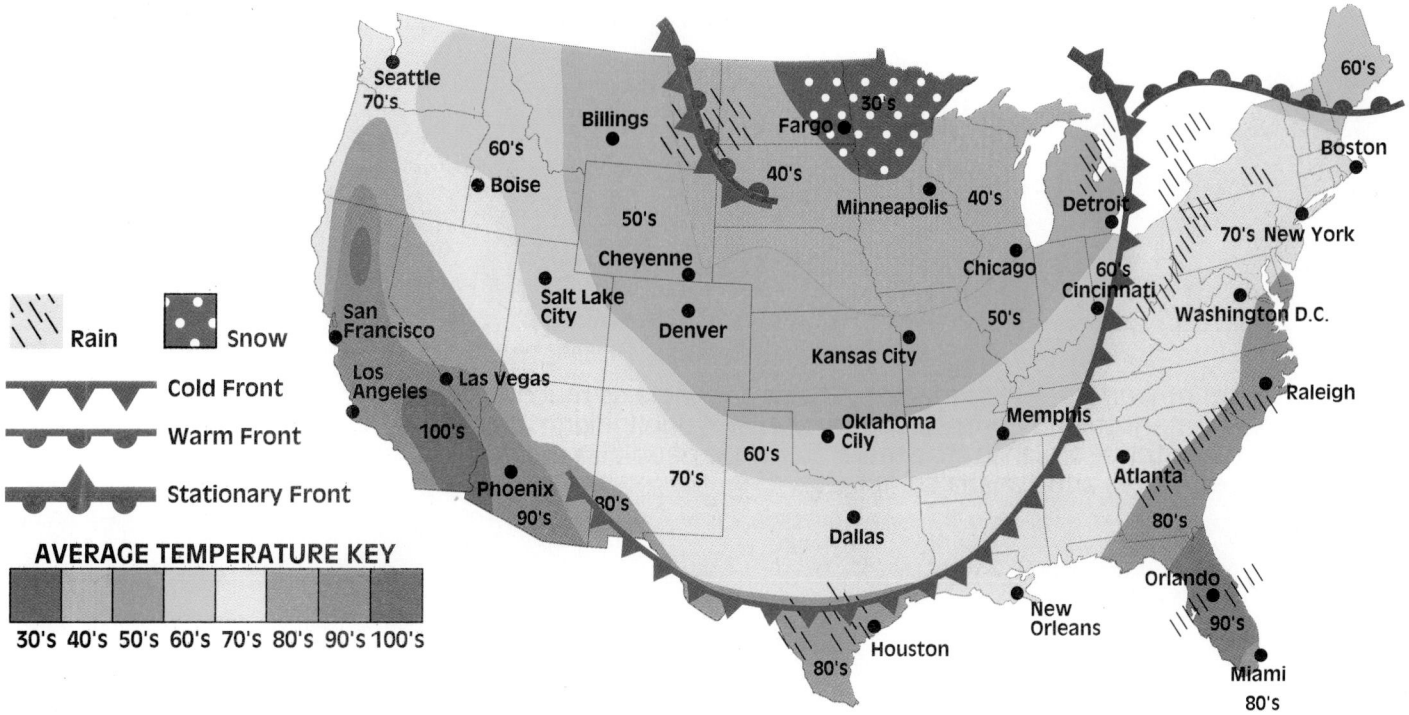

Time Zone Maps

Time zone maps show how the earth is divided into different time zones. (See p. 15 for an example of a time zone map.)

ALTERED STATES:

Cartograms

Cartograms are diagrams in map form. The places on a cartogram are drawn in mathematical proportion to show how much of a particular thing is found in each area mapped.

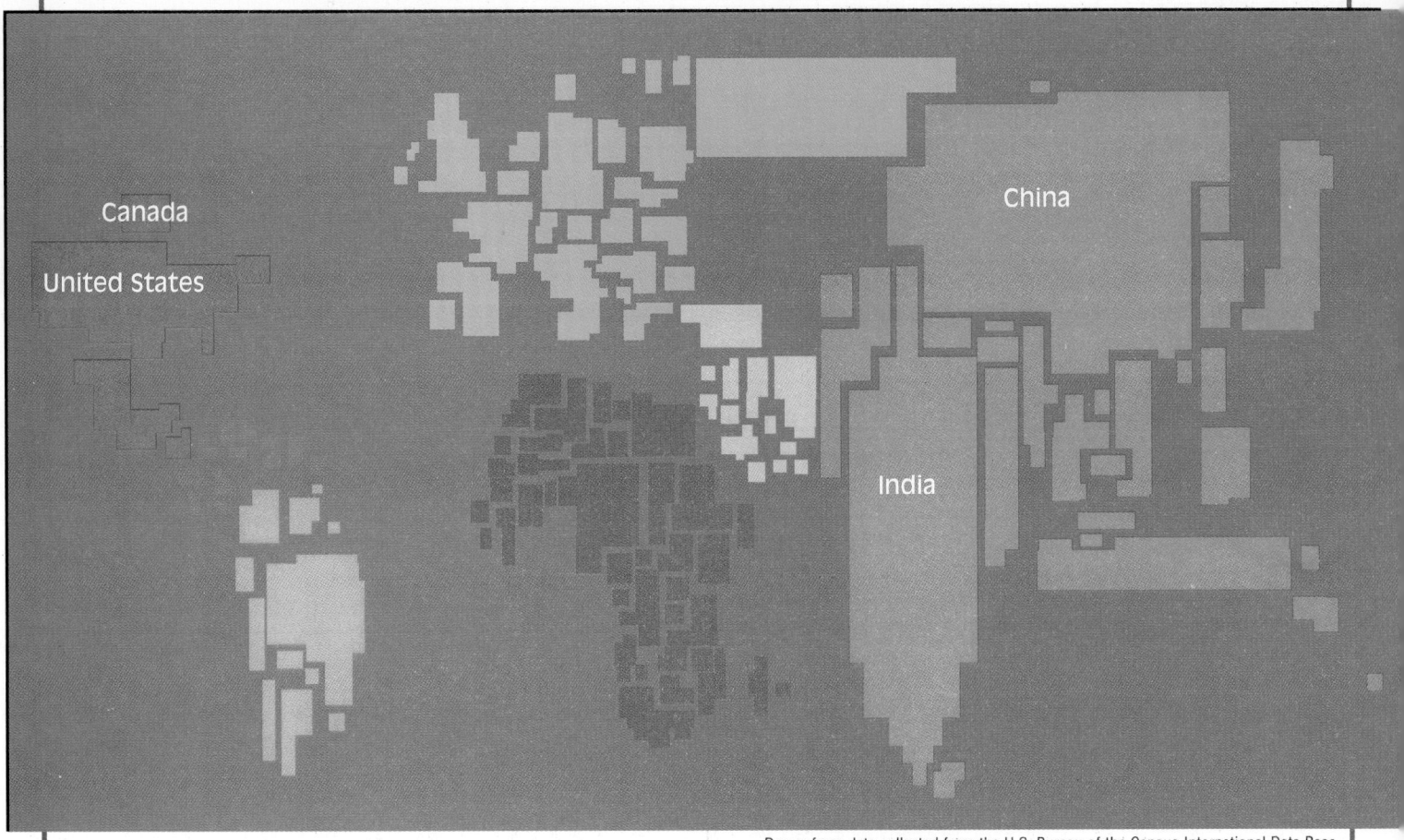

Drawn from data collected from the U.S. Bureau of the Census International Data Base

A cartogram of world population shows China and India as much larger than North American and European countries. Anyone looking at this cartogram can tell at a glance that there are more people in China than in the United States and Canada combined.

Written References:

Geographical Dictionaries and Almanacs

Maps and globes are the most important tools you will need to do your geography homework, but ***geographical dictionaries*** and ***almanacs*** are very useful, too.

Hoth·am, Mount \-ˈhäth-əm\. Mountain in the Darg Plateau, E Victoria, SE Australia, SW of Mt. Kosciusko; 6108 ft.
Ho–t'ien \ˈhō-ˈtyen\ *also* **Kho·tan** \ˈkō-ˈtän\. **1** River, W Sinkiang Uighur, W China; joins the Yarkand to form Tarim river, but dry much of the year.
2 Town, China. See KHOTAN 2.
Hotin. See KHOTIN.
Hot Spring. County in Arkansas. See table at ARKANSAS.
Hot Springs. 1 County in Wyoming. See table at WYOMING.
2 City, ⊗ of Garland co., W cen. Arkansas, in Ouachita Mts. 47 m. WSW of Little Rock; pop. (1970c) 35,631; health and tourist resort noted for its 47 thermal springs. Settled 1807; made, with surrounding area, a U.S. Government reservation 1832, **Hot Springs National Park** 1921 (see UNITED STATES, *National Parks*).
3 City, New Mexico. See TRUTH OR CONSEQUENCES.
4 City, ⊗ of Fall River co., SW corner of South Dakota, in foothills of Black Hills 48 m. S of Rapid City; pop. (1970c) 4434; health resort; thermal and mineral springs; sandstone quarries; mica, feldspar, gold, silver mines.
5 Village, Bath co., W Virginia, 5 m. SW of Warm Springs; mineral springs; Japanese diplomats interned here 1942 at beginning of war with Japan; scene of United Nations Conference on Food and Agriculture 1943.
Hot Springs Peak. Mountain, Humboldt co., NW Nevada; 6450 ft.
Hot Sul·phur Springs \-ˈsəl-fər-\. Town, ⊗ of Grand co., N Colorado; pop. (1970c) 220; hot sulfur springs.
Hotte, Massif de la. See SUD, MASSIF DU.
Hot·ten·tot Point \ˌhät-ᵊn-ˌtät-\. Cape on SW coast of South-West Africa, N of Lüderitz.
Hou·dain \ü-ˈdaⁿ\. Commune, Pas-de-Calais dept., N France, near Béthune; pop. (1962c) 8869; coal; has church (12th and 16th cents.); destroyed in World War I and rebuilt.
Hou·dan \ü-ˈdäⁿ\. Village, Yvelines dept., N France; pop. (1962c) 2358; has 15th–16th cent. church and keep of an early 12th cent. castle; noted for its poultry market, the Houdan breed of domestic fowl originating here.
Hou·deng–Goe·gnies \ü-ˌdäⁿ-gər-ˈnyē\. Commune, Hainaut prov., SW Belgium, on a tributary of the Haine, E of Mons; pop. (1969e) 8947; coal mines, smelting, woodworking, rope making, glassworks.
Houf·fa·lize \ˌü-fə-ˈlēz\. Village, Luxembourg prov., SE Belgium, 10 m. N of Bastogne; pop. (1969e) 1346; taken by Germans in [illegible] phase [illegible] of the Bulge Dec. 1944;

Geographical dictionaries, or *gazetteers*, are made up of alphabetical lists of geographic names. General gazetteers list all kinds of geographical features—including countries, cities, counties, landforms, bodies of water, and more—each followed by a brief description. The description usually tells the size and location of a feature, as well as how to pronounce its name. Gazetteers often define the location of a place by latitude and longitude coordinates, or by the number of miles it is from a well-known location.

New Jersey
(see States, U.S.)
Admission, area, capital.....386,640
Agriculture.....160,161,162,163
Altitudes (high, low).....385
Birth, death statistics.....939
Bridges.....622-624
Budget.....154
Chamber of Commerce.....640
Commerce at ports 674
Congressmen.....74,579,583
Courts, U.S. 596
Debt.....154
Ethnic, racial distribution.....640
Fair.....640
Geographic center 387
Governors 598,601
Income, per capita 640
Interest, laws, rates.....713
Marriages, divorce laws722-723,942
Name, origin of.....388
Population 129

Almanacs, unlike geographical dictionaries, are not organized alphabetically. Instead, they have detailed indexes to help you locate geographic information.

Parts of a Map

Elevation means the height of land above sea level. It is shown on maps using contour lines. Elevation can also be shown using shading or colors.

The **directional arrow** shows the directions—north, south, east, and west, and sometimes northwest, northeast, southeast, and southwest—in relation to the map. These directions show the orientation of the map. Most world maps show north on the top and south on the bottom, east to the right, and west to the left. Maps of smaller areas often use this standard orientation, too. Some directional arrows are plain and simple. Others are decorated.

A **compass rose** is an ornamental directional arrow often used on ship charts and old-fashioned maps. The rose is usually drawn from a circle divided into 360 degrees, and is used to tell directions from magnetic north, or 0 degrees (0°) on the compass.

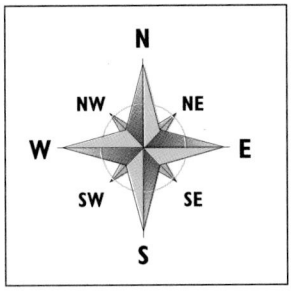

A map **index** is included on some maps. It is a list of place-names, complete with coordinates for finding the places on the map.

Symbols, or **icons**, are used on maps to represent real objects or places. Symbols can be simple dots to indicate cities, pictographs (tiny pictures) to indicate products, or colors to show location. Symbols are explained in the map key or legend.

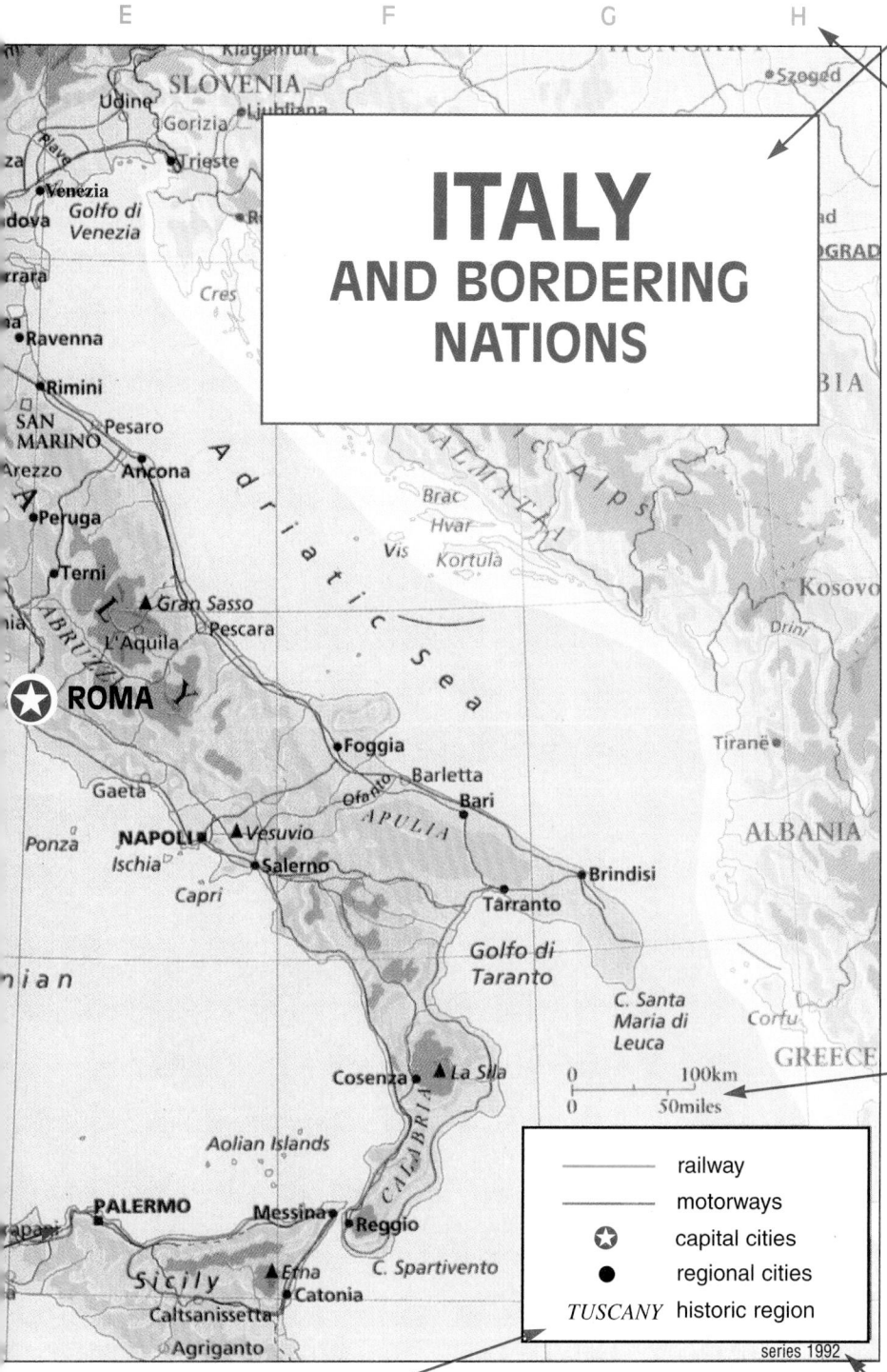

A **title** is included to tell map readers what the map is about.

Coordinates are a set of points or spaces, for example, *G-2*, located by using the map grid. The map index uses a map grid to help the reader find a specific location.

A **map grid** is a grid drawn on a map. You can read the map grid by looking in the margins of the map. The letters *A, B, C*, etc., run along the top and bottom margins. The numbers *1, 2, 3*, etc., run along the left and right margins. If a place is identified at *D–3*, simply find the square on the grid where column *D* and row *3* intersect. The map grid may or may not follow the geographic grid of latitude and longitude. Many highway maps have their own grids.

The map **scale** shows how the size of the map relates to the size of a real place. It may be stated in words, in combinations of words and numbers, and in ratios. For example, if a map's scale is 1 inch=100 miles, one inch on the map represents one hundred miles in the real world.

A **key** or **legend** lists the symbols used on a map and tells what each symbol means. For example, on some maps, cities can be represented by different sized dots. Large dots can stand for large cities and small dots for small cities or towns. Maps and keys are usually set apart from the rest of a map, often in a box.

Dates appear on many maps to tell when the map was drawn.

Understanding and Comparing Maps

To understand a map, you must be able to "read" it.

Once you can read maps, you can compare maps. By comparing the information on different maps, you can learn how many features work together to make a place special. For example, if you compare a map of North American waterways to a map of North American cities, you'll find that most cities are located on waterways. This is important geographical information—it shows that water is one thing people think about when deciding where to live.

Three Steps to Reading Maps

1 **Look at the map title. It will tell you what type of information, as well as which region or location, is shown on the map.**

2 **Look at the map scale. Some maps are very simple. Others show a lot of detail. The amount and type of detail on a map depend on the map scale, or the size of the area shown on the map. For example, it would be difficult to show the location of houses on a map of your state. However, it would be a logical feature on a map of your neighborhood. Successfully reading a map means understanding its scale.**

3 **Look at the legend. The legend will tell you what the symbols on the map mean. In order to understand the map fully, you will need to understand the symbols and the type of information they convey.**

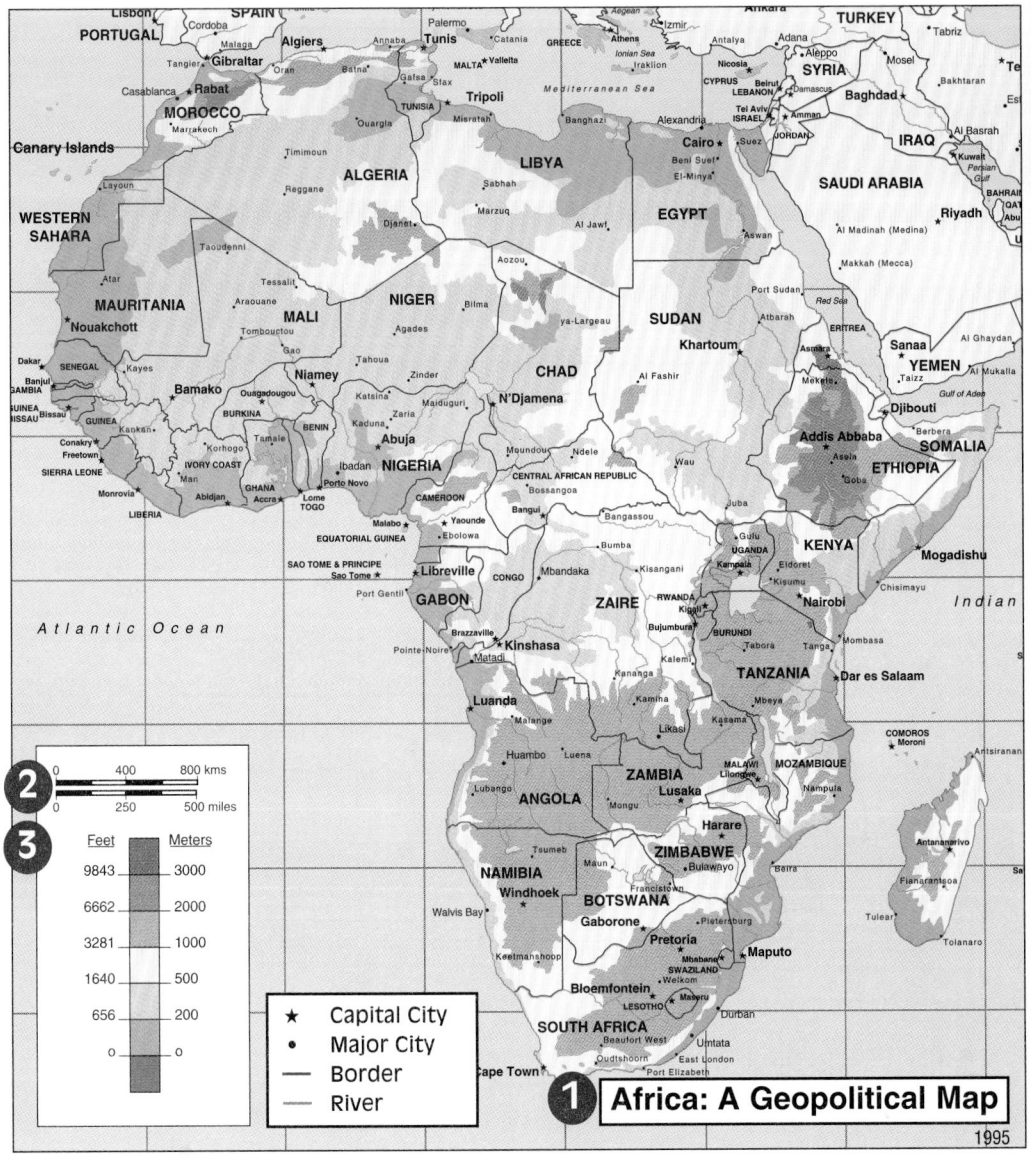

Three Steps to Comparing Maps

1 Choose maps that show information you want to compare.

2 Locate your area of interest on both maps.

3 Use the map symbols to read both maps. Then note how the maps are alike and how they are different. When you are using two or more maps, watch for map scale, the type of projections used (see p. 17), and the date the maps were published.

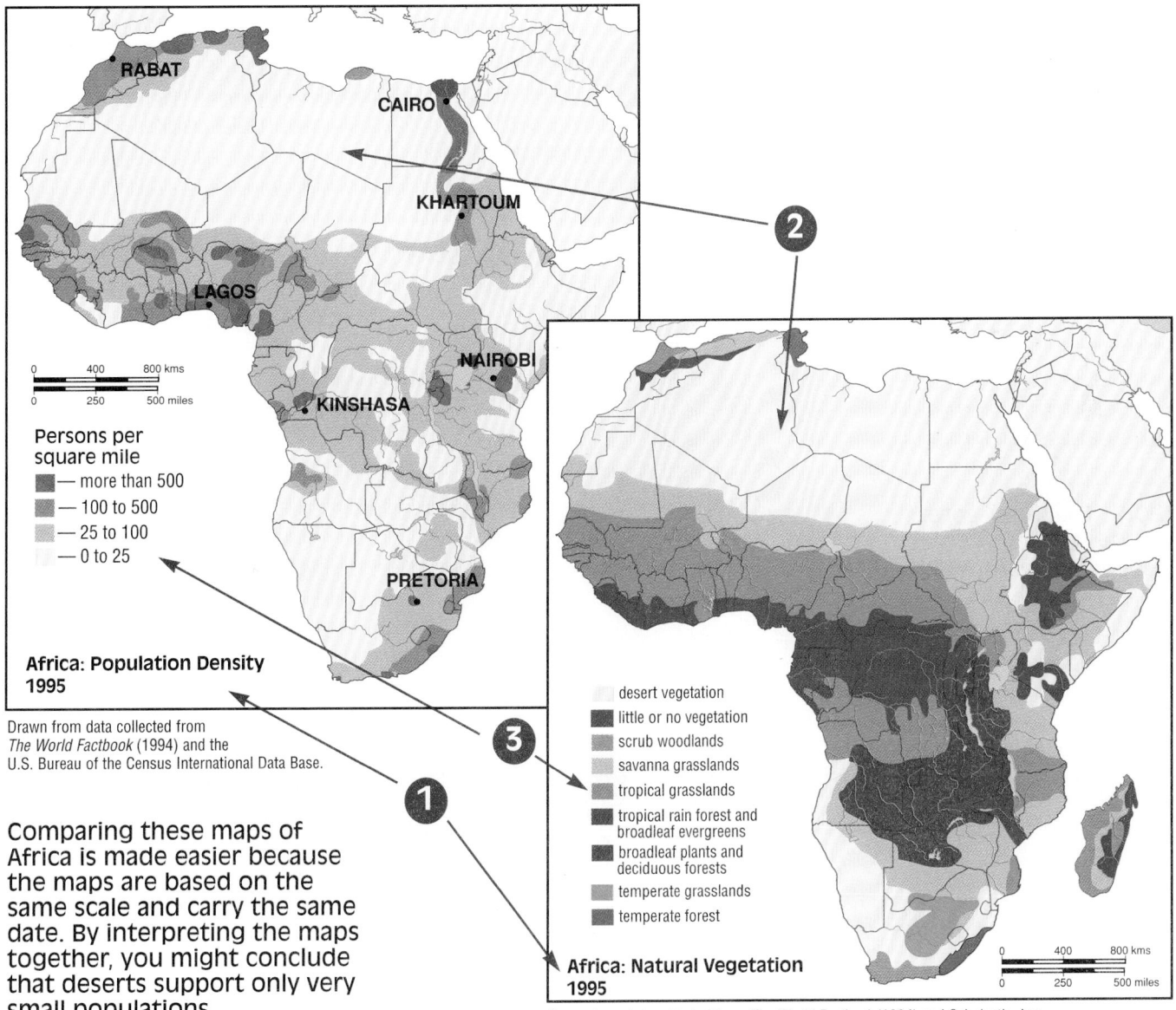

Drawn from data collected from *The World Factbook* (1994) and the U.S. Bureau of the Census International Data Base.

Drawn from data collected from *The World Factbook* (1994) and Scholastic, Inc.

Comparing these maps of Africa is made easier because the maps are based on the same scale and carry the same date. By interpreting the maps together, you might conclude that deserts support only very small populations.

LAND, WATER, AND AIR: THE PHYSICAL WORLD

1 The Land

How the Earth Was Formed

Geographers believe that about 4.6 billion years ago a cloud of dust particles came together to form a ball of melted rock. The ball cooled over several million years, forming the earth.

As the molten rock ball cooled, a thin solid layer formed over the surface of the earth. This layer is called the **crust**. The crust is about 2 miles thick under the deepest parts of the ocean and up to 75 miles thick under the tallest mountain peaks.

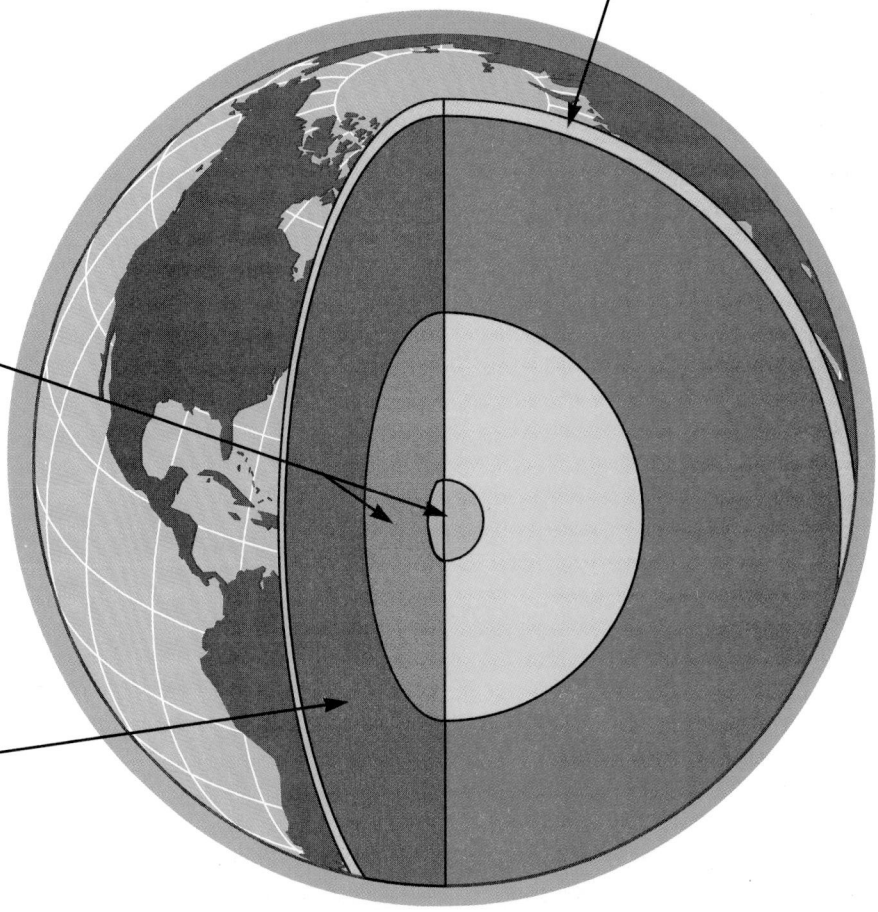

The earth's **core** has two parts: the **outer core** and the **inner core**. The outer core is made up of molten rock. The inner core is solid. The core has a radius of about 2,100 miles.

The **mantle** lies between the earth's crust and core. It is a layer of very hot, sometimes melted rock about 1,800 miles thick.

Plate Tectonics

Continents are the large landmasses on earth: Africa, Australia, Antarctica, North America, South America, and Eurasia. Eurasia is sometimes considered two continents, divided by the Ural Mountains and the Caspian Sea into Europe to the west and Asia to the east.

The crust of the earth is not one solid piece. It is broken into large pieces, called ***tectonic plates***. The plates are like enormous ships that float upon the earth's mantle.

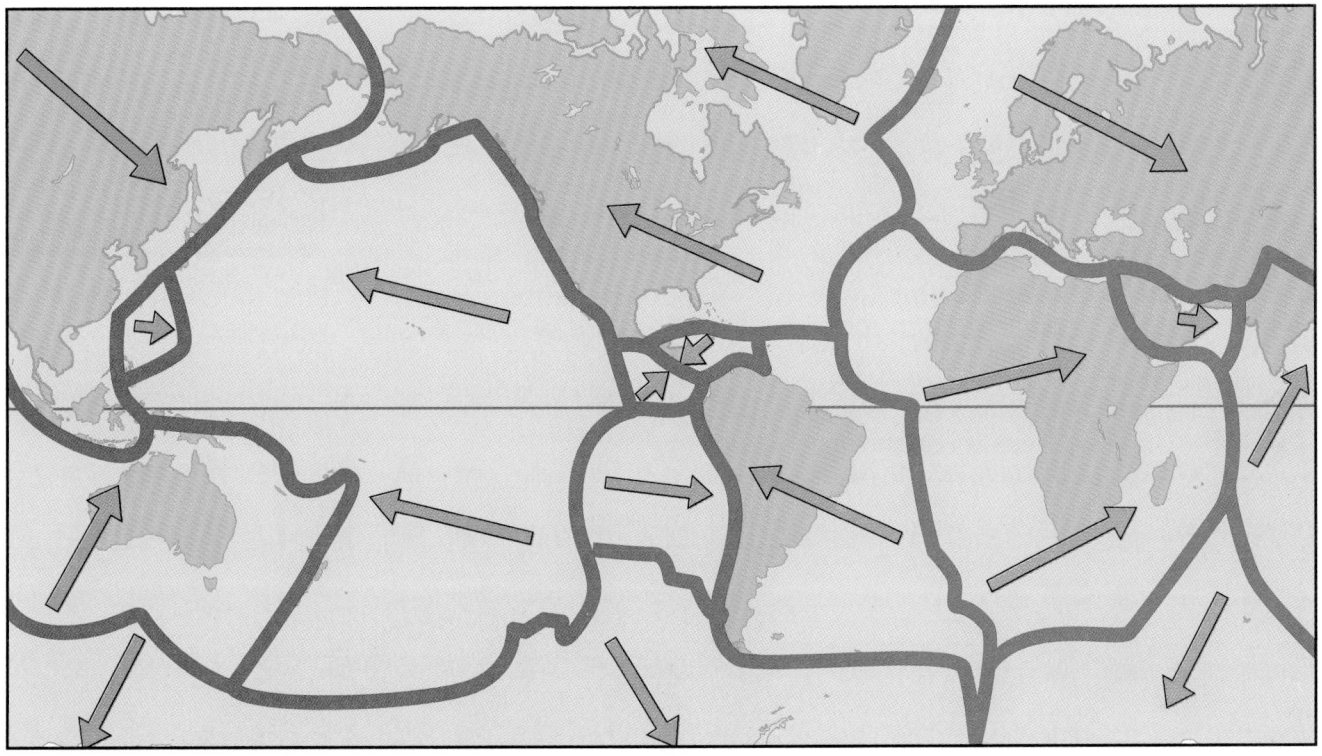

World map showing fault lines and the direction of tectonic plate movement.

Fault Lines

Fault lines occur along the edges where tectonic plates meet. As the plates move, a number of tectonic events occur along the fault lines.

Pangaea and Continental Drift

Scientists believe that about 200 million years ago, all the continents were connected. They formed a supercontinent that scientists call ***Pangaea***.

Then the continents separated at places where the tectonic plates broke apart. Like ships on water, the plates slowly moved apart, and the continents we know today were formed.

The continents are still moving. This movement is called ***continental drift***. In another 200 million years, the continents may be connected again or may have drifted into a completely different arrangement on the planet.

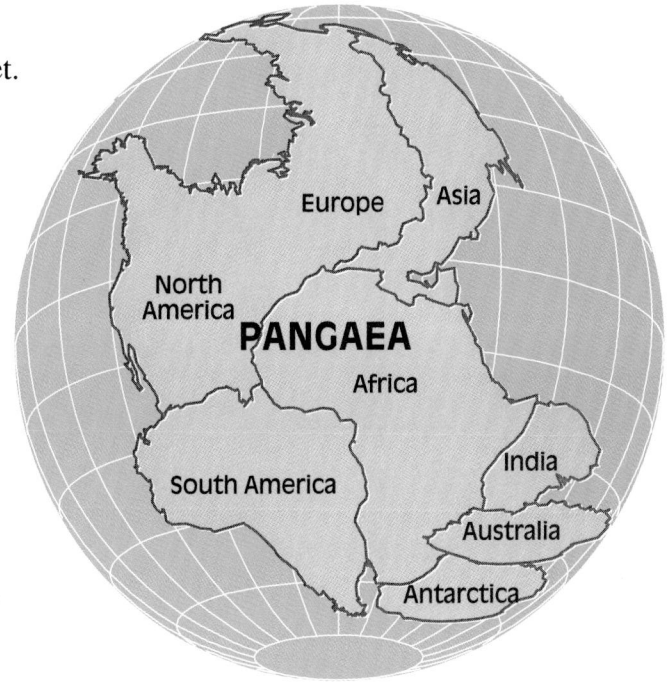

Tectonic Events That Shape the Land

Tectonic plates are moving in different directions at different speeds. The features on the surface of the earth tell us where the plates push beneath each other or collide.

Mountains

Most **volcanoes** form when molten rock from deep inside the earth rises to the surface at or near a fault line or a soft spot in a plate. The molten rock spurts out of the top of the volcano in the form of lava.

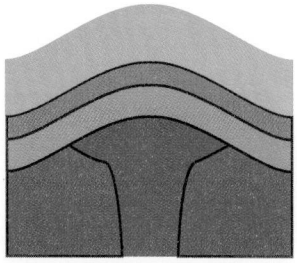

Dome mountains form when molten rock pushes up toward the earth's surface along a fault line but doesn't break through the surface of the earth.

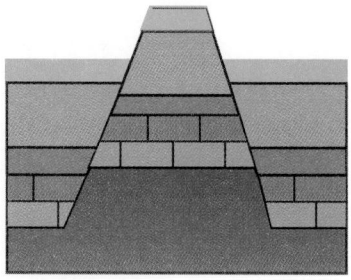

Block mountains form when blocks of rock split along fault lines and slide in opposite directions.

Fold mountains form when tectonic plates move against each other and push and squeeze up the crust of the earth.

VOLCANOES

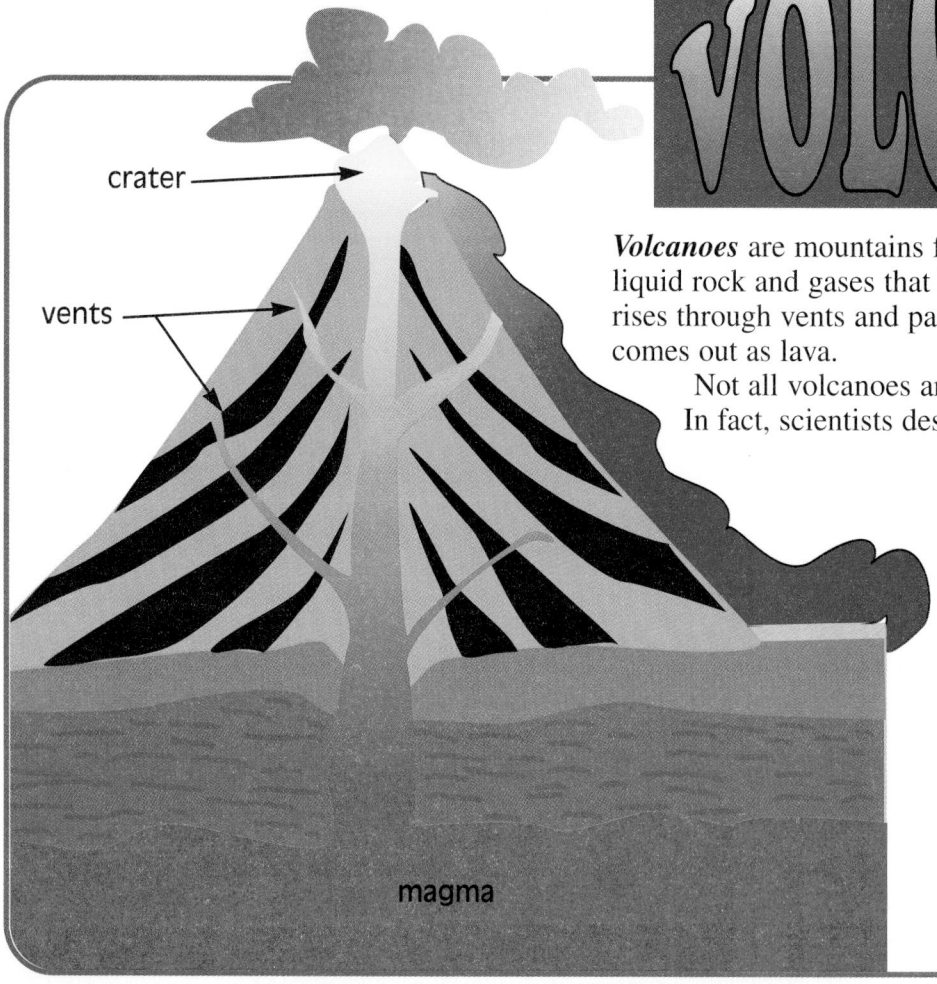

Volcanoes are mountains formed when the ***magma***, or red-hot liquid rock and gases that lie below the surface of the earth, rises through vents and passages in the earth's surface and comes out as lava.

Not all volcanoes are ***active***, or capable of erupting. In fact, scientists describe four types of volcanoes:

active	**erupting constantly**
intermittent	**erupting at regular intervals**
dormant	**inactive, but expected to become active again**
extinct	**inactive for hundreds of years**

Earthquakes

Earthquakes are sudden shifting movements in the earth's surface. Some earthquakes cannot even be felt, yet others are strong enough to knock down skyscrapers and twist highways as if they were ribbons.

Earthquakes happen when tectonic plates collide, separate, or scrape against one another along fault lines.

1

Forces push tectonic plates into one another, causing them to collide or scrape against each other.

2

Over thousands of years, the forces cause the rocks along the fault line to bend and twist.

3

Finally, the force becomes so great that the rocks break loose and jolt past each other, causing an earthquake.

THE RING OF FIRE

Where Volcanoes and Earthquakes Often Happen

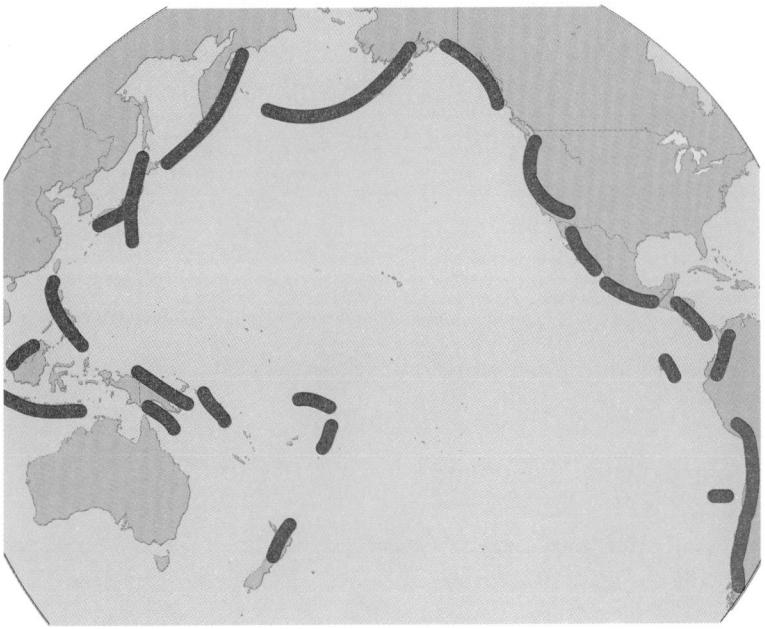

Volcanoes and earthquakes most frequently occur along the fault lines in the earth's tectonic plates. The Ring of Fire in the Pacific Ocean is the world's most active area of earthquake and volcanic activity. Why? The faults in the Atlantic are, for the most part, expanding, or moving away from each other. But in the Pacific, the the plates are colliding, or rubbing up against each other (see above, also p. 31).

Landforms

Landforms are the natural features of the earth's land surface, including mountains, other highlands, plains, and lowlands.

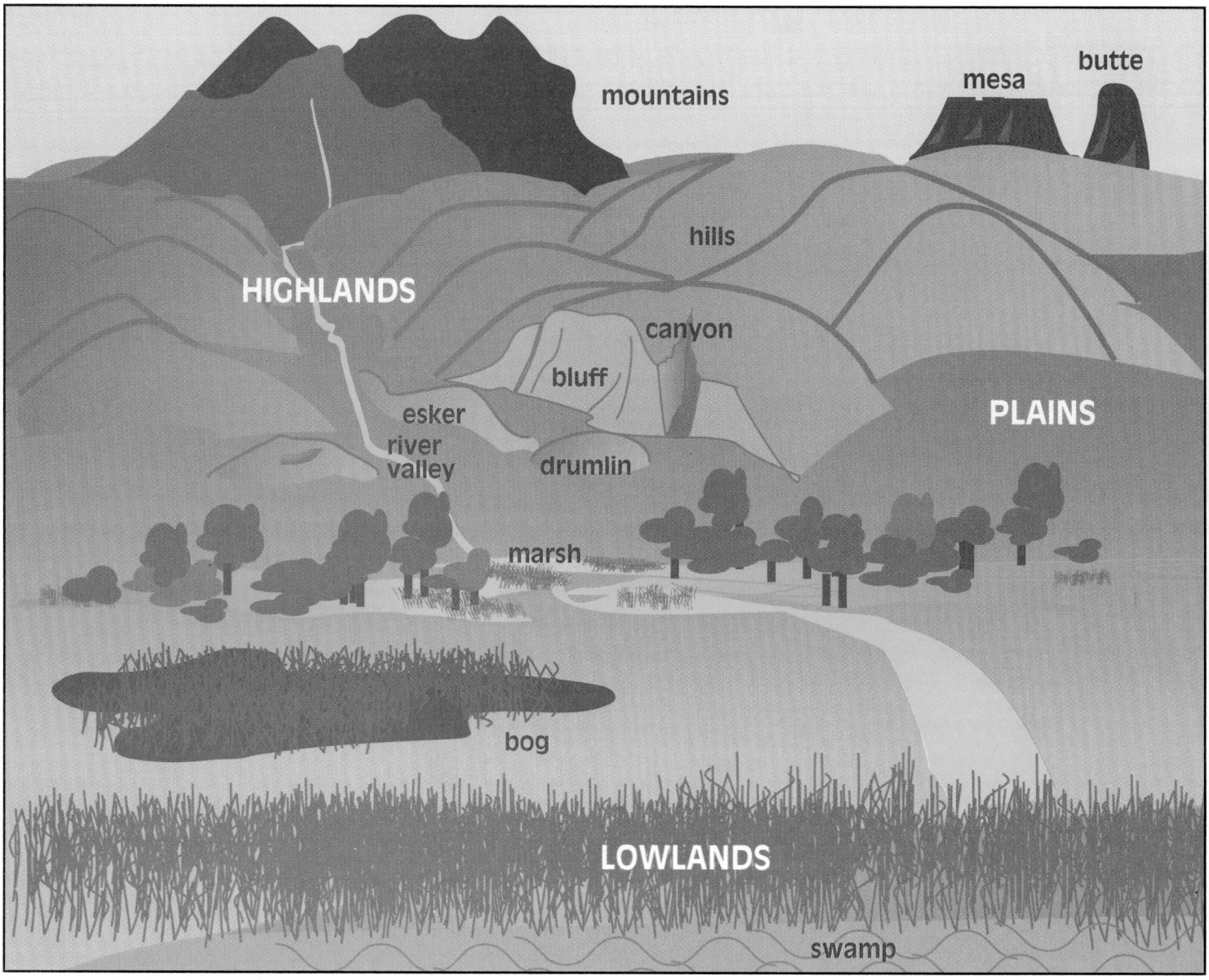

A composite landscape shows many kinds of landforms. (For definitions of the specific landforms, see Glossary pp. 88–99.)

Mountains and High Land

A ***mountain*** is any point on land that rises quickly to at least 1,000 feet above its surroundings. Some mountains are jagged and snowcapped, others are rounded and smooth. Some are volcanoes, with large craters in their tops.

Mountains exist, too, below the oceans. Some of these mountains, while deep under the salty water, rise even higher than Mount Everest, the highest mountain on the continents.

A ***hill*** is an area on the earth's surface that rises above the land, but not more than 1,000 feet above the surrounding area. Any high land that is not a mountain can be classified as a hill. However, geologists and geographers have developed a special vocabulary for high landforms based on how the landforms were created.

Plains

Plains are large, flat, mostly treeless areas of land.

Lowlands

A ***lowland*** is an area of land that is lower than the land surrounding it. Just as geologists and geographers have a special vocabulary for highlands, they have a special vocabulary for lowlands.

A ***valley*** is a natural low place in the earth's surface, often located between mountains or hills. The bottom of a valley is called its ***floor***, the sides its ***walls***. A ridge between valleys is called a ***divide***. Valleys with steep cliff walls are called ***canyons*** or ***gorges***.

Other natural lowlands are ***wetlands***, where the water level stays at or above the land's surface for most of the year. ***Bogs, marshes,*** and ***swamps*** are the most common types of wetlands.

Erosion and Weathering

Erosion is the gradual wearing away of land by the action of wind, water, or glaciers. ***Weathering*** is the gradual breakdown of rocks by weather, including wind, rain, snow, and changes in temperature (see p. 44). Erosion and weathering work together constantly to change the landforms on Earth.

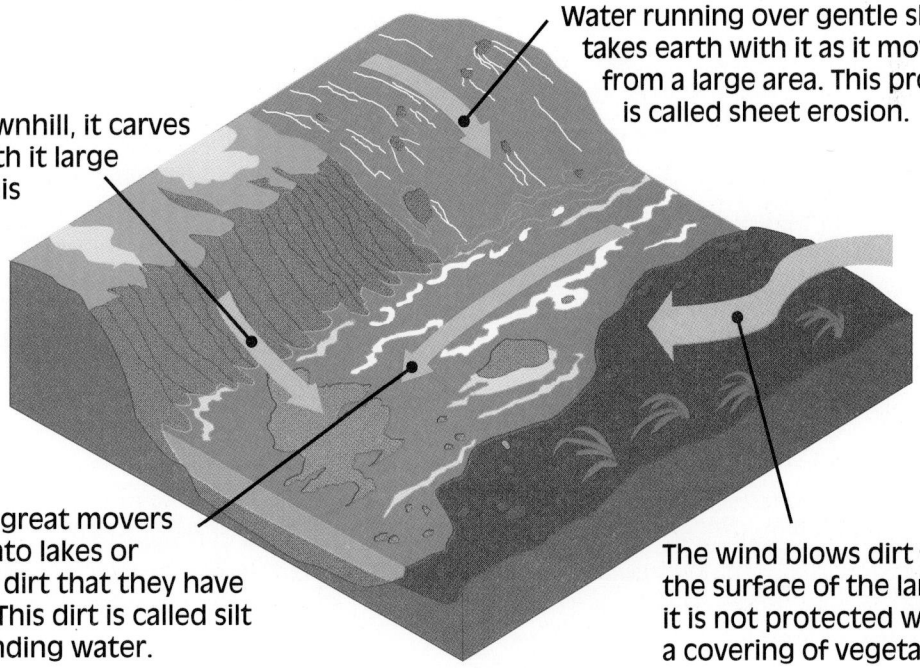

The study of the earth's physical features is called geomorphology.

Glaciers

Glaciers are slow-moving sheets of ice found in high mountain valleys and polar regions. Glaciers cover about six million square miles, or three percent of the earth's surface.

Glaciers form at high latitudes and high elevations, where it is cold enough that more snow falls than melts or evaporates. Over the years, the snow gets deeper and deeper. Pressure from the weight of the snow finally turns the snow into huge sheets of ice. These ice sheets flow, like slow-moving rivers, down mountainsides until they reach warmer air along the oceans or at lower elevations. There the ice sheets melt or break off to form floating ***icebergs***.

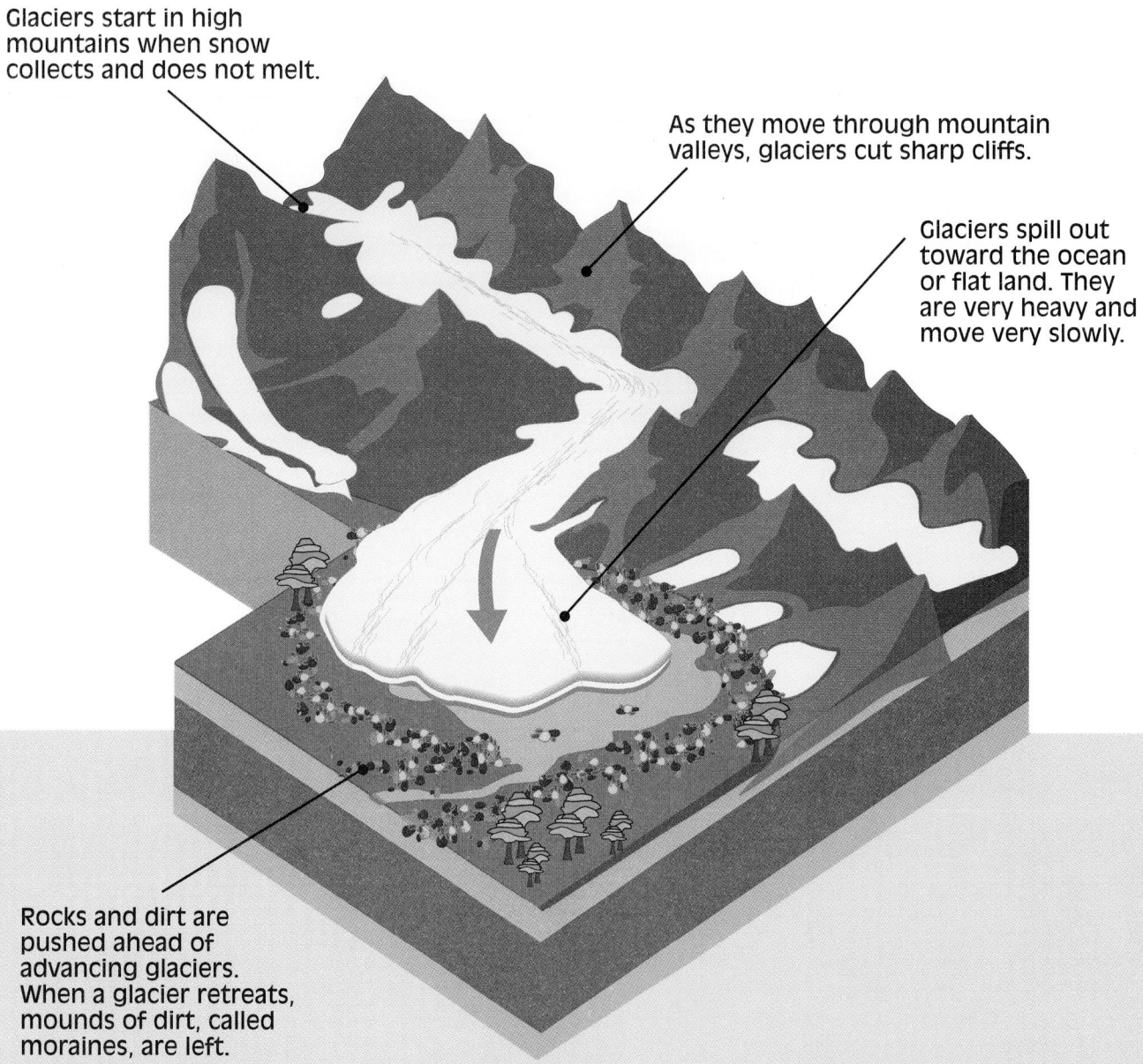

2 The Water

Oceans

Oceans are large bodies of salt water that cover almost three-fourths of the earth's surface.

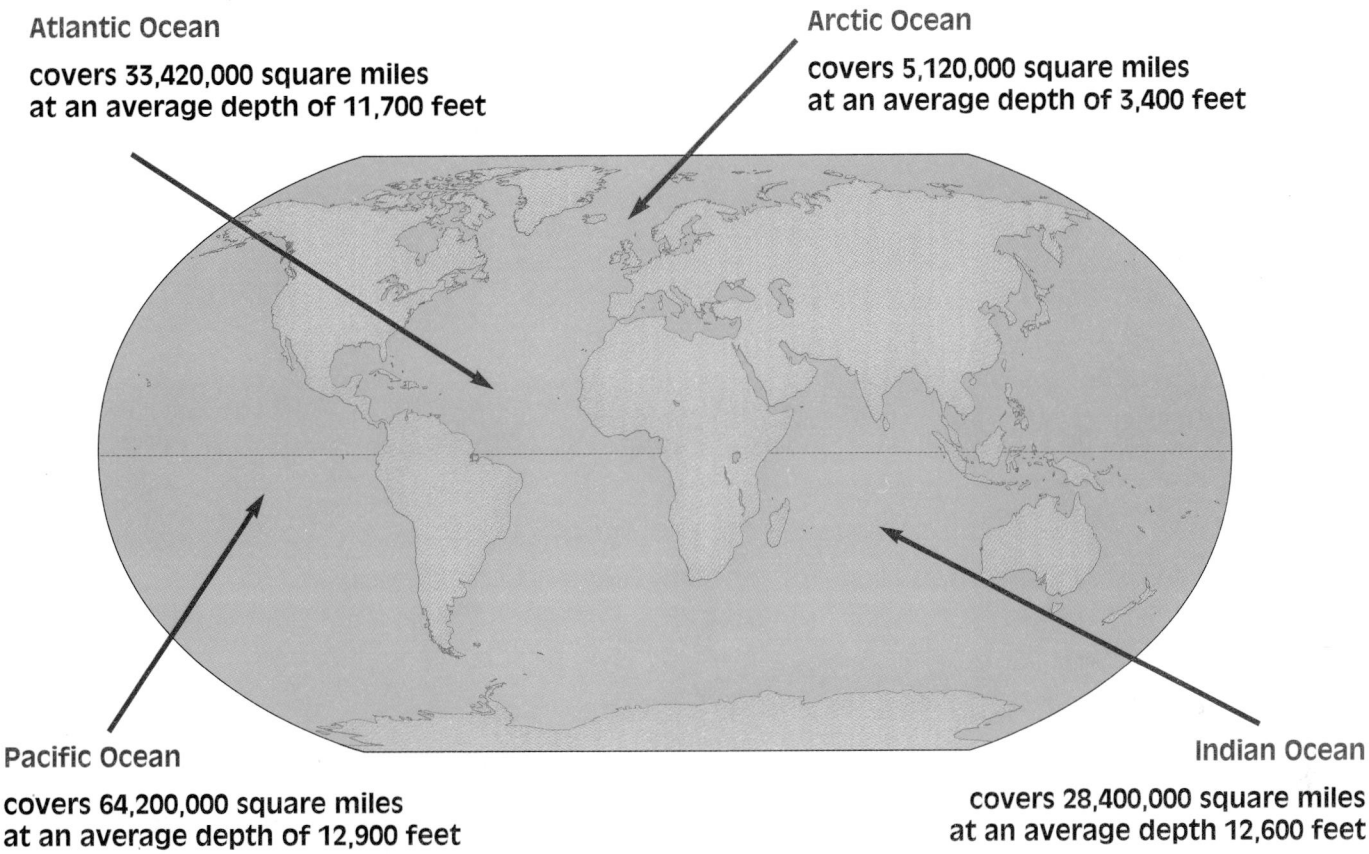

THE BRINY DEEP

	Depth (Feet)	Depth (Meters)
Pacific Ocean		
Mariana Trench	35,800	10,900
Tonga Trench	35,400	10,800
Philippine Trench	33,000	10,000
Kermadec Trench	33,000	10,000
Atlantic Ocean		
Puerto Rico Trench	28,200	8,600
South Sandwich Trench	27,300	8,300
Cayman Trench	24,700	7,500
Romanche Gap	24,400	7,700
Indian Ocean		
Java Trench	23,400	7,100
Ob' Trench	22,600	6,900
Diamantina Trench	21,700	6,600
Vema Trench	21,000	6,400
Arctic Ocean		
Eurasia Basin	17,900	5,500
Mediterranean Sea		
Ionian Basin	16,900	5,200

The ocean floor, like the surface of the land, is made up of many features. Huge trenches drop off deeply from underwater plains. Plateaus and ridges rise thousands of feet to form mountains on the ocean floor. As on the land, the underwater surface is formed by the movements of tectonic plates and shaped by the movement of water (see p. 31 and below).

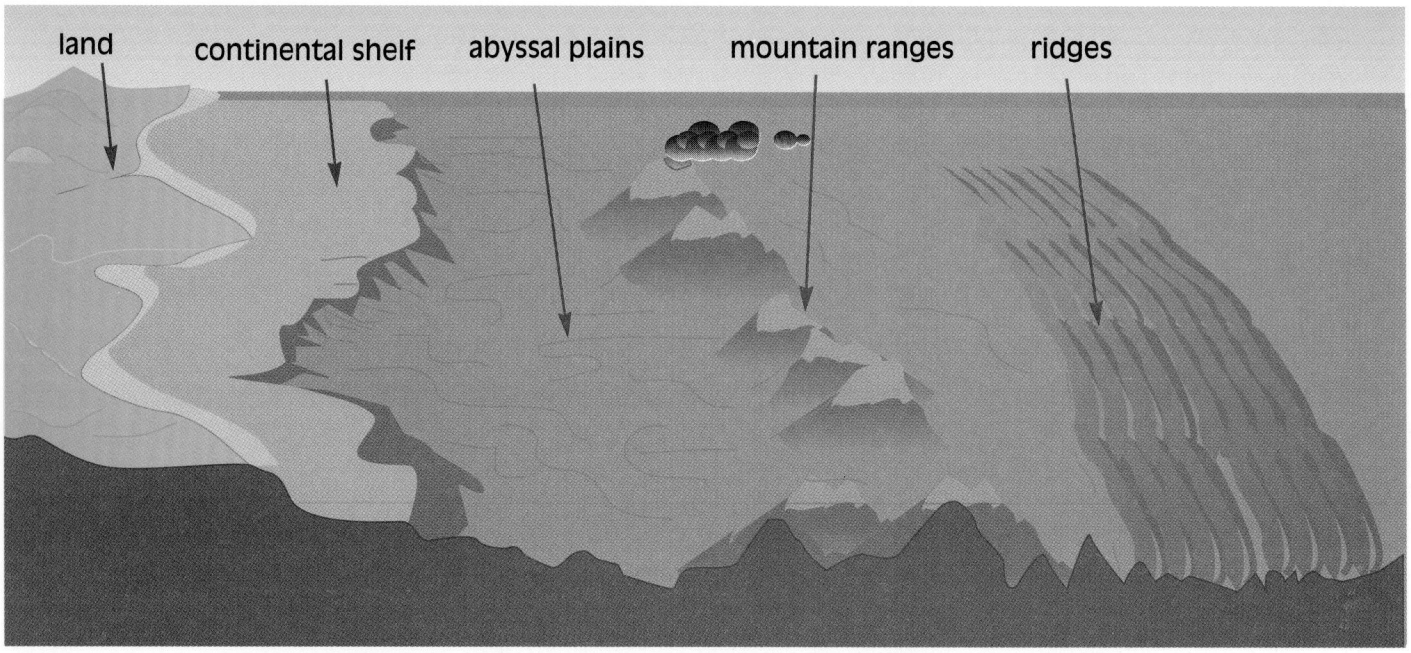

A cross section of the ocean floor shows some of the many features of its landscape.

Ocean currents flow in predictable patterns throughout the major water bodies of the earth.

Natural Events Under Water

As on land, erosion, earthquakes, and volcanoes make regular changes under water.

In addition to changing the ocean floor, underwater volcanoes and earthquakes cause giant surges of water in the ocean. These surges of water aren't noticeable at sea, but when they near shore, they can rise anywhere from six to sixty feet high. When the surge of water, called a ***tsunami***, hits land, it can cause dangerous flooding and wash away homes, roads, and buildings in its path.

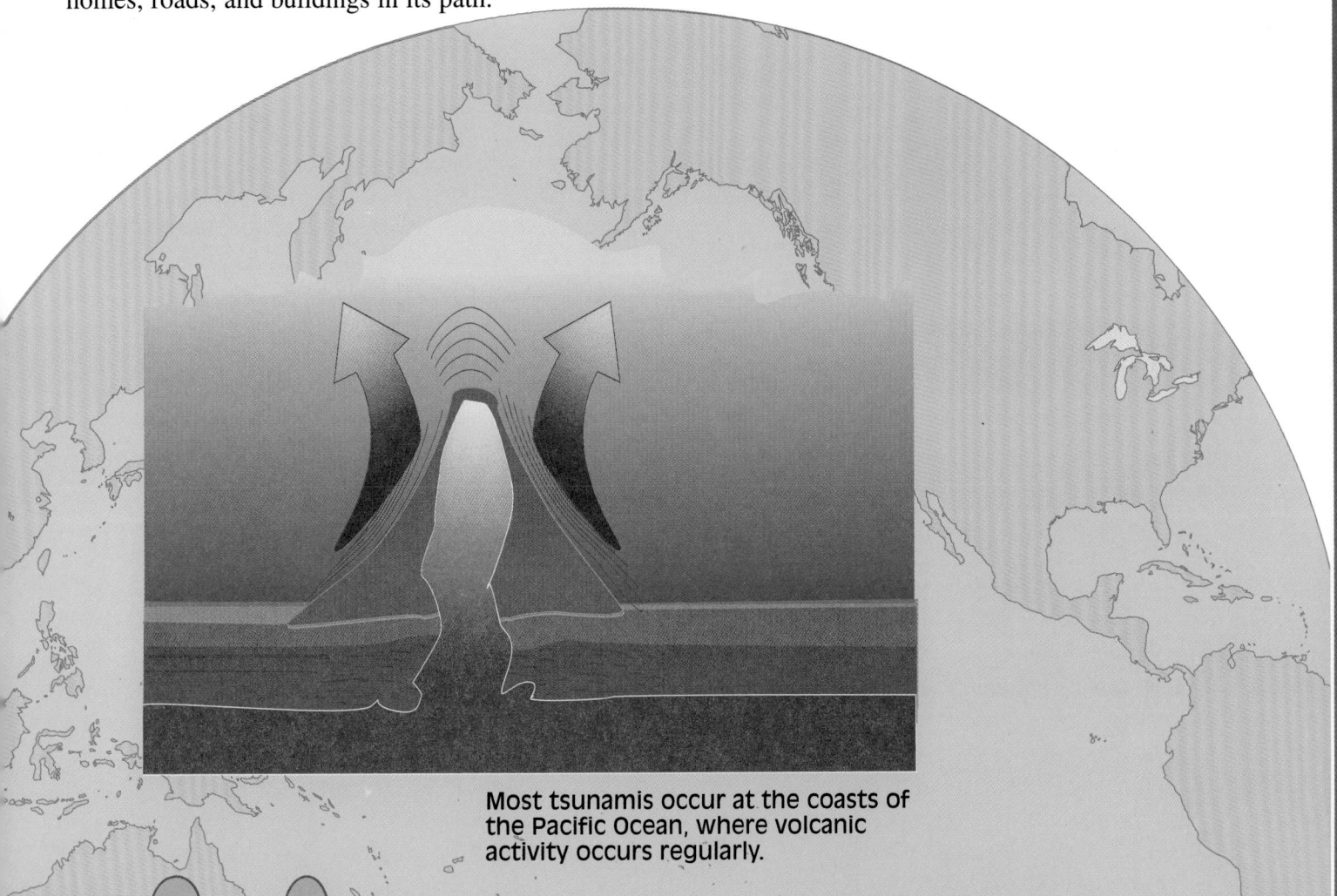

Most tsunamis occur at the coasts of the Pacific Ocean, where volcanic activity occurs regularly.

Tides

Tides are the daily changes in the levels of water in the oceans and seas. They are caused by the gravitational pull of the moon and sun on the earth. The moon affects tides more than the sun does. As the earth rotates on its axis, different parts of the earth face the moon (see pp. 13-14). The energy from gravity moves the water to the part of the ocean nearest the moon, where it piles up, or bulges. Oceans and seas on the opposite side of the earth bulge because of the way the earth spins. The bulges of water travel around the earth from east to west. They bring high tides to ocean and seashores every 12 hours. When the bulge reaches a shore, it is high tide. When it is away from the shore, it is low tide.

Rivers

Rivers are bodies of water than begin at a source and flow downhill between ***banks*** of earth to a ***mouth***, where they empty into a larger body of water. Most large rivers have three parts, or ***courses: upper***, ***middle***, and ***estuary***.

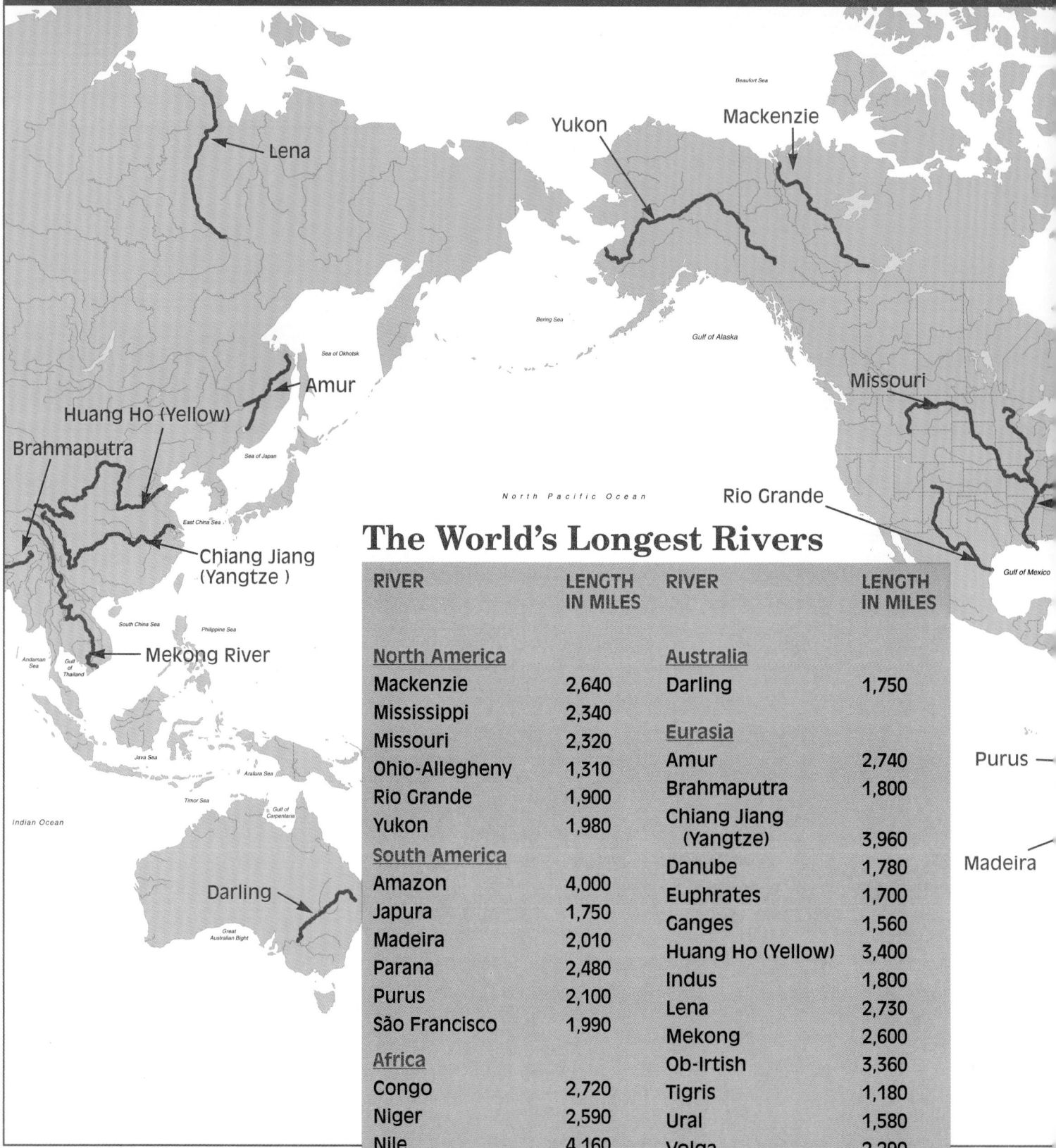

World's Major River Systems

The World's Longest Rivers

RIVER	LENGTH IN MILES	RIVER	LENGTH IN MILES
North America		**Australia**	
Mackenzie	2,640	Darling	1,750
Mississippi	2,340		
Missouri	2,320	**Eurasia**	
Ohio-Allegheny	1,310	Amur	2,740
Rio Grande	1,900	Brahmaputra	1,800
Yukon	1,980	Chiang Jiang (Yangtze)	3,960
South America		Danube	1,780
Amazon	4,000	Euphrates	1,700
Japura	1,750	Ganges	1,560
Madeira	2,010	Huang Ho (Yellow)	3,400
Parana	2,480	Indus	1,800
Purus	2,100	Lena	2,730
São Francisco	1,990	Mekong	2,600
Africa		Ob-Irtish	3,360
Congo	2,720	Tigris	1,180
Niger	2,590	Ural	1,580
Nile	4,160	Volga	2,290
Zambezi	1,700	Yenisey	2,540

Greenland Sea
Baffin Bay
Norwegian Sea
Yenisey
Ob-Irtysh
Gulf of Bothnia
Labrador Sea
North Sea
Baltic Sea
Volga
Ural
North Atlantic Ocean
English Channel
Caspian Sea
Aral Sea
Bay of Biscay
Danube
Black Sea
Ohio-Allegheny
Tyrrhenian Sea
Ionian Sea
Mississippi
Mediterranean Sea
Tigris
Ganges
Persian Gulf
Nile
Euphrates
Gulf of Oman
Arabian Sea
Red Sea
Indus
Bay of Bengal
Gulf of Aden
Japura
Amazon
Niger
São Francisco
Indian Ocean
Congo
South Atlantic Ocean
Parana
Zambezi

Parts of a River

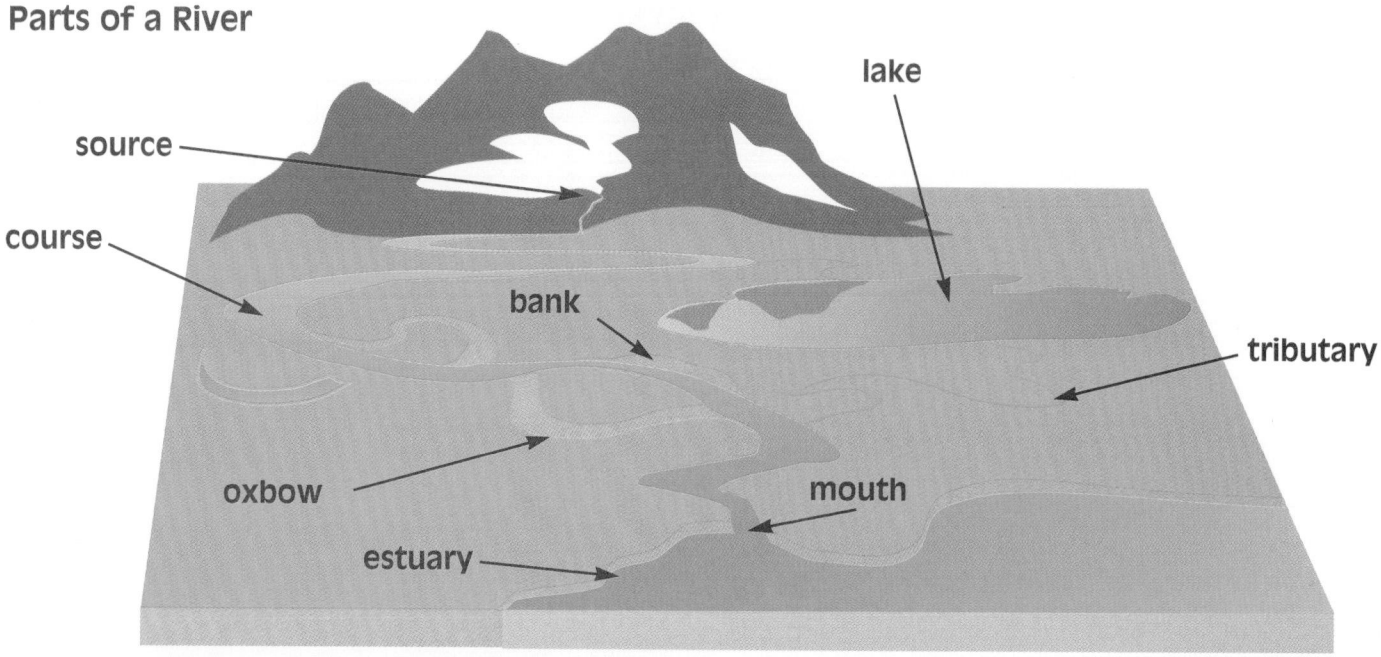

The source of the river shown here is melted water from a glacier, although rivers also form from the waters of highland springs and lakes flowing downhill, and from a combination of these waters. All rivers flow from a source to a mouth, where river waters empty into a larger body of water, sometimes another river, or a bay, gulf, lake, sea, or ocean. (For definitions of specific river parts, see Glossary, pp. 88-99.)

Seas, Gulfs, and Bays

Seas are large bodies of salt or fresh water that are partly or completely enclosed by land. ***Gulfs*** and ***bays*** are large bodies of ocean or sea water that are partly surrounded by land. Bays are usually smaller than gulfs.

Lakes

Lakes are natural and human-made low spots on the land that have filled with water from flooding, melting glacial ice, rivers, and groundwater traveling downhill.

Most lakes hold fresh water, although some hold salt water.

Ponds ***are small lakes.***

Four Kinds of Lakes

Lakes can be divided into four types, depending on how they are formed.

Crater Lake

Water collects in craters left by volcanoes.

Glacial Lake

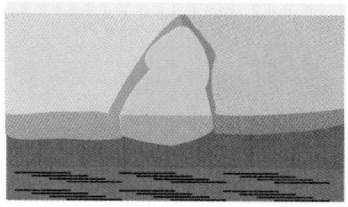

Ice from glaciers carves depressions (low areas) in the landscape. The ice melts and forms a lake.

Rift Valley Lake

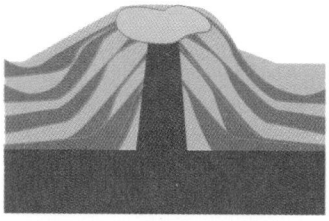

Shifts in plates on the earth's surface form depressions that fill with water.

Artificial Lake

Lakes are created artificially by building dams on rivers or by digging depressions and filling them with water from nearby sources.

3 The Air: Atmosphere, Weather, and Climate

The Atmosphere

The ***atmosphere*** is the air that surrounds the earth. It is made up of five main layers. Although we don't pay much attention to the atmosphere most of the time, it is taller than any mountain, it extends past the horizon, and it is a very important element in the earth's geography. Without the atmosphere, the many variations in weather and climate that we know on the earth would not occur, and without those variations, different natural regions would not exist (see p. 50). Also, weather and climate affect the landforms physically through the processes of erosion and weathering (see p. 35).

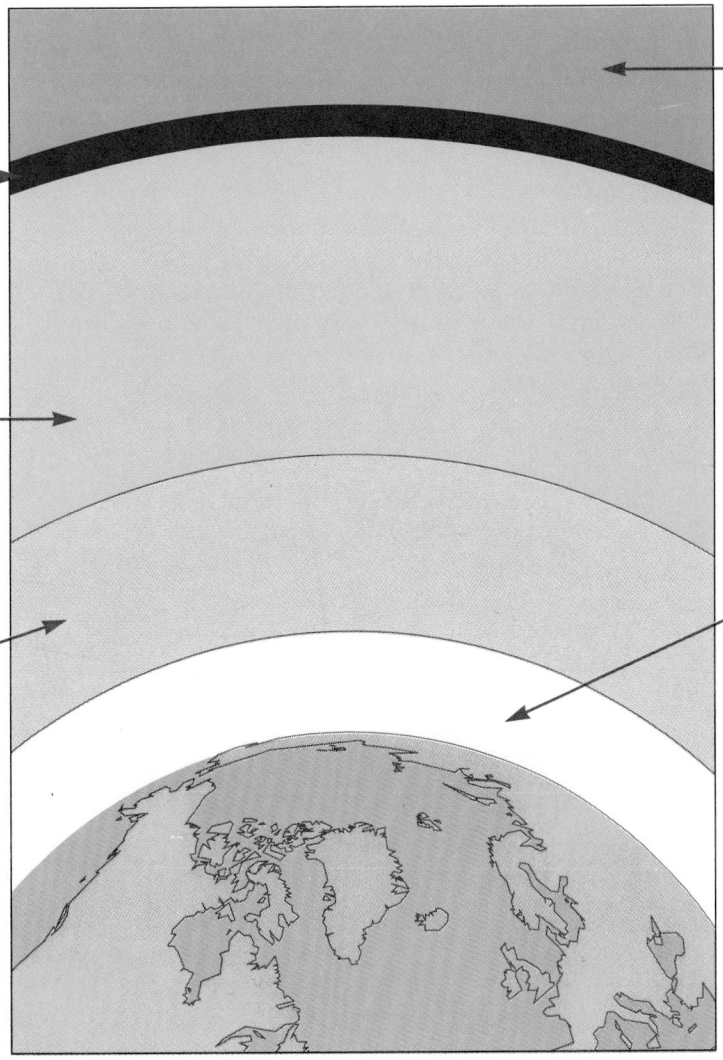

Exosphere

The border between the earth and space at about 310 miles. Satellites revolve around the earth in the exosphere.

Mesosphere

Ranges to about 50 miles. Temperatures drop to under -100°F.

Stratosphere

Stretches to about 30 miles. Icy winds blow through the lower parts, speeding supersonic jets like the Concorde to their destinations. Above the clouds, the air is usually dry and clear. The ozone layer, which absorbs harmful ultraviolet rays from the sun, is here.

Thermosphere

Ranges to about 400 miles above the earth's surface. Within the thermosphere, electrically charged particles called ions make up the ionosphere. Radio waves beamed up through the atmosphere bounce back to earth from the ion layers.

Troposphere

About 12 miles thick at the equator and 5 miles thick at the poles. More than half the atmosphere's gases, water vapor, and dust particles are in the first 4 miles. We live here. Clouds and weather form here, too.

Weather and Climate

Weather is the day-to-day change in the atmosphere around us. The weather in a place varies constantly. It can be sunny and warm one day, cool and cloudy the next. Some days it rains, others it snows. Although many elements make up weather, two of the most important are temperature and precipitation (rain, snow, sleet, hail, or drizzle). The third most important element is wind.

Climate is the usual weather in an area over a long period of time. Some words that describe different climates are tropical, temperate, and arctic. (See also Biomes, pp. 51-56).

Heat

Most of the heat on Earth comes from the sun. (The rest radiates outward from the very hot interior of the earth.) The heat from the sun begins as sunlight passing through the atmosphere and being absorbed into the earth. It then changes to heat and rises from the surface of the earth to warm the atmosphere. This warming of the atmosphere near the earth's surface helps create wind systems and the patterns of weather.

The most important cause of weather is heat in the atmosphere. But not all sunlight that enters the earth's atmosphere is converted to heat. Some of the light is reflected back into space from the white tops of clouds and tiny particles of ice and water in the atmosphere. Some of the light reaches the surface of the earth and reflects off snow, water, and other reflective surfaces. Plants with green leaves absorb some of the light and change it into sugar and starch in the process called ***photosynthesis***. The rest of the light is absorbed into the earth, converted into heat, and radiated back into the atmosphere, where its rising and cooling help create wind and weather.

Air Pressure

The weight of the atmosphere pressing down on the earth is called ***air pressure***. Because warm air is less dense than cold air, warm air forms areas of low air pressure and cold air forms areas of high pressure. High pressure usually means clear skies and sunny weather. Low pressure usually means cloudy, rainy (or snowy) weather.

Dalol, Ethiopia, has the highest annual average temperature on Earth—94°F. Nedostupnosti Polyus, Antarctica, has the coldest annual average temperature—-72°F. Nedostupnosti Polyus means "inaccessible pole."

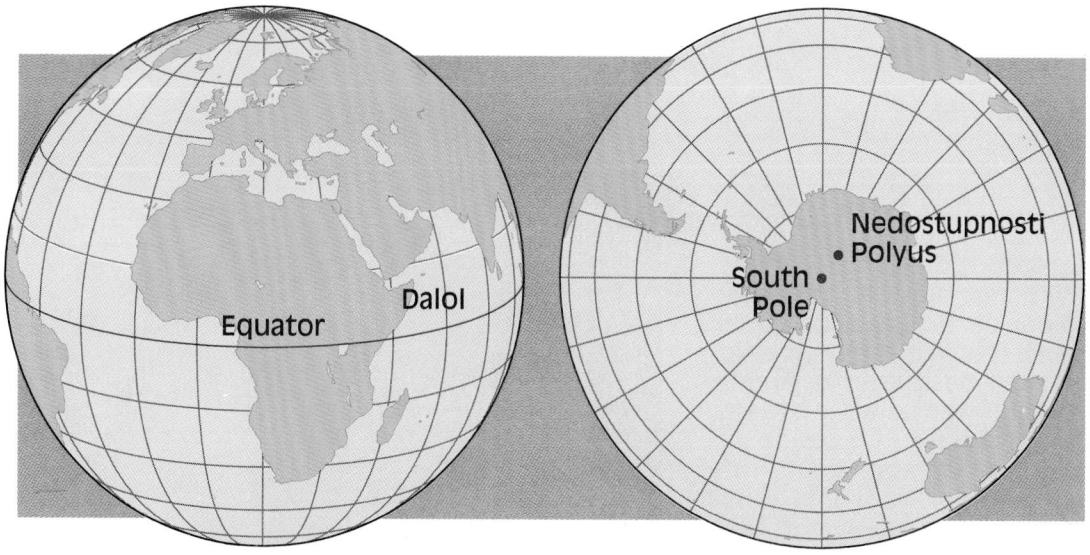

Weather Fronts

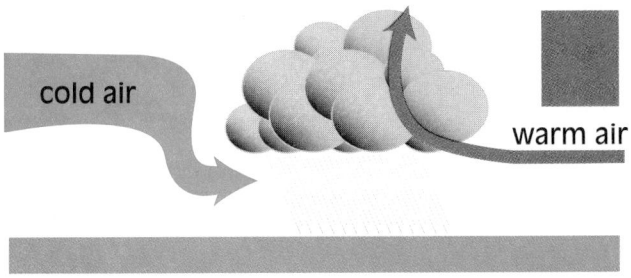

Cold Front

Cold air moves in on an area of warm air. The heavier cold air slides in underneath the lighter warm air mass and pushes it up. ***Clouds*** and ***thunderstorms*** often form.

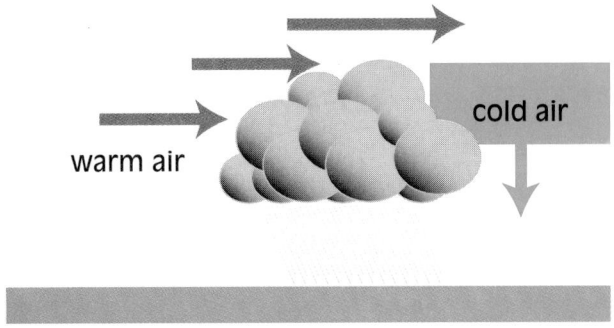

Warm Front

Warm air moves in on an area of cold air. The lighter warm air slides over the heavy, cold air, creating a front with a gentle slope. Clouds form, usually leading to some form of ***precipitation.***

Stationary Front

Cold and warm air masses meet, but neither moves on the other. Clouds often form at the boundary.

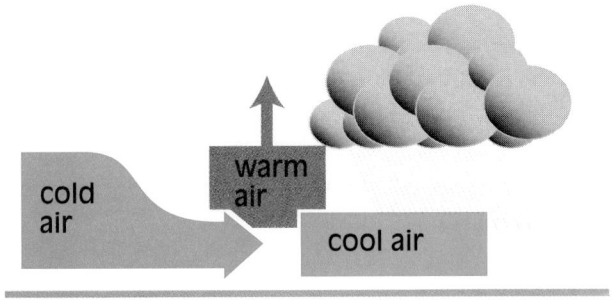

Occluded Fronts

When warm air is trapped between cold and cool air, it is forced upward. Clouds and precipitation usually result.

In places where the sun's rays reach the earth most directly and for the longest periods of time, the climate is warmer than in other places. Likewise, the coldest places are located where the sun's rays reach the earth less directly and for shorter periods of time.

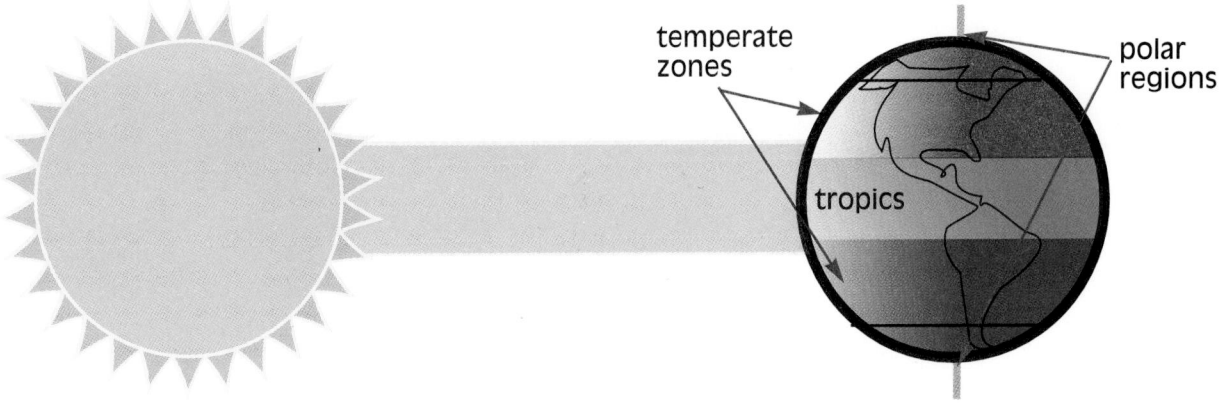

Water Heaters: Land and Ocean Temperatures

Oceans heat up more slowly than landmasses. They also cool down more slowly. That means that in the summer the ocean is cooler than the land. It cools the air above it. This cool ocean air moves across the coastal land, keeping it cool. In winter, the water is warmer than the land, so the ocean air helps warm the air over coastal land. Temperatures vary less from summer to winter near oceans than they do in the middle of continents.

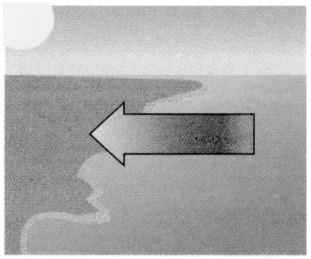

In summer, the cooler water cools the air that moves from the sea to the coast.

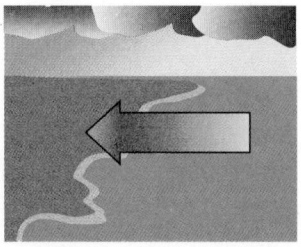

In winter, the warmer water warms the air that moves from the sea to the coast.

Air

When air moves between areas of high and low pressure, ***wind*** results. The greater the difference in the pressure, the greater the speed of the wind. But air doesn't move in a straight line from one area to another. Instead, winds circle areas of high and low pressure, moving in opposite directions.

Warm air rises at the equator, and winds move in from north and south to take its place. The warm air cools and falls at around 30 degrees of latitude north and south, returning to the equator to replace other rising air. This circulation helps to cause similar air movements between 30 and 60 degrees latitude and between 60 degrees and the poles. The winds do not blow directly north and south because Earth's rotation skews them at an angle.

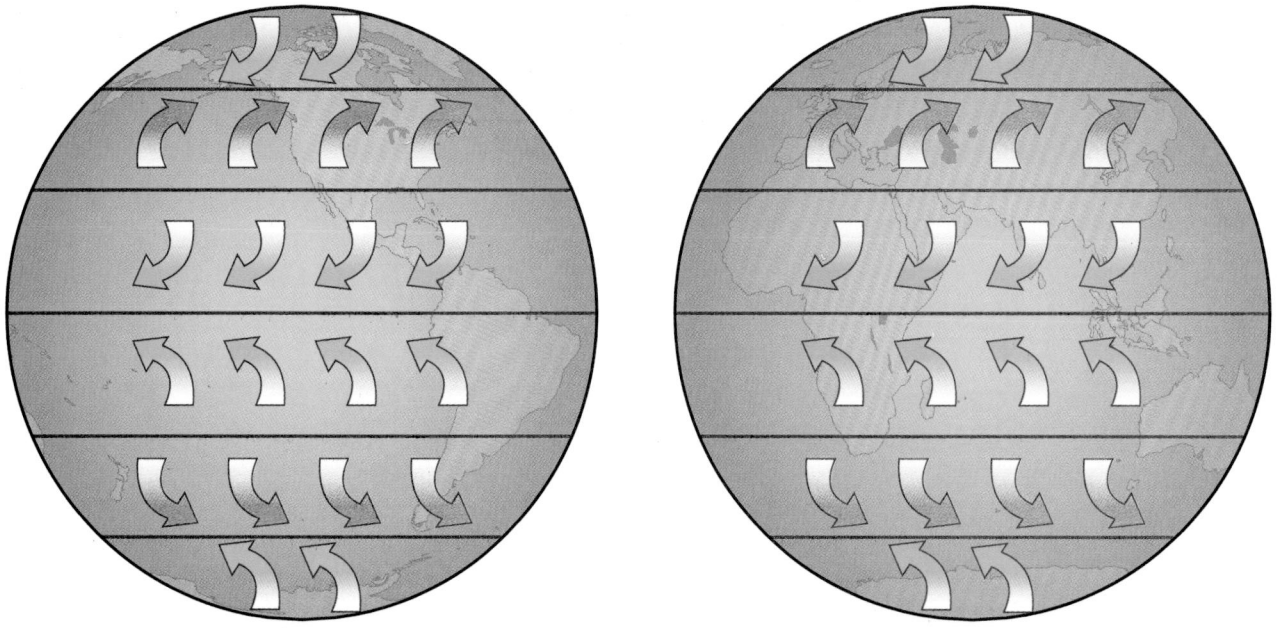

Prevailing wind patterns around the earth.

HURRICANES, TORNADOES, TYPHOONS, AND CYCLONES

Hurricanes, tornadoes, typhoon, and cyclones are spirals of air moving around areas of intense low pressure.

Tornadoes are small, tightly spiraling storms that occur over land, most often forming over the Great Plains and in the upper midwest of the United States from late spring until fall. They also occur infrequently in many other parts of the world.

Hurricanes, typhoons, and ***cyclones*** are three names for large spiraling storms that form over water and then sometimes move onto land, causing great damage. They can topple trees and lift houses off their foundations. When these storms occur in the North Atlantic Ocean, Caribbean Sea, Gulf of Mexico, or in the eastern North Pacific near Mexico and Central America, they are called hurricanes. When they occur in the North Pacific, west of the International Date Line, near China, Japan, and Southeast Asia, they are called typhoons. When they occur in the South Pacific or the India Ocean, they are called cyclones.

The word ***cyclone*** also means any circling air, from fast-moving, tiny dust devils to slow-moving, thousand-mile-wide areas of low pressure, so tornadoes, hurricanes, and typhoons are all sometimes called cyclones.

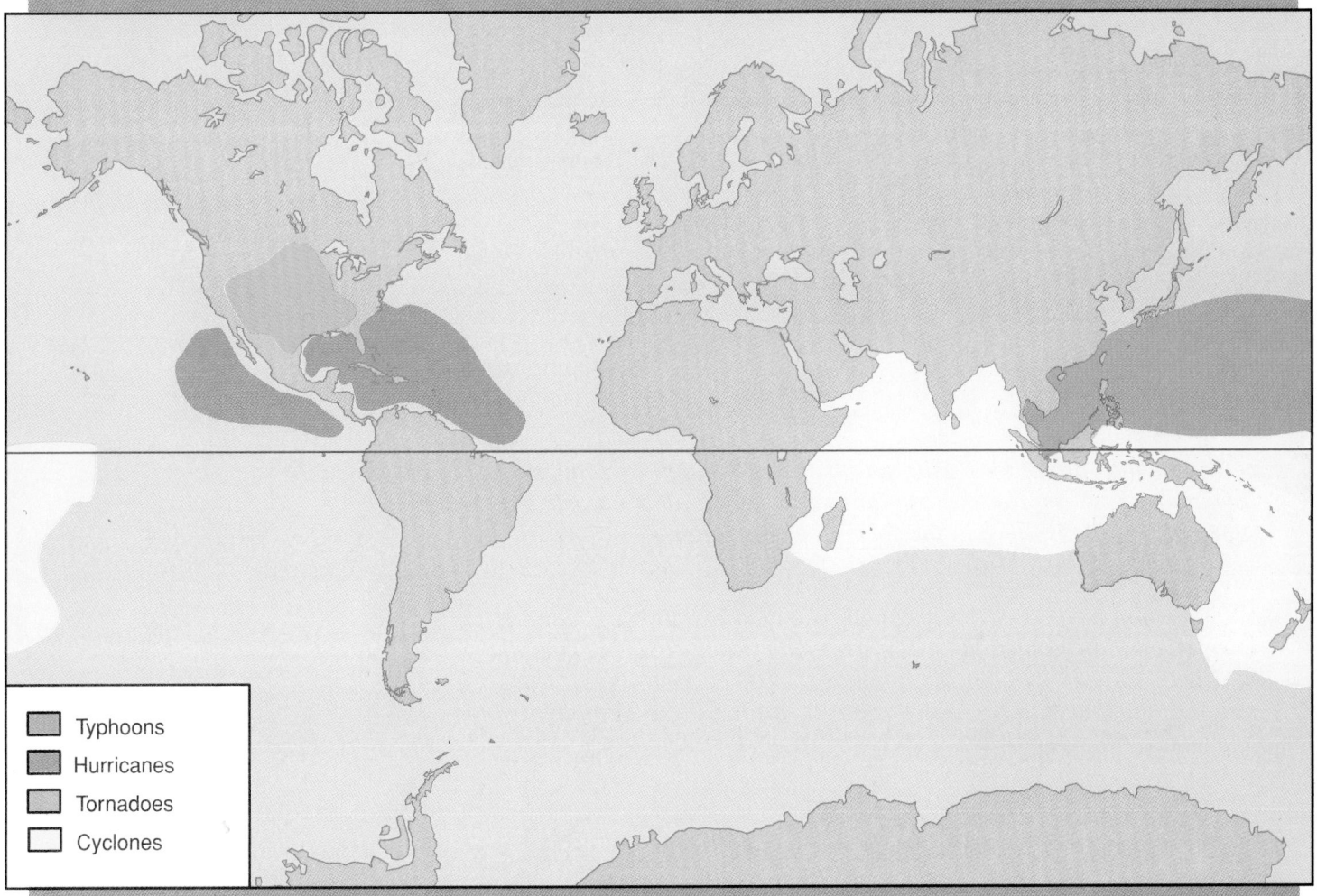

Water in the Air

Water and heat work together to create different weather conditions. Heat warms water in lakes, rivers, and oceans. The water ***evaporates***, or changes from liquid to a gas called ***water vapor***. Water vapor cools and condenses into droplets in the atmosphere to form clouds, fog, or ice crystals. These droplets grow heavier and fall back to the earth in the form of precipitation—rain, snow, sleet, hail, or drizzle. Warm air can hold more water vapor than cold air. That means that the humidity—or the amount of water vapor in the air—is usually greater on warm days than on cold ones.

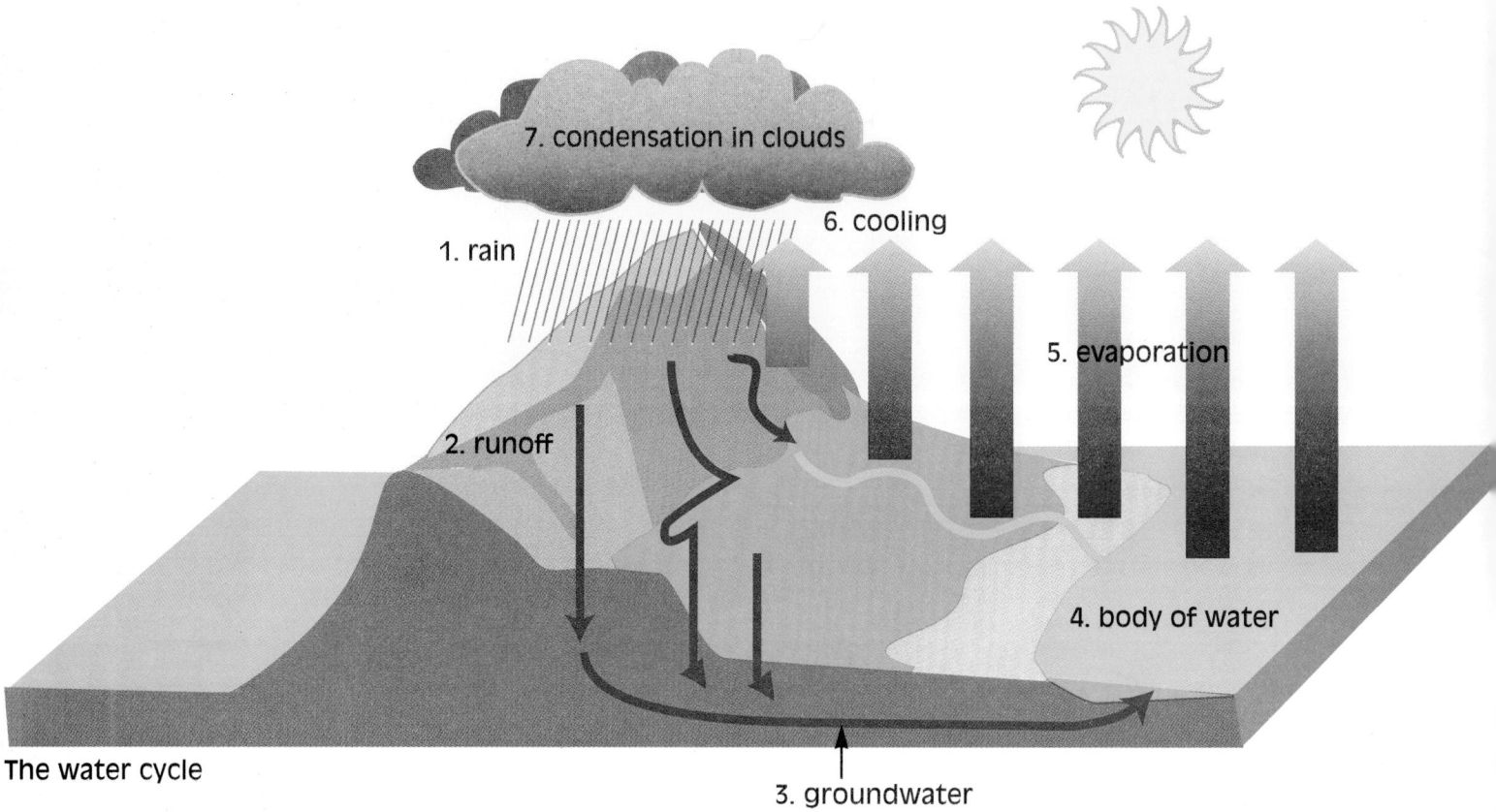

The water cycle

On any day, about four trillion (4,000,000,000,000) gallons of water—about ten times the amount of water in all the world's rivers—are in the atmosphere in the form of water vapor.

The amount of moisture in the air is called **humidity**. *Humidity is referred to in percentages. For example, when the air is completely filled with water vapor, the humidity is 100 percent. When the air is holding about half the water vapor it can hold, the humidity is measured at 50 percent.*

INSULATION: CLOUDS AND CLIMATE

Insulation prevents heat from passing into or out of an area. Your coat insulates your body, keeping your body heat in. The thick walls of a refrigerator keep the cold air inside and prevent the warm air outside from getting in.

Clouds insulate the earth. During the day they act as shields reflecting the sun's light and keep much of it from reaching the surface of the earth. At night, they act as blankets reflecting heat leaving the earth's surface downward again. So cloudy skies tend to bring smaller swings of temperature from day to night than clear skies.

Winds at Sea

The warm and cold winds that blow across the earth don't just move air. They also push surface water along as waves. These become ocean currents, some warm and others cold. Warm and cold currents, like winds, affect the weather and climate in different places on the earth. (See also ocean currents map, p. 38.)

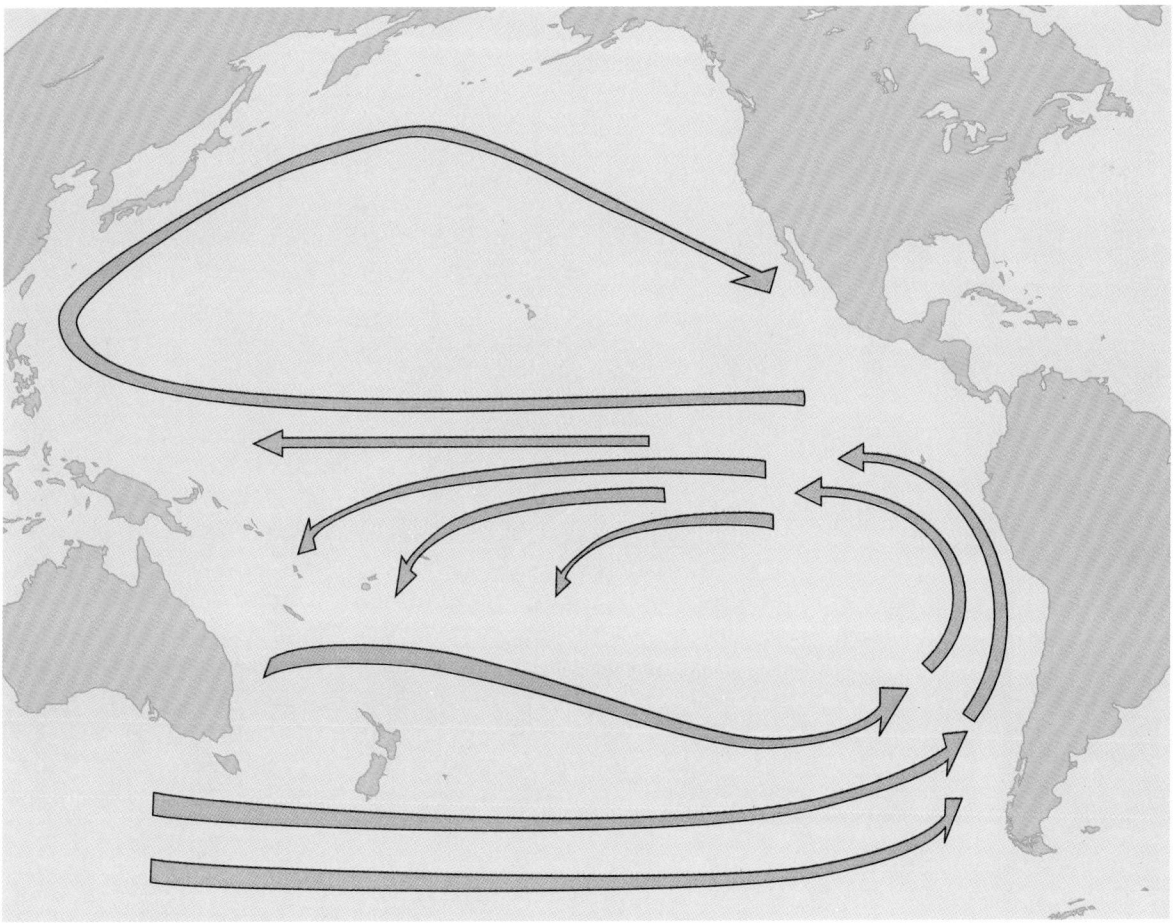

This map shows the pattern of winds over the Pacific Ocean.

PLANTS AND ANIMALS

1 The Natural Regions of the World

Land Biomes

The earth can be divided into about ten different natural regions, or ***land biomes***. Each biome is unique, with a special mixture of physical features—landforms, bodies of water, and climate—and their own forms of plant and animal life.

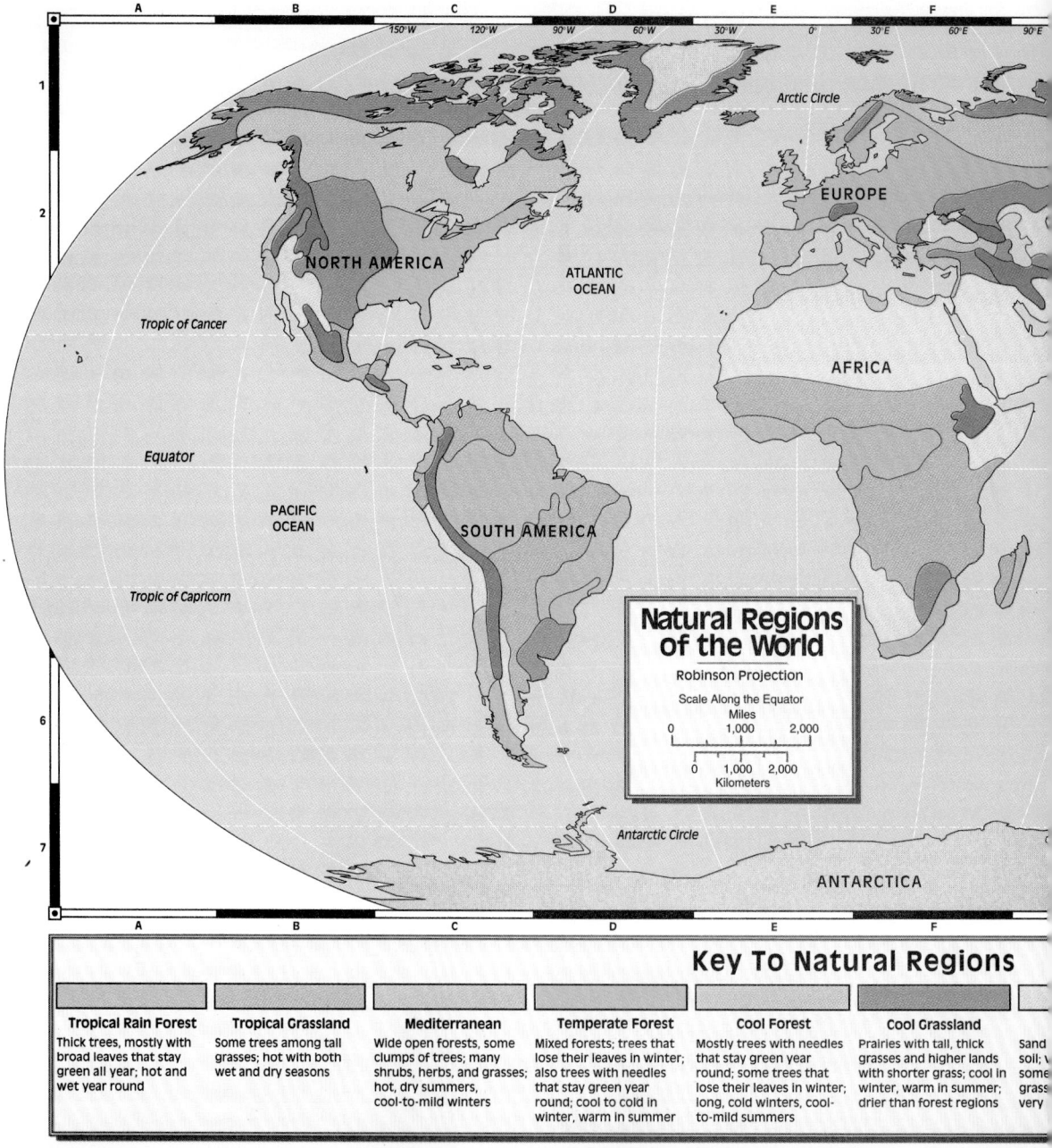

2 The Biomes

Tropical Rain Forests

Tropical rain forests are warm, wet biomes near or at the equator, where more species of plants and animals flourish than in all other biomes combined.

Hundreds of varieties of trees grow in tropical rain forests, most of them hardwoods. Although the warm, wet conditions encourage luxurious growth, the trees grow so close together that they have to fight for the light they need to grow. To catch more light, trees grow very tall, and the upper branches spread out over a wide area. The tops of trees grow close together, weaving a thick layer of leaves and branches called the forest canopy. The canopy is so thick that little sunlight gets through to the rain forest floor. Between the canopy and the floor grows a layer of shrubs and small trees that rises about 10 to 50 feet above the floor. This layer is called the understory. Some trees are very tall, and their branches and leaves tower at the top of the canopy. These are emergent trees, and are usually hardwoods, such as mahogany, rosewood, and ebony.

Because the floor of the rain forest is dark and damp, plants that require sunlight do not grow quickly. The few plants that grow there have broad, flat leaves to absorb as much sunlight as possible. Their leaves have waxy surfaces and pointed tips to allow water to run off easily. Other plants along the floor include vines that grow on top of understory shrubs and up tree trunks toward the light in the canopy.

Since the plant life is richer in the canopy than on the floor, so, too, is the animal life. Reptiles, amphibians, birds, and mammals live together in the treetops of the rain forest. These tree-dwelling, or ***arboreal***, animals include frogs, snakes, termites, eagles, toucans, parrots, flying squirrels, leopards, bats, and monkeys.

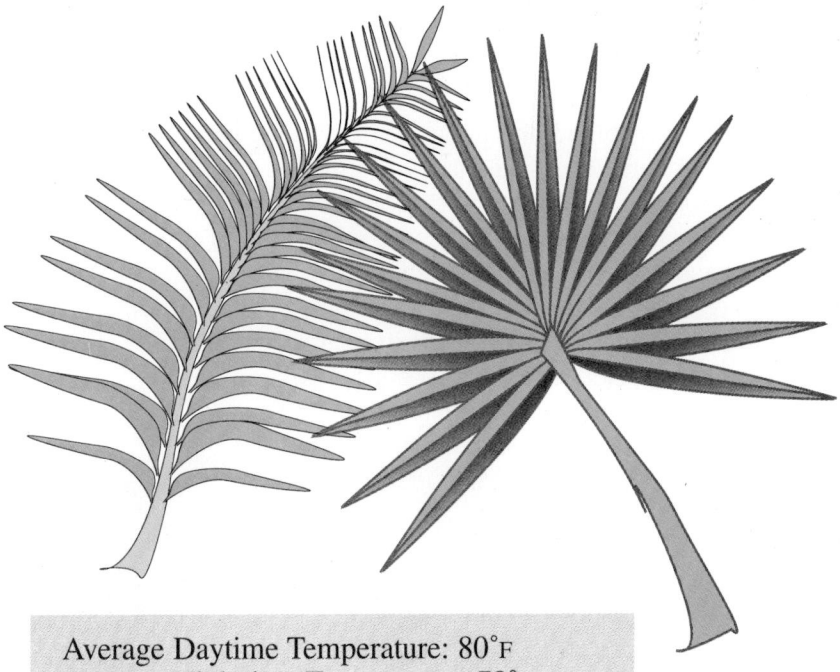

Average Daytime Temperature: 80°F
Average Nighttime Temperature: 70°F
Average Annual Rainfall: 100–200 inches

Tropical Grasslands

Tropical grasslands, often called ***savannas***, are biomes located inland at or near the equator.

The seasons in tropical grasslands are called the wet season and the dry season. Because it's hot all year round, the seasons are determined by variations in rainfall, not temperature.

Few plants survive here except for tough grasses and a few hardy types of trees, among them baobabs and acacia, which have thick trunks, deep roots, and waxy, spiny leaves. These features allow them to survive the extreme drought of the dry season.

The thick grasses are food to the millions of savanna animals, among them antelopes, wildebeests, zebras, giraffes, gazelles, rhinos, buffalos, and elephants. Enormous herds of these grazers roam up and down the grasslands following the rains and searching for water and fresh grasses. Other animals, including cheetahs, leopards, and lions, follow the grazers to prey on them. Still others, including hyenas and jackals, scavenge the remains of dead or dying animals. The savannas also support hundred of species of birds, from tiny sunbirds to eagles, and unique reptiles, amphibians, and insects.

Average Daytime Temperature: 80°F
Average Nighttime Temperature: 55°F
Average Annual Rainfall: 10–40 inches

Mediterranean Regions

Mediterranean regions, also called ***chaparrals***, are coastal biomes that are cool and moist in the winter and hot and dry in the summer. These biomes support clumps of trees and some widely spread forests.

During hot summer months, drought-resistant evergreens prove the hardiest plants in this scrubland and grass biome. The leaves and stems provide moisture and nutrition for a variety of animals, most of them small enough to seek cover beneath the low branches as they nibble on leaves. Here is a home for rodents—tiny mice and rabbits—and their predators. Underground or deep in shade, lizards wait out the heat of the day. Foxes and hawks, and other predator mammals and birds, stalk and circle to make a meal on the small local fare.

The chaparral is a different place in winter months when it is cooler and wetter. Then plants grow more abundantly and the animal populations surge as well. Even large grazers, such as deer, gather to nibble on the winter foliage.

Average Daytime Temperature:
90°F summer, 55°F winter
Average Nighttime Temperature:
70°F summer, 40°F winter
Average Annual Rainfall: about 10 inches

Temperate Forests

In the areas between the cold polar regions and the hot tropics of both hemispheres are ***temperate forests*** with warm summers and cool winters.

These temperate forests are dominated by deciduous trees, such as oak, elm, ash, maple, and birch. Evergreens are also present in these forests, including the giant sequoias of the temperate forests in northern California.

In spring and summer, the leaves of the trees provide shade for the forest floor, so temperatures remain cool. Although winters can be cold—often below freezing—the forest remains an inviting environment for many types of plants and animals, from earthworms and insects to songbirds, predator birds, deer, and foxes.

Average Daytime Temperature:
68°F summer, 32°F winter
Average Nighttime Temperature:
58°F summer, 18°F winter
Average Annual Rainfall: about 40 inches

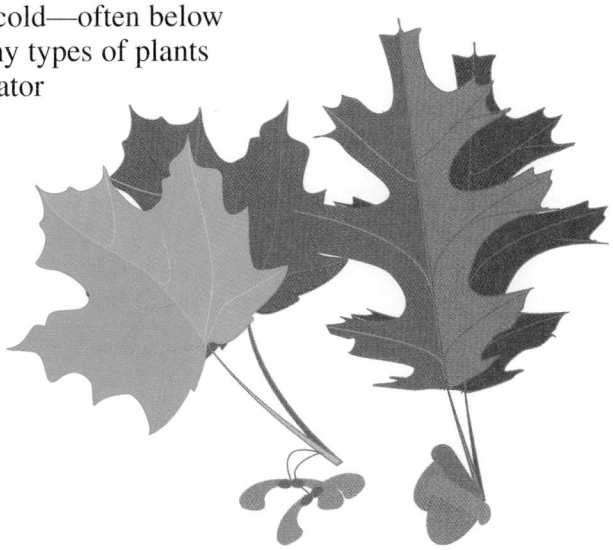

Cool Forests

Also called ***boreal*** forests, ***cool forests*** are made up mostly of coniferous (cone-bearing) trees. The conifers grow better than other trees in these cold regions located in the extreme temperate zones and into the polar regions, where summer is short and winter is long and dark. Pine, spruce, and hemlock trees grow here, supplying cover to a few year-round residents, including birds; small mammals such as rodents, rabbits, and squirrels; and large animals such as moose, elk, caribou, and bears.

In the winter, the boreal residents tuck themselves away into natural shelters, many to graze only an hour or two each day in the freezing temperatures, others to hibernate during the months of deepest chill.

But spring brings a full complement of migratory animals, particularly birds, who seek the mild temperatures and abundant food in the cool forest summer. These animals will stay until, as summer turns to autumn, instinct tells them to move back to their tropical winter homes.

Average Daytime Temperature:
65°F summer, 20°F winter
Average Nighttime Temperature:
50°F summer, 10°F winter
Average Annual Rainfall: about 20 inches

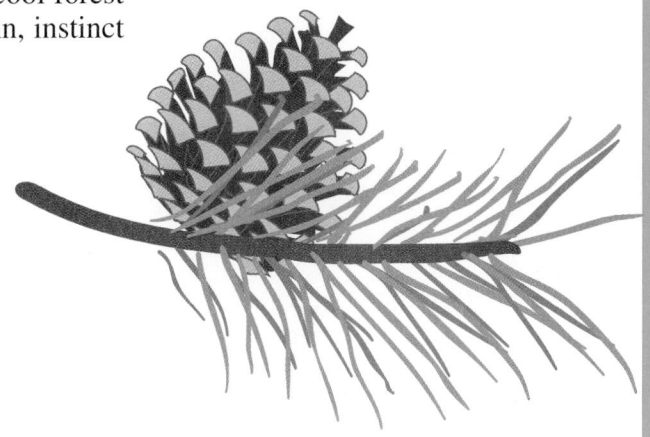

Cool Grasslands

Cool grasslands include ***prairies*** covered in tall grasses and other regions with shorter grasses. These grasslands are drier than cool forest regions, but experience similar summer and winter temperatures.

Few of the cool grassland biomes have been left by human beings in their natural state. That's because the grasslands are excellent for farming both livestock and crops.

Instead of serving as natural grazing lands for large herds of wild animals, the grasslands are now covered in wheat, barley, oats, soybeans, and other grain crops. Populations of cows, sheep, horses, goats, and other domesticated animals feed on the coarse grasses.

Average Daytime Temperature: 75°F summer, 20°F winter
Average Nighttime Temperature: 60°F summer, 0°F winter
Average Annual Rainfall: under 25 inches

Deserts

Deserts are regions—hot or cold—where the land is covered in sand or bare soil and precipitation totals are very small, less than 10 inches each year.

In most hot deserts, temperatures vary greatly, from extremely hot days to cool, even freezing, nights.

Plant and animal life in deserts is well adapted to the harsh environment. Cacti and euphorbia are typical desert plants. Called ***succulents***, these plants store water in their waxy leaves and stems. To avoid the hot days, many animals in the desert are ***nocturnal***, or active only at night. These animals burrow deep into the earth to spend the daylight hours away from the burning sun. They search for food during the cool nighttime hours. Certain types of lizards and snakes thrive in the hot desert sun, as do animals that need only a little water.

Although we often think of deserts as hot places, not all deserts are hot. The far north of Siberia in Russia and much of Antarctica are cold deserts.

Average Daytime Temperature: 100°F summer, 65°F winter*
Average Nighttime Temperature: 75°F summer, 45°F winter*
Average Annual Rainfall: under 10 inches

*Averages represent hot deserts located in tropical and temperate regions, not frozen deserts.

Tundra

Tundra biomes are extreme climates, too cold for trees to grow. While the top of the ground thaws during the warm season, a layer beneath it, about 10 inches of frozen ground, never melts. It is called ***permafrost***.

In this harsh biome, winter is particularly cruel. Yet a few animals remain after the others have migrated south for the winter. Lemmings, ermines, arctic foxes, wolves, musk oxen, reindeer, and polar bears grow heavy winter coats or huddle into dens to keep warm through the long, dark winter.

During the few short months of warm weather, low-growing tundra flowers bloom. Birds and insects newly arrived from the south feast on these, as do herds of moose and caribou that have traveled to the tundra from their winter homes farther south.

Average Daytime Temperature: 55°F summer, 30°F winter
Average Nighttime Temperature: 40°F summer, -10°F winter
Average Annual Rainfall: 30–45 inches

Polar Regions

The ***polar regions*** are frozen deserts covered in ice all year long. Because it is over land instead of water, the Antarctic is much colder than the Arctic.

The Arctic polar region (around the north pole) is a solid mass of frozen ocean water. The Antarctic polar region (around the south pole) is a mass of frozen land covered in ice and snow. Together, the areas surrounding the north and south poles are known as the ***polar ice caps***.

Powerful icy winds blow across the polar ice caps, causing blizzards of snow and ice blown up from the surface. However, little snow actually falls from the skies over the ice caps because the air temperatures are too cold for moisture to evaporate and form clouds.

Only migrating animals, such as polar bears and arctic seals, are found on the Arctic ice mass. Very few animals are hearty enough to survive conditions in Antarctica. The few that do manage it live along the coasts of the continent, relying upon the sea for food and shelter. Among these remarkable animals are such birds as petrels, gulls, terns, albatrosses—and penguins. Penguins are insulated with a thick coat of feathers over skin protected by a thick layer of fat.

In the icy north arctic seas live Arctic mammals. Here dolphins, porpoises, whales, and seals, protected by thick layers of oily fat called ***blubber***, swim in the near-freezing waters.

Average Daytime Temperature:	Arctic: 30°F summer, -10°F winter
	Antarctic: 7°F summer, -80°F winter
Average Nighttime Temperature:	Arctic: 10°F summer, -20°F winter
	Antarctic: -50°F summer, -95°F winter
Average Annual Rainfall:	5–20 inches

Mountain Biomes

Because of the changes in altitude (or height above sea level), high mountain environments support a variety of different climates. Depending on the location of the mountain ranges, biomes on high mountains can range from tropical rain forest to tundra and frozen desert. Mountains also help create different biomes. As warm, moist air flows from coastal regions up against mountain ranges on their ***windward*** sides, the air pushes upward and cools. The cooled water vapor condenses into droplets in the form of clouds. Often these droplets become large enough to fall as rain. Because moisture carrying air is blocked by the mountain ranges, drier climates, such as plains or deserts, often form on the ***leeward*** sides.

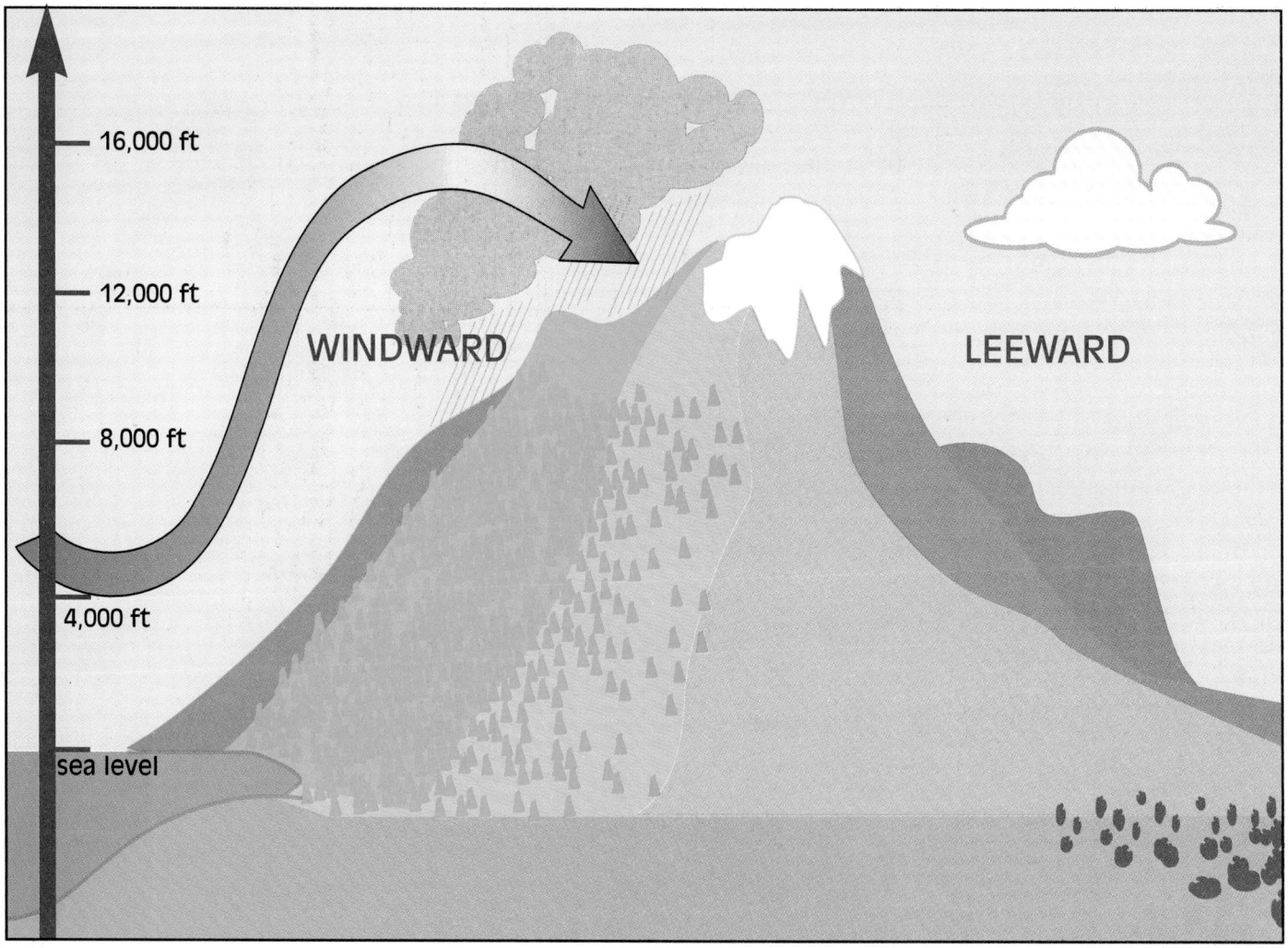

PEOPLE ON LAND AND WATER

1 Location and Place

What Are Location and Place?

Location is where something—for example, a house, a school, a store, an airport, a mine, or a crop field—is created or built. Location is described in absolute terms (latitude and longitude) or relative terms (north of the road or near the playground). A location becomes a ***place*** when it is described in terms of its human or physical characteristics.

Climate and landscape, as well as religion, schools, politics, opportunities to make a living, and environmental surroundings give character to a place.

A farm and a factory are two kinds of places. Farms are usually located in the countryside. The factory on the left is located at the intersection of 4th and Main streets.

2 Counting People: Population

Population

Population is the total number of people who live in a particular place. Geographers study population to understand where people live and why they live there.

World Population Growth

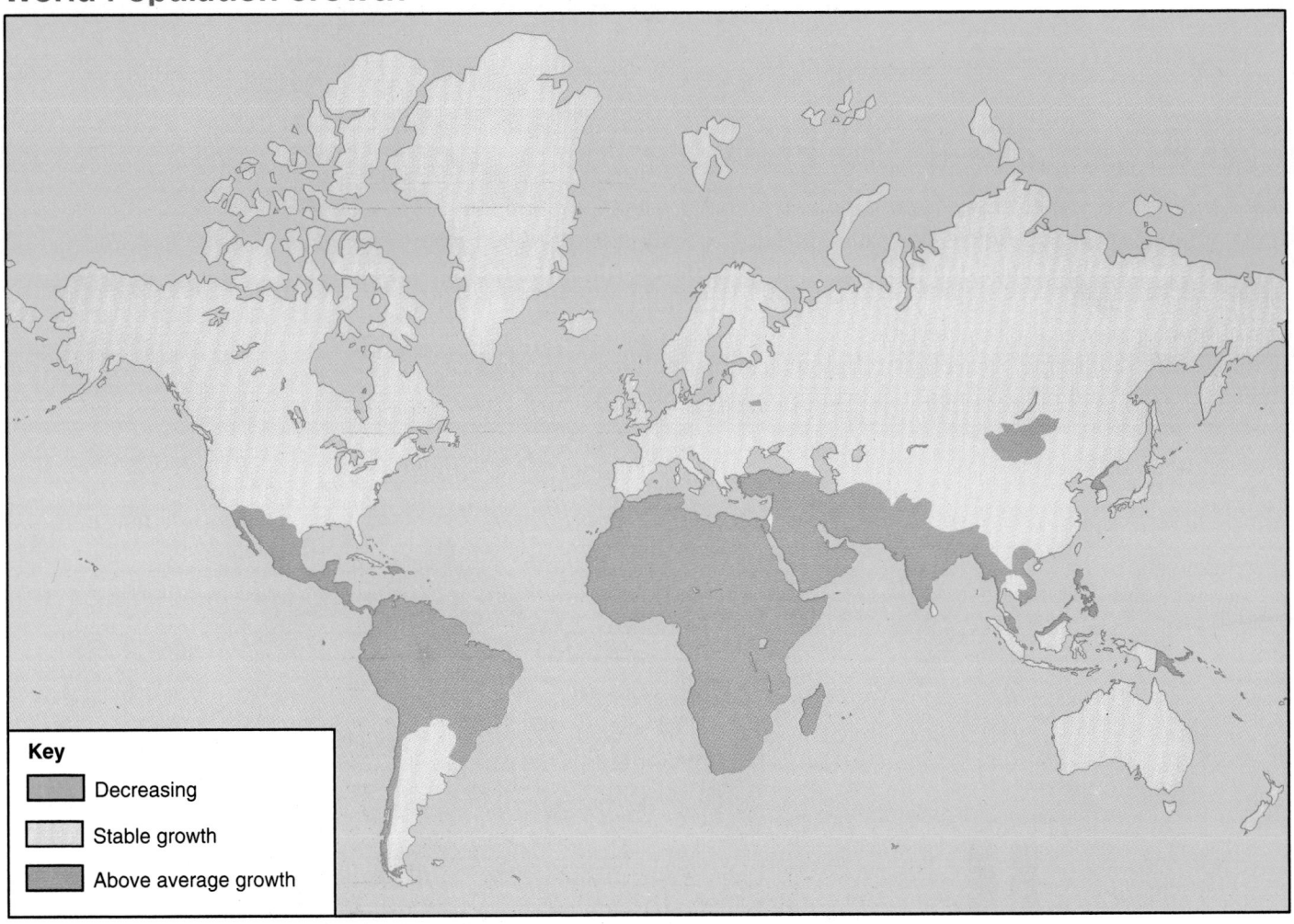

Drawn from data collected from the U.S. Bureau of the Census International Data Base

A map of world population growth shows areas where the number of people is growing, decreasing, or remaining about the same.

The study of population is called **demographics.**
The scientists who study demographics are called **demographers.**

World Population Growth, 1600–Present

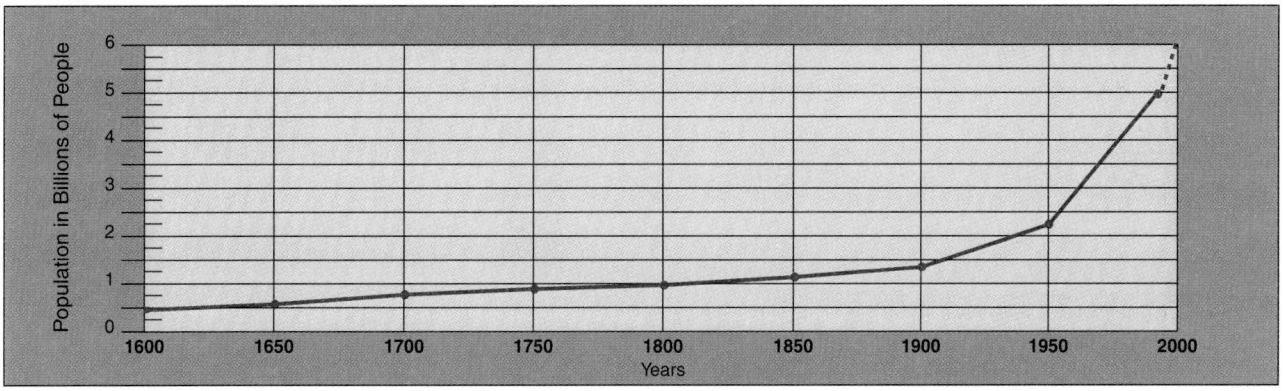

This graph shows world population in billions of people over the last 400 years.

Population Data

In studying human populations, geographers use a lot of different information called ***population data***. These data include basic facts about human populations—past, present, and projected into the future.

Some Types of Population Data

1	Average family size	The average number of children in a family in a particular culture group or region
2	Birthrate	The number of babies born per year per thousand people
3	Death rate	The number of people who die per year per thousand people
4	Doubling time	The time needed for a population to increase 100 percent, or to double
5	Life expectancy	The average number of years people live
6	Population growth rate	How quickly a population grows each year measured in percent
7	Population structure	The makeup of a population by age and gender (male or female)

The world's population increases by about three people every second. That's nearly 200 people a minute, 10,000 people an hour, and 240,000 people a day!

Population Pictures

Profiles and Pyramids

Geographers use graphs to compare populations in different areas. Two of the most common graphs are the ***population profile*** and the ***population pyramid***.

Population Profile

A ***population profile*** is a bar graph that shows the different age groups of a population that shares something in common, such as language, dog ownership, or a school.

Population Pyramid

A ***population pyramid*** is a bar graph that depicts a total population by breaking it down into age groupings and gender.

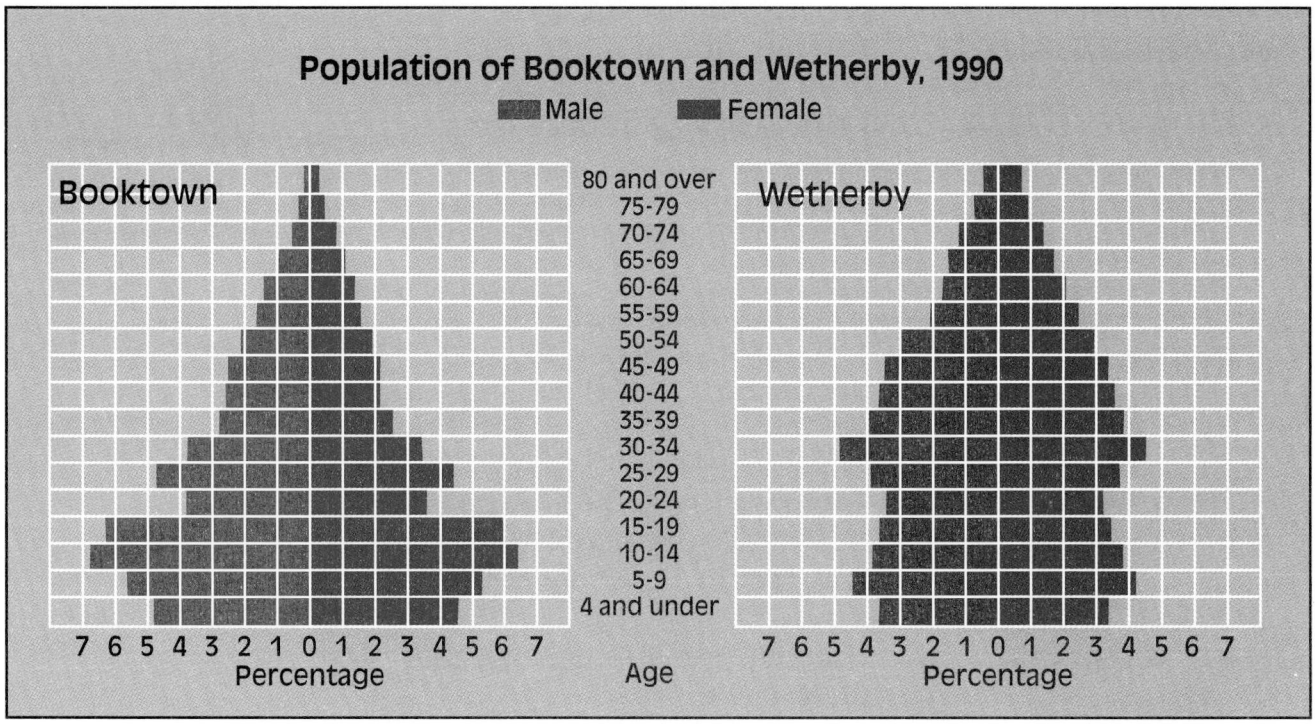

By comparing the population pyramids for Booktown and Wetherby, you can see that a larger percentage of Booktown's population is aged 10–19 than Wetherby's. That is because the Boys Academy of Reading, an all-male middle and high school, brings hundreds of school-age boys into Booktown each year, skewing the population in that age group.

Population Density and Distribution

Population density means how close together people live in a particular place. To find population density, divide the number of people in a place by the total area of that place.

Population distribution or ***patterns*** tell geographers where most people live within a place or region.

Maps show both population density and distribution. This map shows the population density and distribution in the state of Wisconsin. More than half of the 5,000,000 residents live in cities located in the southeastern and south central parts of the state. Located in these areas are the largest cities in the state: Milwaukee, Madison, and Green Bay.

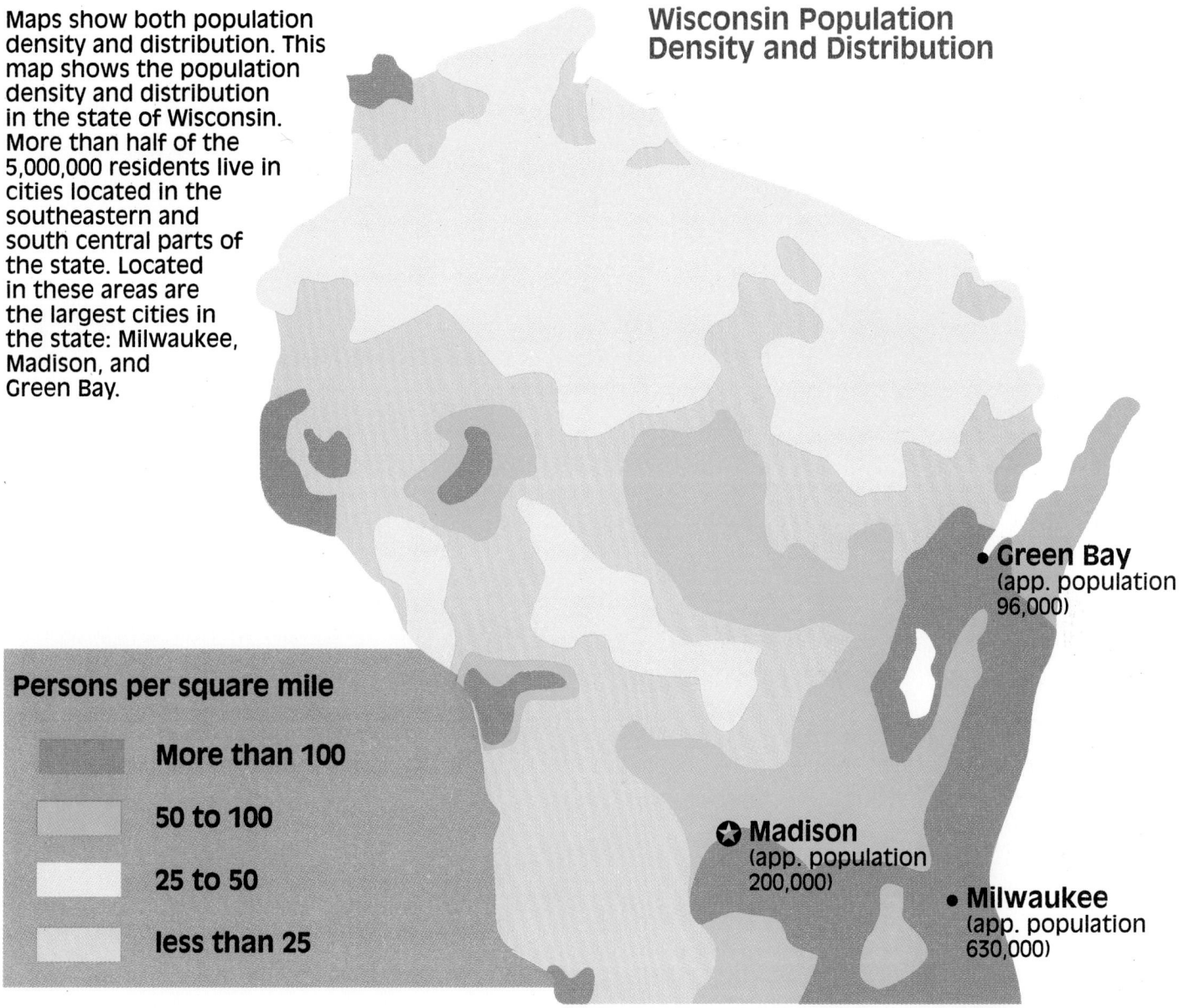

Drawn from data gathered by the U.S. Bureau of the Census

Urban vs. Rural

About half the earth's people live in cities and towns, called ***urban areas***. The other half live on farms or in countryside villages, called ***rural areas***.

Population patterns: Urban vs. Rural

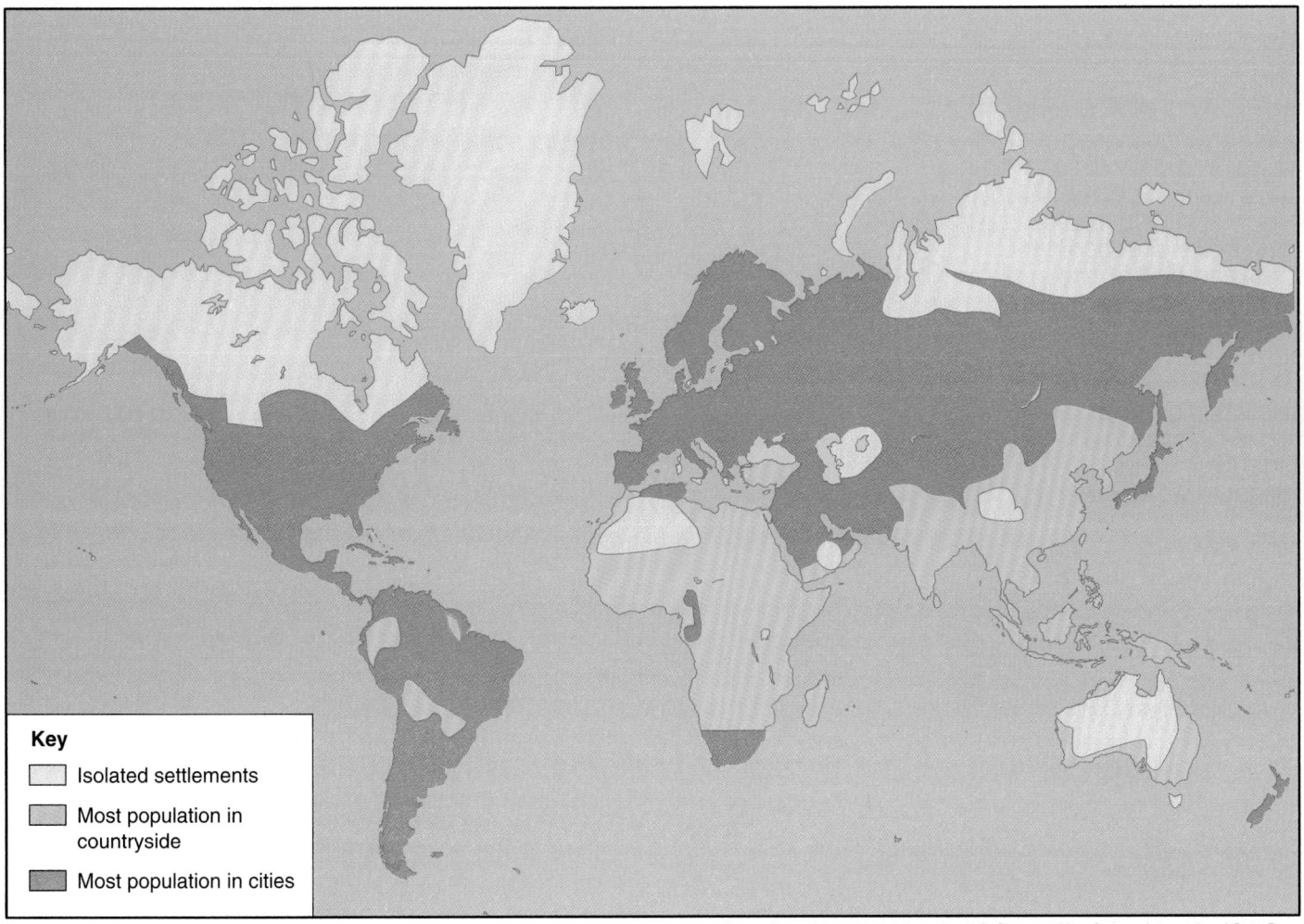

Drawn from data collected from the U.S. Bureau of the Census International Data Base

A map of population patterns shows where people live mostly in cities (urban) and where people live mostly in the countryside (rural).

A Model City, A Model Countryside

A ***city***, or ***metropolis***, is a large or important town. Sometimes a city grows so large that it grows into a neighboring city, forming a ***megalopolis***. But no matter how big it is, a city is made up of a variety of areas.

Businesses and industries are located in the ***commercial areas*** of a city. Stores and service businesses often are located in ***downtown*** commercial areas, or the main business area of a city, called the central business district (CBD). Manufacturing and heavy industry (see p. 75) are usually located along the outer edges of a city on major transportation routes (roads, waterways, trains, airports, etc.).

People's homes are located in the ***residential*** areas of a city. Homes are also found in the ***suburbs***, or the residential districts lying just outside a city or town. Like the people who live in the residential areas of a city, people who live in the suburbs usually work in the city and benefit from the services the city offers. Beyond the suburbs are ***exurbs***, sparsely populated residential areas.

Most cities are divided into ***neighborhoods***, each with its own special cultural makeup. Some neighborhoods are made up of people with the same ethnic or religious backgrounds. For example, many U.S. cities have Chinese, Italian, Korean, or African-American neighborhoods. Other neighborhoods are unique because of their architecture or the era in which they were built. Many U.S. cities have preserved their "historical districts" or the "old cities" where the oldest buildings in the city stand. Still other neighborhoods are defined by physical features. Terms such as "riverside," "highlands," and "flats" are often used to describe neighborhoods within cities.

Outside cities are small towns, villages, and other rural communities, as well as farmland, forests, parks, and other tracts of land. Highways, smaller roads, waterways, railroads, and other transportation routes connect rural areas to each other and to nearby cities, states, or even foreign countries.

Towns ***are usually smaller than cities, but both are thickly populated areas with fixed boundaries and local governments.***

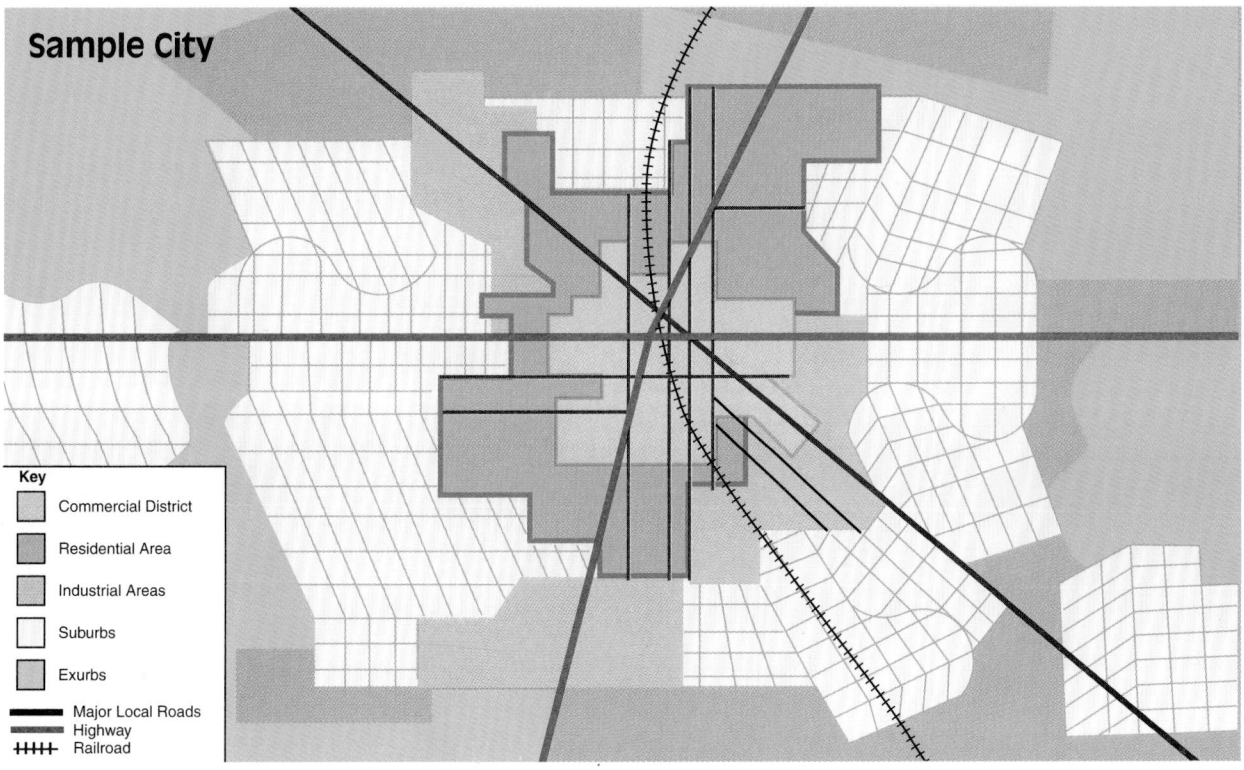

Like most cities, Sample City is made up of several distinct areas, including a downtown, industrial district, residential neighborhoods, and suburbs.

World Birthrates: 1910–1990

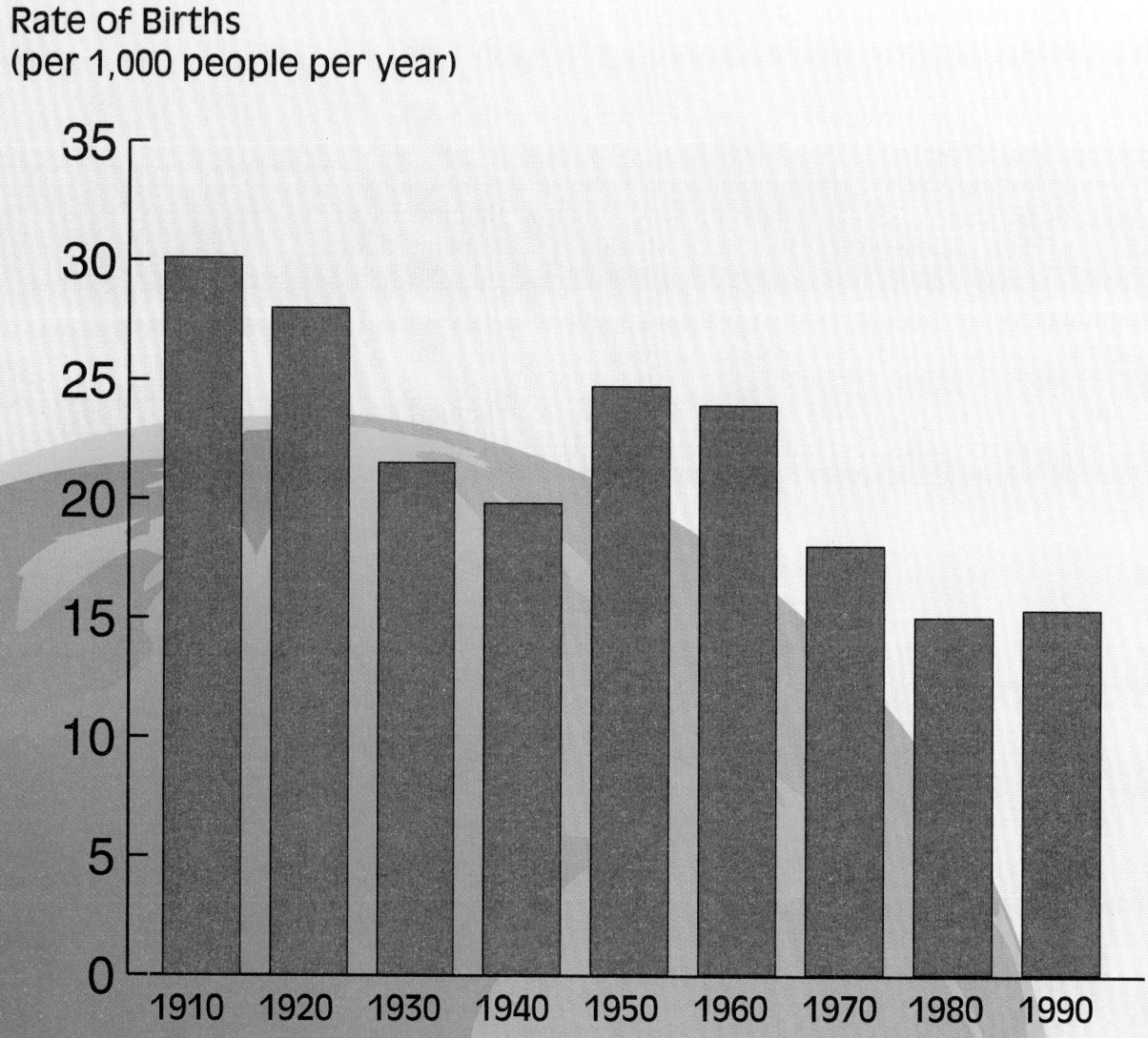

3 Culture

What Is Culture?

Culture is a word used to describe how groups of people act: how we live, what we eat, what we believe, and how we change our environment to create communities.

Geographers who study culture try to explain how people behaved in the past compared with how we behave today. They compare the way people in different areas live their lives. They study languages, beliefs and traditions, political systems, and the technologies that bind communities together or make them different from other communities.

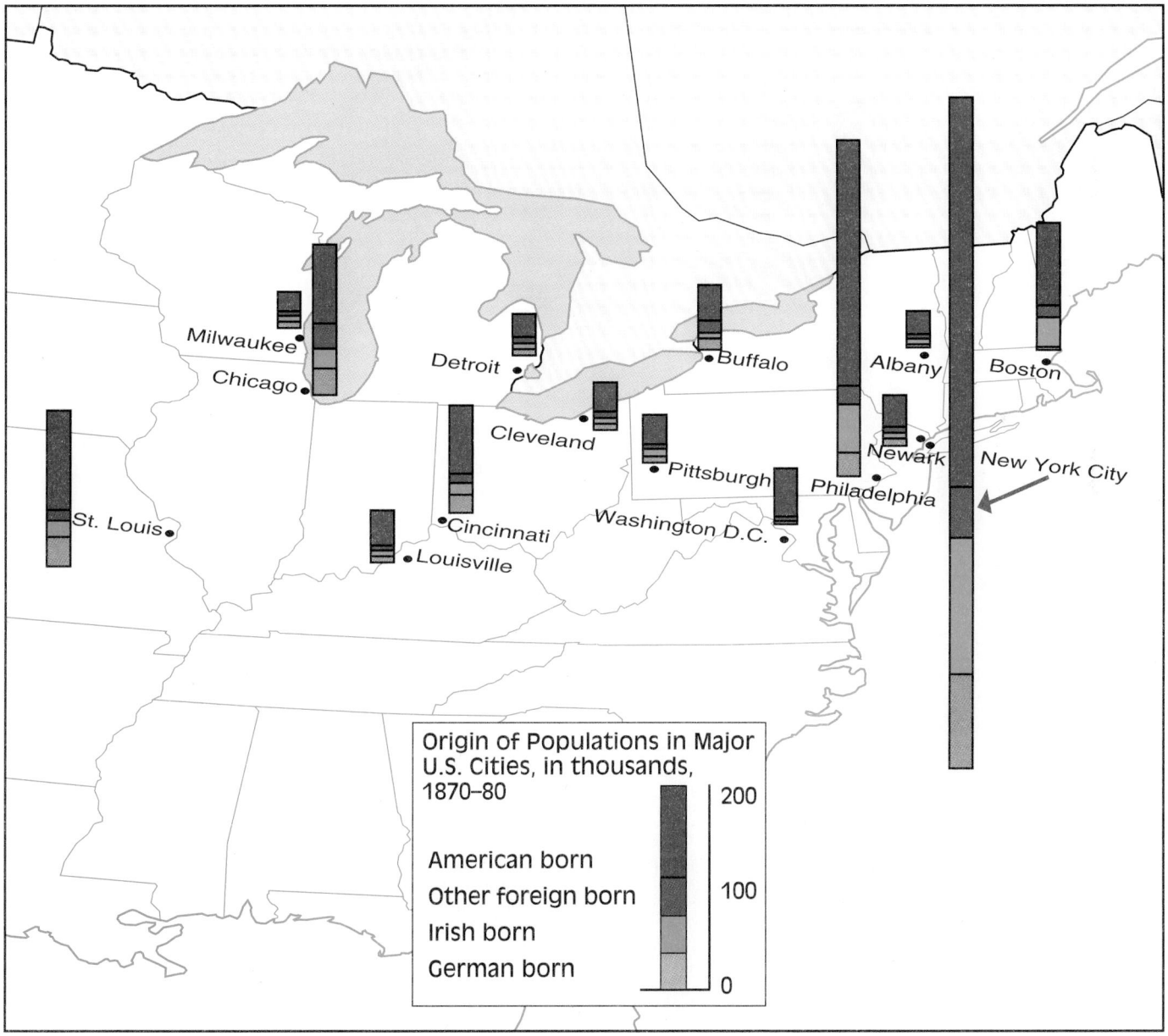

This cultural map compares the Irish and German populations to other foreign-born and American-born citizens of major northern and midwestern American cities over 100 years ago.

Local culture refers to the special culture of a particular place. The place could be as large as the entire United States or as small as a fishing community on the Maine coast.

The Cultural Mosaic

Geographers consider each culture group to consist of different pieces, like the pieces in a ***mosaic***, a picture made by fitting together separate tiles, stones, or glass pieces. Viewed together, the pieces that make up a culture create a picture of that culture, called a ***cultural mosaic***.

Elements of the cultural mosaic can be witnessed in a typical American suburban backyard. The types of clothes we wear, the food we eat, the games we play, and the architecture of our homes are all pieces of our cultural mosaic.

Culture Basics

1. Language (see below)
2. Beliefs and traditions (see pp. 68-70)
3. Arts and crafts (see p. 71)
4. Political systems (see p. 74)
5. Technologies (see p. 75)

Language

Language is the use of voice sounds, gestures, and written symbols to communicate thoughts and feelings.

The five languages most spoken in the world today are Mandarin Chinese, English, Hindi, Russian, and Spanish.

Language Families

More than 2,800 languages are spoken in the world today. These languages have been grouped into several ***language families***. Here are some of the main groups.

FAMILY	APPROXIMATE NUMBER OF SPEAKERS	PRINCIPAL LANGUAGES
Indo-European	2.6 billion	Latvian, Lithuanian, Belorussian, Bulgarian, Czech, Macedonian, Polish, Russian, Serb, Croatian, Slovak, Slovenian, Ukranian, Irish, Scots Gaelic, Dutch, English, German, Norwegian, Danish, Swedish, Icelandic, Bengali, Gujarati, Hindi, Marathi, Punjabi, Urdu, Iranian, French, Italian, Portuguese, Romanian, Spanish
Sino-Tibetan	1.2 billion	Chinese, Thai, Burmese, Tibetan
Black African	440 million	Includes Niger-Kordofanian, Nilo-Saharan, and Khoisan Language families
Malayo-Polynesian	275 million	Indonesian, Tagalog, Maori
Afro-Asian	220 million	Arabic, Hebrew, Berber, Amharic
Dravidian	220 million	Tamil, Telugu
Japanese and Korean	200 million	Japanese and Korean
Uralic-Altaic	165 million	Finnish, Estonian, Hungarian, Turkish
Mon-Khmer	110 million	Khmer and Laotian

Slang *is language used instead of standard vocabulary. It is usually used to provide emphasis or humor in speech and, sometimes, in writing. A* **dialect** *is a variation of a standard language spoken by a particular group of people. A dialect differs from standard language in grammar, vocabulary, or pronunciation, or in any combination of the three.*

Language Barriers

Throughout early history, mountains have stopped the spread of language. So have large bodies of water, deserts, and thick jungles. Because people couldn't cross these barriers easily, groups of people on opposite sides developed languages separately. So, people on one side of a geographic barrier might speak a language different from people on the other. Today these boundaries are no longer difficult to cross, yet they help explain the diversity of world languages.

More than 1,000 Native American languages are spoken in isolated areas throughout the Americas.

World Language Families

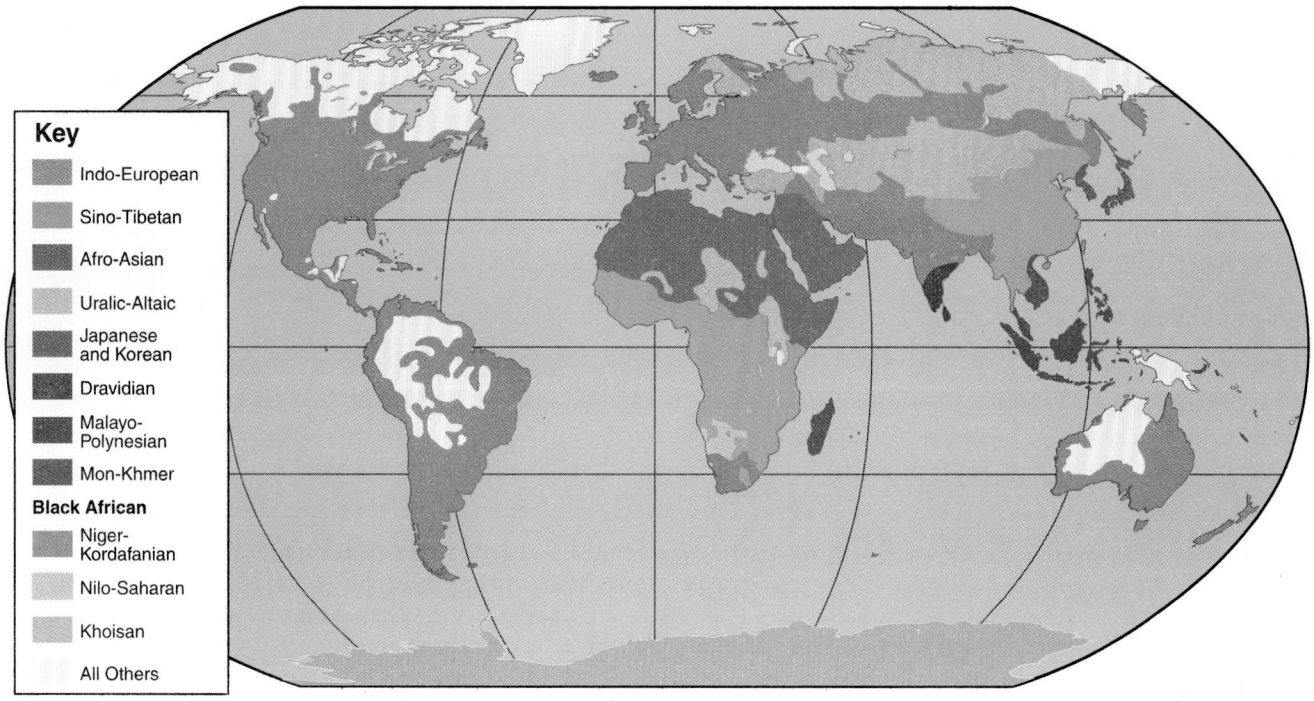

Beliefs and Traditions: Religions, Customs, and Arts and Crafts

Beliefs are the attitudes, ideas, and world views held by a person or a group of people. Every culture has a set of beliefs, or a ***belief system***. This system is made up of three basic elements:

1 Religion	**A belief in and legends about a god or gods who created the world and affect peoples' lives**
2 Customs and manners	**The traditions people have or ways people act or behave in a group**
3 Arts and crafts	**The clothing, music, arts, architecture, tools, etc., used by a group**

Religion

Over the centuries, people have believed in many religions. Today, dozens of religions are practiced in the world. However, five major religions are the most widely practiced.

Major World Religions

1 Hinduism	Begun about 1500 B.C. in India. Hindus believe in many gods and in reincarnation (rebirth of the soul after death). Today, Hinduism is practiced by 764,000,000 people primarily in India, Nepal, Malaysia, Guyana, Suriname, and Sri Lanka.
2 Judaism	Begun about 1300 B.C. among the Hebrew people in the Middle East. Judaism was the first religion founded on a belief in one god rather than a group of gods. Today, Judaism is practiced by 13,500,000 people throughout the world, primarily in Israel, Europe, and the United States.
3 Buddhism	Begun about 525 B.C. by Siddhartha Gautama (Buddha), c. 563–480, in India. Buddhists follow the Hindu belief in reincarnation, and they work to gain inner peace, called Nirvana. Today, Buddhism is practiced by approximately 338,500,000 people throughout Asia, from Sri Lanka to Japan.
4 Christianity	Begun in the first century in the Middle East among Jews who believed that Jesus of Nazareth was the divine son of god. Today, Christianity is practiced by approximately 1,900,000,000 people throughout the world, primarily in Europe, North America, South America, and Africa, as well as in pockets of Asia.
5 Islam	Begun in A.D. 622 in the Middle East by followers of Muhammad. Islam includes many of the features of Judaism and Christianity, including the belief in one god, which Moslems call Allah. Today, Islam is practiced by 1,033,450,000 people, primarily in the western and northern countries of Africa, throughout the Middle East, Central Asia, western China, Malaysia, Indonesia, the Philippines, and the United States.

The rest of the world's population, approximately 1,600,000,000 people, practices other religions or no religion.

Customs and Manners

Customs are the usual habits of a group of people. ***Manners***, or norms, are the habits considered to be polite among a group of people. Both customs and manners are the result of what a group considers important: its values. For example, when a young person offers a seat to an older person, the custom demonstrates the value of respect for one's elders.

GREETINGS!

Manners, Meanings, and Cultural Differences

What is accepted as polite behavior in one place isn't necessarily so in another.

In the United States, people often shake hands as a greeting or when they are introduced to new people. In Japan and India, touch is not used in greetings. In Japan, people bow to acknowledge new contacts or to express respect to old friends. In India, people touch their palms together, prayer-style, to show welcome.

Waving with the palm of the hand facing out is a gesture of greeting in America and most European cultures. In Turkey and Greece, however, the gesture is called "The Hand of Moutza," and is considered a serious insult.

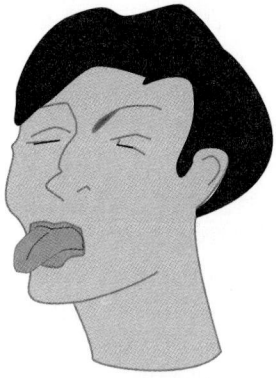

Sticking out the tongue is considered rude in the United States, but among the Aborigines in Australia, it is a sign of greeting and affection. In China, it is a sign of embarrassment.

Arts and Crafts

Art communicates the values and beliefs of a culture in what that culture finds beautiful. It can include paintings, sculpture, plays, poems, dance, photographs, movies, novels, and music.

Crafts refers to useful items and the methods used to make them. Crafts include sewing, weaving, tools for cooking, farming, mining, manufacturing, and the design and construction of buildings (architecture).

All the art forms—visual arts, music, literature, and dance—together are called the **fine arts.**

Culture Crafts

Hand-woven baskets, woolen blankets and rugs, pottery, and ivory needles—among many other items—have been used for centuries in different cultures throughout the world. Created for everyday use, many of these items are now considered art objects. That means their value is measured both in their usefulness and their beauty.

Home, Sweet Home

The Architecture of Houses

Plantation-style houses have been built around the world by European settlers. This particular style of house, however, is most often seen in agricultural or tropical regions.

People in different culture groups tend to build different kinds of houses. The differences include:

1. Building materials: Some cultures build homes of wood, some of stone, some of earth. People build homes with the materials available in their geographical regions.
2. Beauty: People build homes that look pleasing to them, homes that fit their idea of beauty. In Europe, even new homes are built to look like those that have stood in villages for hundreds of years. Among the Bedouin of North Africa, homes are not permanent structures, but brilliantly colored tents festooned with tassels and fringes.
3. Use: People build homes primarily for shelter but also to fit the way they live. A Masai cattle herder needs a place within his home, or ***shamba***, to corral livestock. An Inuit needs shelter from the Arctic winds yet access to fishing. An American suburbanite needs to be near transportation to the city. Homes are also designed to suit different climates and amounts of space. For example, many houses in cold climates are insulated between the inside and outside walls, floors, and ceilings. In tropical climates, walls made of a single layer of bamboo or reeds provide shelter from the hot sun.

Teepees were once homes to some of the members of the Plains Nations of Native Americans.

Houses built along the rivers and rice paddies of Asia are often built on stilts to protect dwellers from rising and falling water levels.

Food! Glorious Food!

What people in a group eat is part of their culture. The food culture is created by tastes and influenced by religion and customs. A group's diet is also determined by what it can grow or raise. Climate, too, influences how people build their kitchens and prepare their foods.

Location determines dietary factors in many cultures. However, nowadays, because of excellent transportation and storage, canned goods are found in the homes of Arctic Inuits and frozen meals in the homes of people in desert regions.

Cuisine ***means a particular style of cooking or preparing food. Cuisine is determined by everything from taste to climate, farming, and location. For example, the cuisines of Asia use rice as a main ingredient. In Italian cuisine, wheat flour noodles called pasta are common. Cuisine is another way of saying "food culture." Today, with mass communication, migration, and transportation, many cuisines are available all over the world. Chinese and Italian cuisines, for example, are enjoyed by people in restaurants all over North America. Once an American phenomenon, fast foods, such as hamburgers and fries, are available in cities as far apart as Beijing, China, and São Paulo, Brazil.***

Political Systems

Political systems are governments, or the ruling bodies of the world's peoples. People who live under one government form a ***country*** or ***nation***.

What Is Government?

Political systems or ***governments*** provide a set of laws and rules. There are many types of political systems, including:

Anarchy	**No government or organized authority.**
Confederacy	**An alliance of separately governed states.**
Democracy	**A nation in which power rests with the people and is exercised directly by them or their elected representatives.**
Dictatorship	**A nation in which absolute power is controlled by a person whose position is not inherited.**
Empire	**A group of nations or territories ruled by one leader or country.**
Monarchy	**A nation ruled by a supreme sovereign, such as a king, queen, or emperor. In most monarchies, the rulers inherit their power. A constitutional monarchy is a system in which a king or queen is the head of state in a country ruled by a separate government.**
Parliamentary Government	**An assembly of persons, not necessarily elected, who make up the laws of a nation or state.**
Republic	**A nation without a monarch and, in modern times, usually led by a president.**

4 How People Live

The Hunter-Gatherers

In ancient societies, people lived as ***hunter-gatherers.*** In some places today, they still do. That means they hunt, fish, and forage from the wild to find food.

Subsistence Farmers

To feed themselves, humans learned to sow plants and grow crops as well as to hunt and gather food. Over time, farmers learned to raise enough food to feed themselves.

Farmers who raise just enough food to feed themselves and their families are called ***subsistence farmers***. Subsistence farming is still common in several parts of the world. In other parts, farming has become an industry or commercial activity (see below).

INDUSTRY & TECHNOLOGY

Industry means making products not simply for your use or your family's, but for sale to other people. Industries are divided into two categories: light and heavy.

Light industries **use lightweight raw materials to make clothes, food products, plants and flowers, furniture, and other consumer goods.**

Heavy industries **produce machines that do big jobs, such as cranes, oil derricks, cars, ships, airplanes, and farm equipment.**

There are many different types of light and heavy industries, but most fall into one of five categories:

1. Agriculture

2. Mining

3. Forestry

4. Fishing and fishery

5. Manufacturing

Technology is the use of scientific knowledge, usually to improve industry and commerce. Technology includes the machines and other tools used to work in a variety of industries, manufacturing (see p. 81), and arts and crafts (see p. 71).

Agriculture

Agriculture means farming. Farming began more than 10,000 years ago. Unlike hunter-gatherers who roamed from one place to another to find food, farmers built permanent homes and farmed the same land in the same area year after year.

Most of the food we eat and many of the materials for the things we use are grown on farms.

Some farms only grow plants, or crops, for food (fresh vegetables and fruits) or manufacture (wheat for flour, soybeans for meat substitutes, cotton for fabrics, corn for feed, etc.). Other farms use the land to graze animals. These are called livestock farms, and include farms where animals are grown to be processed into meats or where they are grown to provide milk for dairy products (milk, cream, butter, cheese) and eggs. Some farms produce both crops and livestock. (These are called mixed farms.)

Old MacDonald Had a Farm

Old MacDonald had a farm—but just what kind of farm was it?

cooperative farm	Farm owned and operated by a group of farmers for the benefit of each individual involved.
corporate farm	Farm owned by a corporation, usually producing goods for sale in stores under a company label.
crop farm	Farm that raises crops for harvest, such as vegetables, fruits, or grains.
dairy farm	Farm specializing in the production of milk, cheese, butter, and other dairy products.
family farm	Farm owned and operated by a family as a private business.
livestock farm	Farm specializing in growing animals, such as chickens, pigs, cows, goats, or buffalo, for egg, dairy, or meat production.
mixed farm	Farm where both livestock and crops are grown.
ranch	Farm specializing in one type of crop or livestock, such as a cattle ranch, mink ranch, or deer ranch.
subsistence farm	Farm on which food and other products necessary for life are grown by one family for its own use.
commercial farm	Farm specializing in products for sale to a wide market and intended to make profits from sales instead of products for family use.
plantation	Large farm or estate in tropical or semitropical areas, often specializing in commercial crops, such as cotton, tobacco, rice, sugar cane, coffee, or tea.
truck farm	Farm close to a city that specializes in vegetables, fruit, and other cash crops.
herding farm	Farm that uses large areas of land, usually arid, for herding goats, camels, sheep, and/or cattle.

World Agriculture

World Agricultural Work Force

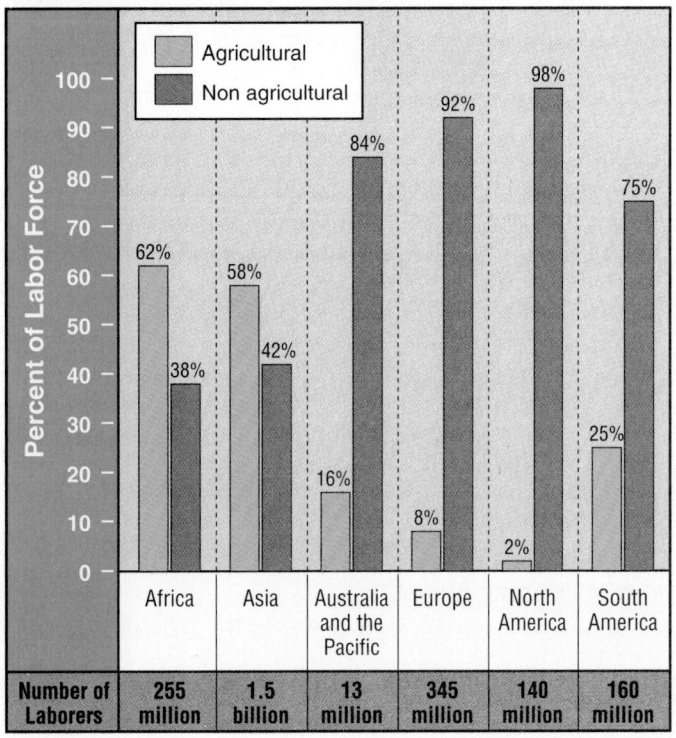

World Crop Production by Continent

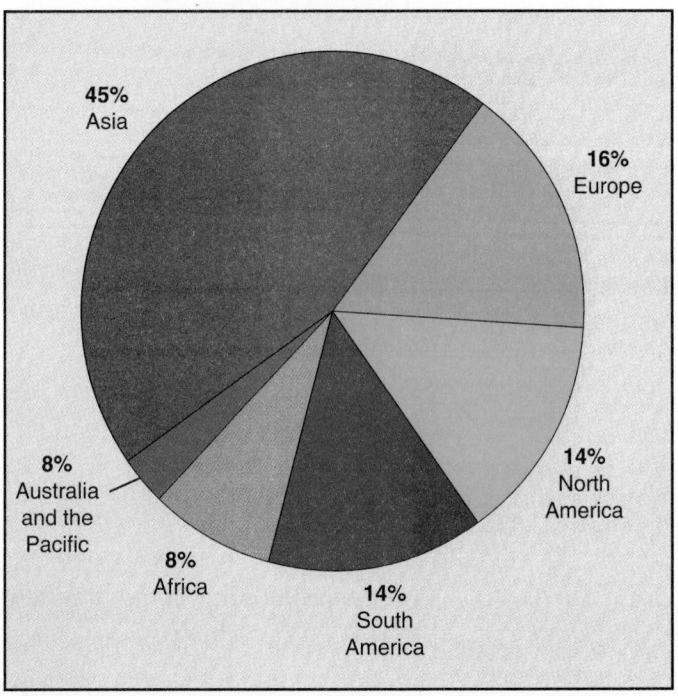

Both charts drawn from data collected from the Food and Agriculture Organization of the United Nations (1992)

More than half the labor force—or more than 1 billion people—in Asia and Africa work in agriculture, whereas only approximately 12%—or about 75 million people—work in agriculture in the rest of the world. Yet these 75 million people produce almost half the world's crops. By comparing these graphs, you might conclude that most of the farming in Asia and Africa is subsistence farming, not commercial farming.

Mining

Mining means taking rocks and minerals out of the earth. Many different rocks and minerals are mined, although they all fall into one of four categories:

Category	Example
metals	iron, lead, gold, silver, platinum
gemstones	diamonds, emeralds, rubies, sapphires, amethyst, lapis lazuli, jade
fossil fuels	natural gas, oil, coal
conglomerates	rock, sand, gravel

Some rocks and minerals are harder than others. The hardness is measured on the Mohs scale, a scale devised by the German scientist Friedrich Mohs. It ranks all rocks from 1 to 10.

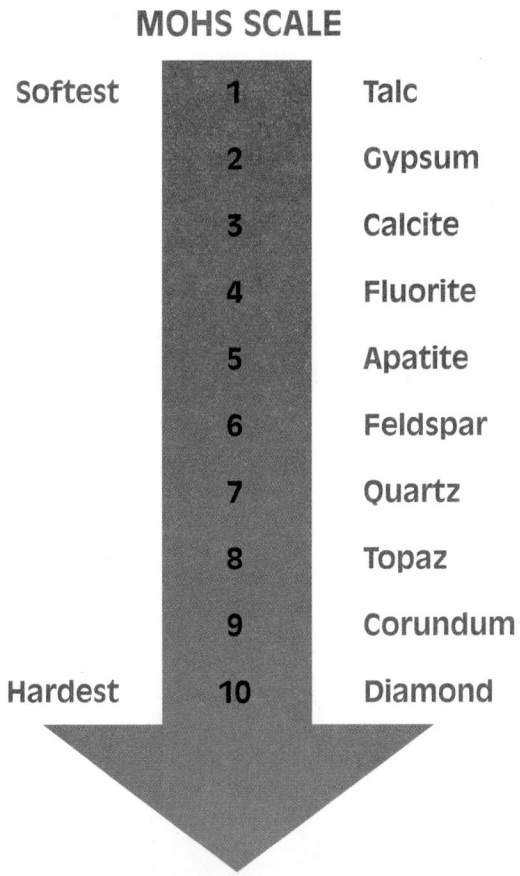

Which Mine Is Mine? Different Types of Mining

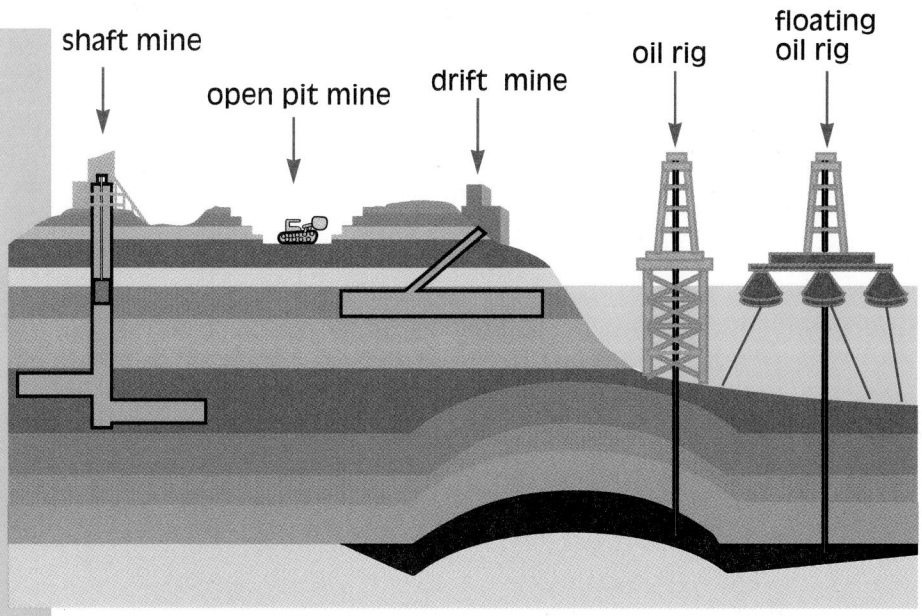

Mining occurs above ground, deep underground, and even in the land under seas and ocean.

Some mineral resources are running low. If we continue to use minerals at our current rate, silver, gold, copper, natural gas, oil, iron ore, and uranium could be in short supply by 2050. However, because we recognize the danger, some people are using minerals more carefully. Also, geologists are searching for new deposits of these precious minerals, on land and in the oceans.

Forestry

Forestry is the growing, maintaining, and harvesting of forests. Forests provide us with wood, which is used for building materials, furniture, paper, fuel, gums and resins, waxes, and medicines.

The world's forests come in many sizes and are filled with many different types of trees.

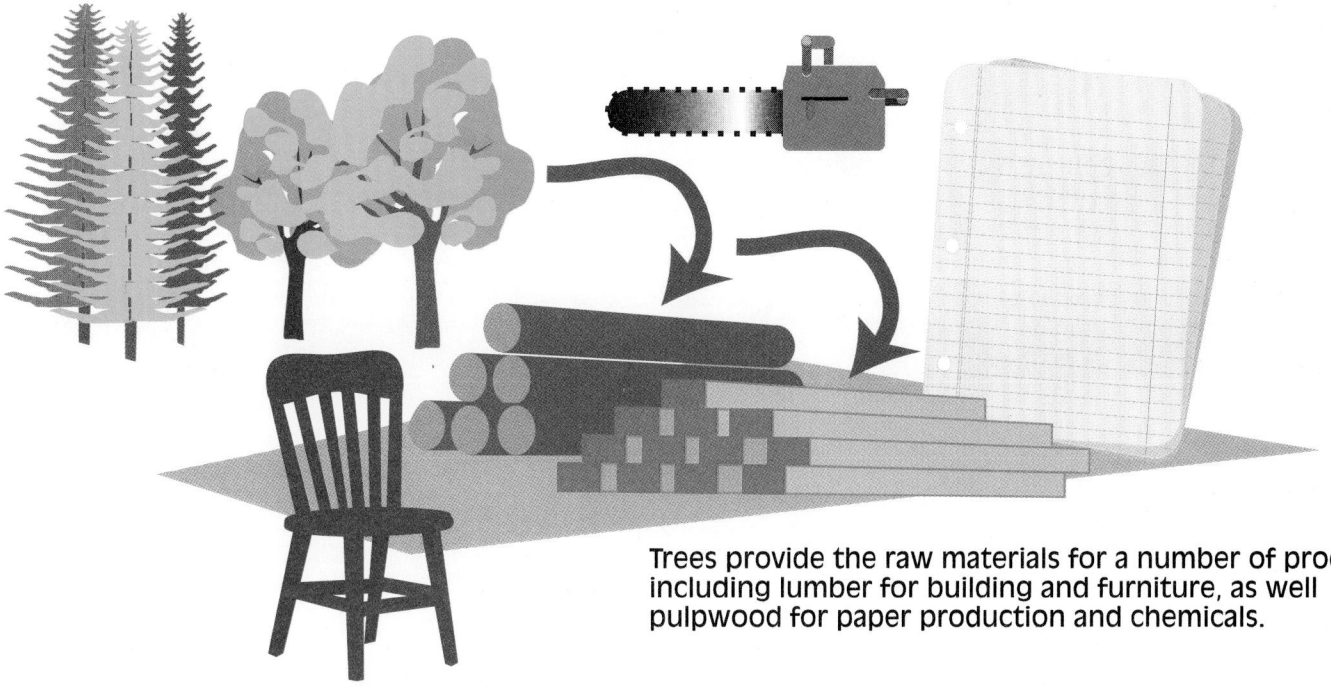

Trees provide the raw materials for a number of products, including lumber for building and furniture, as well pulpwood for paper production and chemicals.

Fishing and Fisheries

The business of fishing is called ***fishery***, and includes not only the catching and farming of fish and other aquatic animals, but also their processing and selling. Fishing is big business around the world. Nearly 80 million tons of sea animals are caught each year.

Manufacturing

Manufacturing means making new products from both raw materials and recycled materials. ***Raw materials*** are the natural products used to make new products. ***Recycled materials*** are the glass, metal, plastic, and paper collected from trash that are processed and reused to make new products.

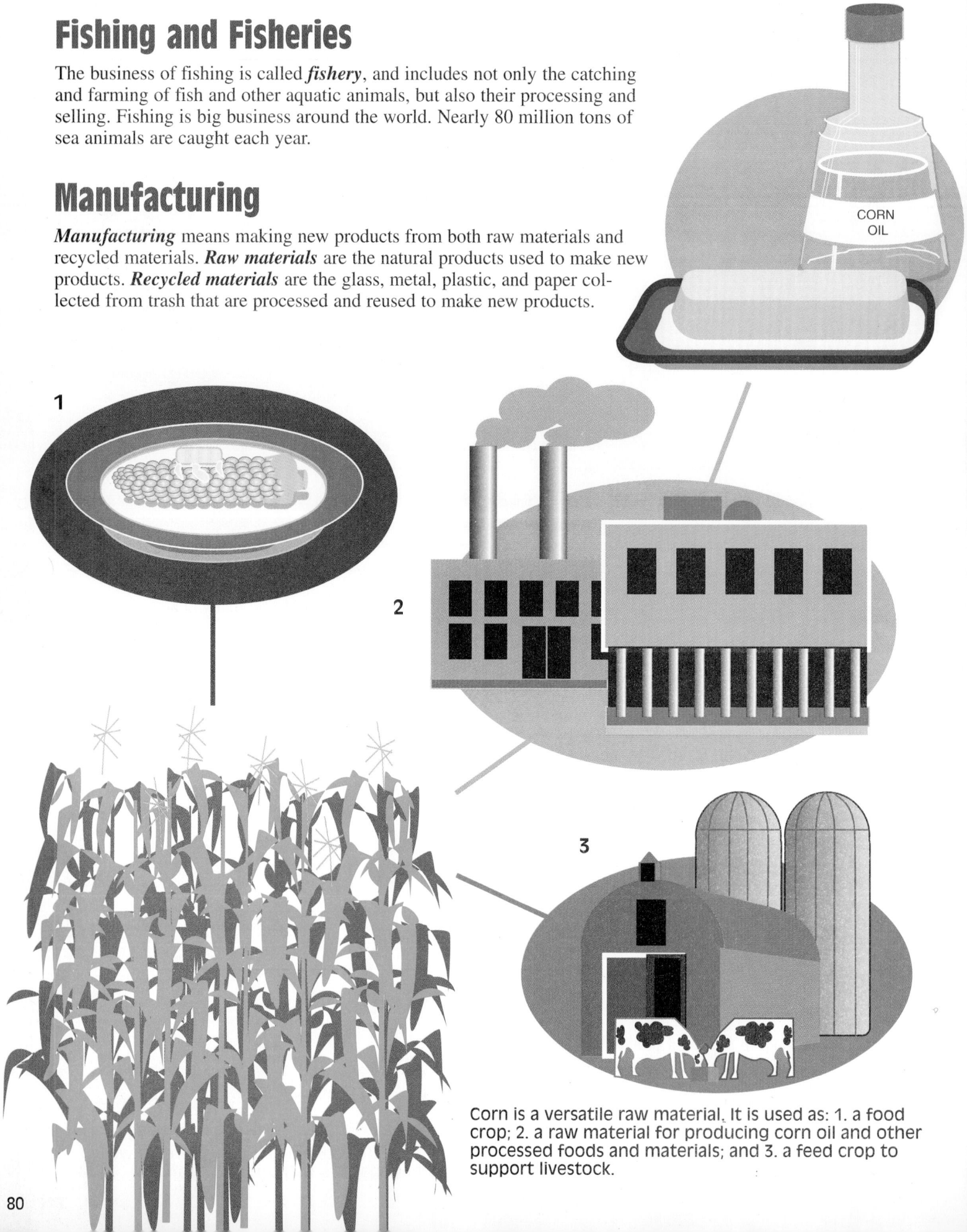

Corn is a versatile raw material. It is used as: 1. a food crop; 2. a raw material for producing corn oil and other processed foods and materials; and 3. a feed crop to support livestock.

A Brief History of Manufacturing

Machines such as the spinning wheel made cottage industries possible.

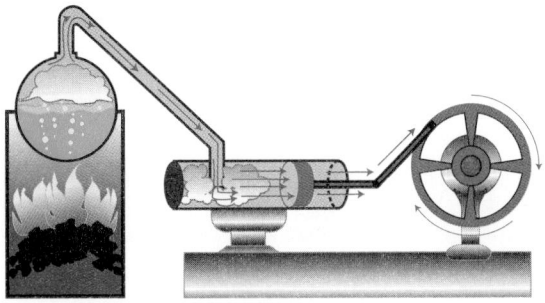

James Watt patented his steam engine in 1769, and the Industrial Revolution began.

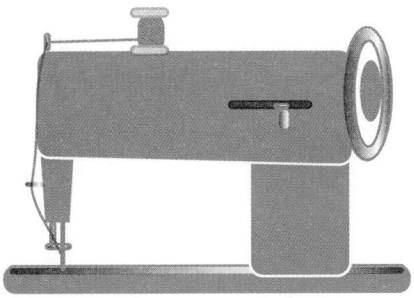

The sewing machine made the creation of clothes easier for homemakers. It also made possible the garment industry because clothes could be mass-produced with the aid of this time-saving machine.

Before the 1700s, most people manufactured goods for their own use in their homes. People wove fleece and plant fibers into fabrics and made their own clothes. They caught fish and raised crops, and preserved and canned them. They cut trees to burn as fuel and to use as lumber to build houses, barns, fences, and more.

Later, people made things for other people from within their homes. For example, a tailor would sew not only for himself or herself, but also for those who paid for the service. A farmer might grow extra crops to sell at a farm stand, or a lumberer might fell logs for other people to build with or burn as firewood. People still manufacture products in their homes or in small local factories. These home-based manufacturing operations are called ***cottage industries***.

In Europe, the early 1700s brought machines that made work easier and the production of manufactured products quicker and cheaper. The most important of these machines was improved and patented by the British inventor James Watt in 1769. It was the steam engine, and it brought about a change in the way people in Europe and the New World made products. This period of change is called the ***Industrial Revolution***.

With the Industrial Revolution came many changes in the world of manufacturing and business. For example, instead of making one product at a time, the machines of the Industrial Revolution allowed for ***mass production***, or the creation of many of the same product at the same time.

Many factory owners earned a great deal of money by selling mass-produced products. They built huge factories to make more and more products. To operate these factories, they hired many people. In fact, huge numbers of people moved into cities and factory towns during the Industrial Revolution to find work, live, and raise families.

Then, as today, businesses built or bought up other factories in different towns, cities, or even different states or countries. Companies with factories in two or more countries are called ***multinational companies***.

Many items are produced on assembly lines, where different workers are responsible for separate tasks in the creation of a product. Cars are mass-produced, usually on assembly lines.

150°W
120°W
90°W
60°W
30°W
0°
30°N
0°
30°S
60°S
Beaufort Sea
Baffin Bay
Greenland Sea
GREENLAND (KALAALLIT NUNAAT) (DENMARK)
Arctic Circle
ALASKA (U.S.)
Gulf of Alaska
Hudson Bay
CANADA
UNITED STATES OF AMERICA
ATLANTIC OCEAN
PACIFIC OCEAN
Tropic of Cancer
Equator
Tropic of Capricorn
Antarctic Circle
HAWAIIAN ISLANDS (U.S.)
TAHITI (FRANCE)
MEXICO
Gulf of Mexico
CUBA
BAHAMAS
HAITI
JAMAICA
Caribbean Sea
BELIZE
GUATEMALA
EL SALVADOR
HONDURAS
NICARAGUA
COSTA RICA
PANAMA
VENEZUELA
COLOMBIA
ECUADOR
PERU
BRAZIL
BOLIVIA
PARAGUAY
CHILE
URUGUAY
ARGENTINA
FALKLAND ISLANDS (ISLAS MALVINAS) (U.K.)
Cape Horn
DOMINICAN REPUBLIC
PUERTO RICO (U.S.)
VIRGIN ISLANDS (U.S., U.K.)
ST. KITTS AND NEVIS
ANTIGUA AND BARBUDA
DOMINICA
ST. LUCIA
ST. VINCENT AND THE GRENADINES
BARBADOS
GRENADA
TRINIDAD AND TOBAGO
GUYANA
SURINAME
FRENCH GUIANA (FRANCE)
ICELAND
NORWAY
DENMARK
THE NETHERLANDS
BELGIUM
UNITED KINGDOM
IRELAND
LUXEMBOURG
SWITZERLAND
LIECHTENSTEIN
SLOVENIA
CROATIA
MONACO
ANDORRA
BOSNIA AND HERZEGOVINA
PORTUGAL
SPAIN
FRANCE
SERBIA AND MONTENEGRO
ALBANIA
MACEDONIA
MOROCCO
CANARY ISLANDS (SPAIN)
WESTERN SAHARA (disputed)
ALGERIA
CAPE VERDE
MAURITANIA
MALI
SENEGAL
GAMBIA
GUINEA-BISSAU
GUINEA
SIERRA LEONE
LIBERIA
BURKINA FASO
CÔTE D'IVOIRE
GHANA
TOGO
BENIN
SÃO TOMÉ AND PRINCIPE
EQUATORIAL GUINEA
ANTARCTI

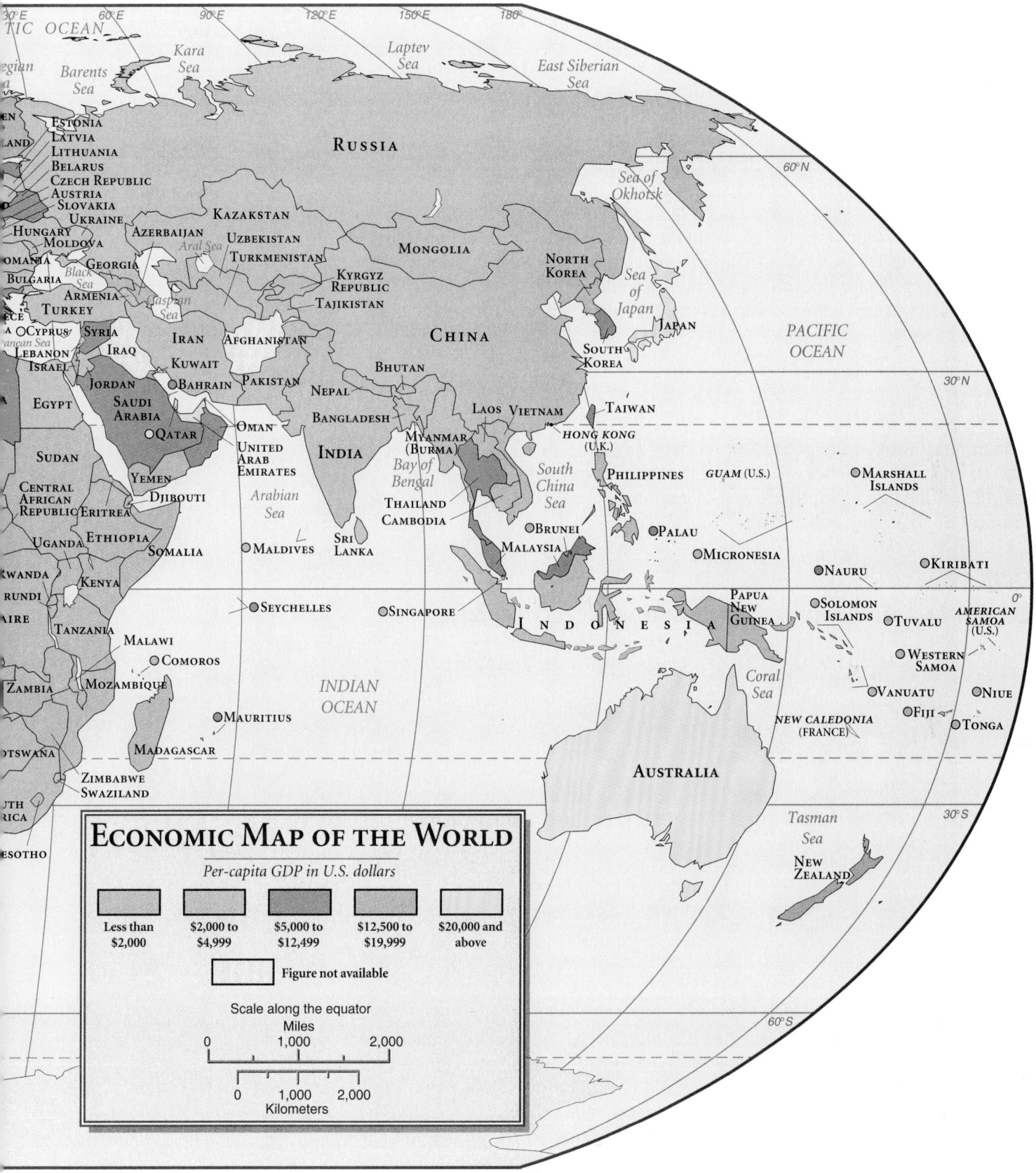
ECONOMIC MAP OF THE WORLD
Per-capita GDP in U.S. dollars
Less than $2,000
$2,000 to $4,999
$5,000 to $12,499
$12,500 to $19,999
$20,000 and above
Figure not available
Scale along the equator
Miles
0 1,000 2,000
0 1,000 2,000
Kilometers
RUSSIA
CHINA
INDIA
INDONESIA
AUSTRALIA
PACIFIC OCEAN
INDIAN OCEAN
Barents Sea
Kara Sea
Laptev Sea
East Siberian Sea
Sea of Okhotsk
Sea of Japan
Aral Sea
Black Sea
Caspian Sea
Bay of Bengal
Arabian Sea
South China Sea
Coral Sea
Tasman Sea
Estonia
Latvia
Lithuania
Belarus
Czech Republic
Austria
Slovakia
Ukraine
Hungary
Moldova
Georgia
Bulgaria
Armenia
Turkey
Cyprus
Syria
Lebanon
Israel
Iraq
Jordan
Egypt
Saudi Arabia
Qatar
Kuwait
Bahrain
Oman
United Arab Emirates
Yemen
Djibouti
Eritrea
Sudan
Central African Republic
Ethiopia
Uganda
Somalia
Kenya
Rwanda
Burundi
Tanzania
Seychelles
Malawi
Comoros
Zambia
Mozambique
Mauritius
Madagascar
Botswana
Zimbabwe
Swaziland
Lesotho
Kazakhstan
Uzbekistan
Turkmenistan
Kyrgyz Republic
Tajikistan
Mongolia
North Korea
South Korea
Japan
Iran
Afghanistan
Pakistan
Nepal
Bhutan
Bangladesh
Maldives
Sri Lanka
Laos
Vietnam
Taiwan
Hong Kong (U.K.)
Myanmar (Burma)
Thailand
Cambodia
Brunei
Malaysia
Singapore
Philippines
Guam (U.S.)
Palau
Micronesia
Marshall Islands
Nauru
Kiribati
Papua New Guinea
Solomon Islands
Tuvalu
American Samoa (U.S.)
Western Samoa
Vanuatu
Niue
Fiji
Tonga
New Caledonia (France)
New Zealand
60° N
30° N
0°
30° S
60° S
30° E
60° E
90° E
120° E
150° E
180°

Measuring Economies

An **economy** *is the system used by a state, region, or country to manage its resources, including its money, labor, and natural and human-made materials.*

Geographers study and compare the economies of different places. One way they measure an economy is by how much industry, sometimes called industrial development, a place has. Some countries, such as Taiwan and Russia, have lots of factories to turn natural resources into manufactured goods. They are considered ***industrially developed***.

Other places, such as Mexico, are considered ***developing countries*** because they have some industry but need more. Still others, such as those of Chad or Cambodia, have little industrial development. Geographers consider the natural resources underused, or underdeveloped, in these ***pre-industrial economies***.

Geographers sometimes use the term ***postindustrial*** to describe industrialized countries, such as the United States and Japan, no longer dominated by heavy industry. These postindustrial countries employ many workers to gather information, manage communications, and perform various services, such as banking or sales.

The Geography of Production

Geographers look at the goods and services a country produces, including the tons of crops, the number of cars, and the number of people working in different jobs. Added together, the output of a country is called its ***gross domestic product*** (GDP). (See also pp. 82–83.)

High GDPs

Countries with advanced machinery and technology:

1. **Need fewer people to produce goods and supply services.**
2. **Create goods and provide services quickly and efficiently.**

Low GDPs

Countries without advanced machinery and technology:

1. **Need more people to produce goods and supply services.**
2. **Create fewer goods and provide services more slowly and less efficiently.**

Development and the Standard of Living

While GDP measures how productive a country is, geographers use another measurement when they look at how well individual people live. The ***standard of living*** shows how well the average person is able to find a job, a place to live, food, and an education. Generally, the more industrialized a country, the higher its standard of living. But this is not always true. For example, the standard of living in Kuwait, which has lots of oil but little other industry, is very high. On the other hand, one reason people in the former Soviet Union were dissatisfied is that they had a very low standard of living although their nation had a lot of industry.

5 Migration, from Exploration to Settlement

An Overview of Migration

Scientists who study migration hypothesize that the first humans were born in Africa more than two million years ago and spread out from there into other parts of the world.

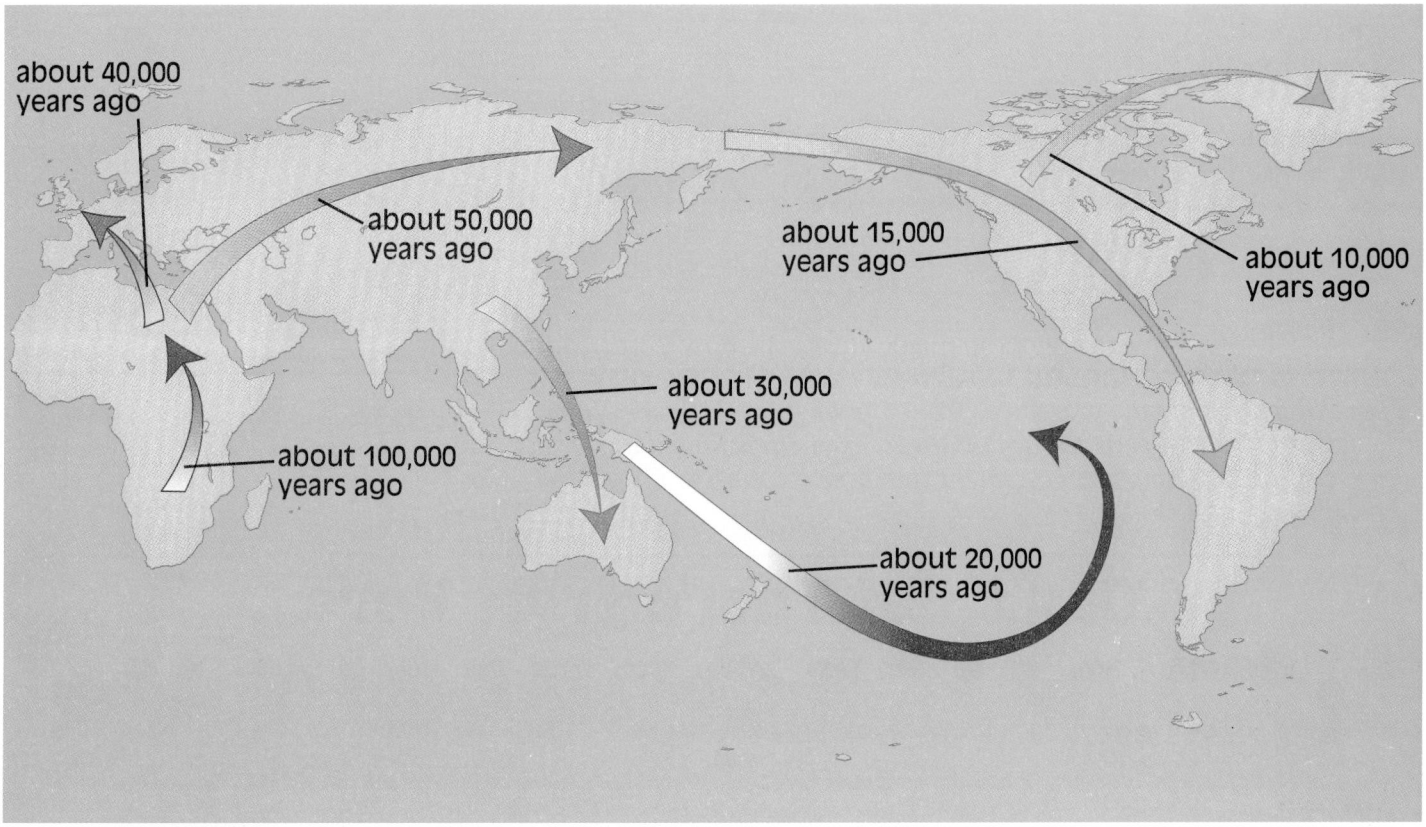

Many scientists and geographers believe that humans moved from Africa into Europe and Asia between 40 and 50 thousand years ago, then, over the next 30,000 years, spread further to inhabit all the continents, except Antarctica, and many Pacific islands.

CONQUEST AND EMPIRE

In Europe in the late 1400s, an era called the Age of Exploration began. During this era, explorers made voyages to areas unknown to Europeans. Soon Europeans began to colonize and settle in many new places.

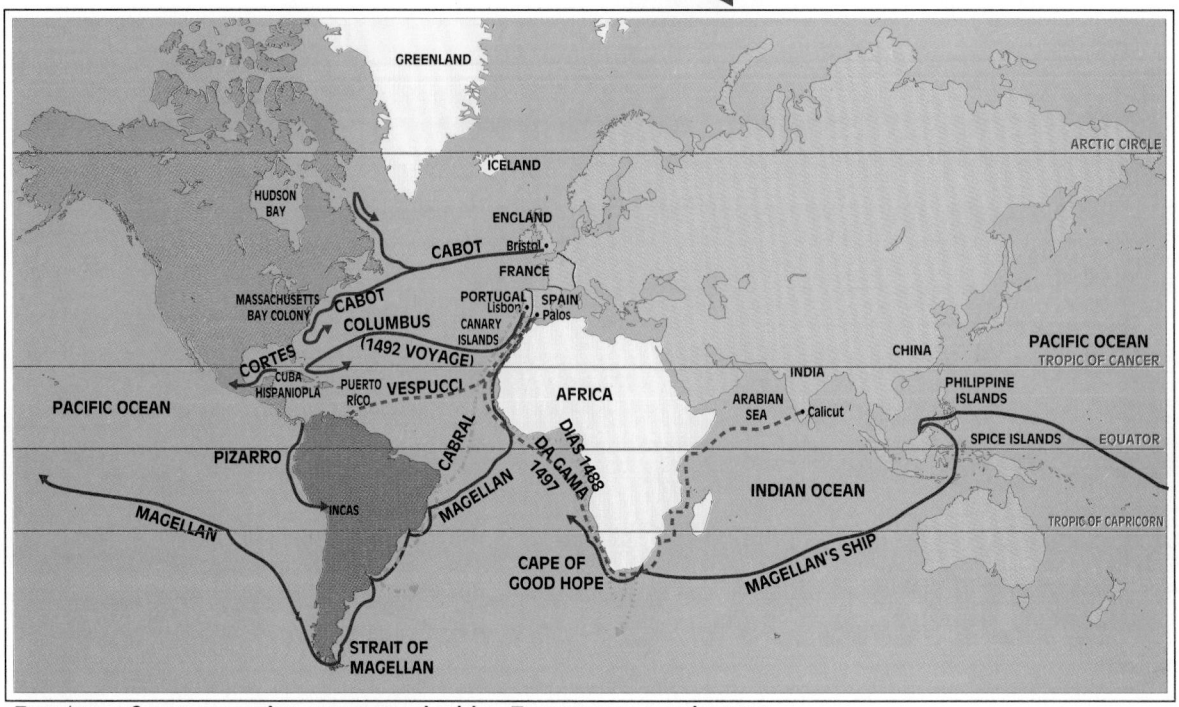

Routes of some major voyages led by European explorers.

Migration *means movement from one place to settle in another.*
Emigration *means movement* **away** *from one's homeland.*
Immigration *means movement* **into** *a new country.*

Can't Get There from Here:

TRANSPORTATION

In order for people to move from one region to another, they need ***transportation*** for themselves and their possessions. Early transportation was by foot. People simply walked from one place to another. Later, animals—horses, mules, and oxen—were tamed and used to carry passengers or packages, as well as to pull carts, sleds, and carriages.

With the Industrial Revolution (see p. 81) came the invention of machines to transport people farther in less time.

One of the products of the Industrial Revolution was the automobile.

Why Move?

People usually move from one place to another in search of a better place to live. Although there are many things that make one place better or worse than another, these things fall into two main categories:

1. Economics
2. Politics

People move away from:	To:	
Poverty	Areas of greater wealth	Economic Reasons
Overcrowded conditions	Greater space and comfort	
High cost of living	Affordable goods, services, and housing	
Lack of jobs	More work opportunities	Economic and Political Reasons
Poor schools	Greater educational opportunities	
Poor health care	Available, higher quality, health care	Political Reasons
Intolerance of race, culture, or religion.	Tolerance	
Political oppression	Political choice and rights	
War or crime	Peaceful, safe life	

APPENDIX

1. Glossary of Geographical Terms

acid rain — Rain that is polluted by acid in the atmosphere and damages the environment.

agriculture — Using the land to grow crops and raise animals; farming (see p. 77).

Antarctic Circle — A line of latitude that lies 66 degrees 30 minutes (66° 30′) south of the equator. From September 21 to December 21, the area north of the Antarctic Circle has daylight more than 12 hours a day. On December 21 it is daylight for 24 hours at the Antarctic Circle. Then the days get shorter until there is darkness for 24 hours on June 21.

aquifer — A layer of rock that holds water in its pores.

archipelago — A group of small islands.

Arctic Circle — A line of latitude that lies 66 degrees 30 minutes (66°30′) north of the equator. From September 21 to December 21, the area north of the Arctic Circle is increasingly in darkness. It has 24 hours of darkness on December 21 and then daylight begins at the Arctic Circle and moves north to the pole. On March 21 the area within the Arctic Circle has 12 hours of daylight and 12 hours of darkness. From March 21 the hours of daylight increase until the sun rises for 24 hours on June 21.

arid — Land that is arid is extremely dry because very little rain has fallen on it.

arroyo — A dry streambed.

art, fine — Visual, literary, and movement arts that communicate what a culture finds beautiful.

atoll — A horseshoe-shaped island formed by coral and surrounding a lagoon.

bank, river — The land along the sides of a river or canal.

basin, river Land drained by a river or a river system.

bay A curved area along a coast or shore where the water juts into the land. A bay is usually smaller than a gulf and usually has a smaller opening.

bayou A system of swampland with slow-moving streams flowing through it, found in the southern United States.

bedrock The solid rock that lies beneath the soil on the earth's surface.

beliefs Attitudes, ideas, and world views held by a person or group of people.

birthrate The number of babies born alive as a proportion of the population in a specific place in a specific amount of time.

blizzard Heavy snowfall with high wind.

bog A small, very acidic body of water that has no natural inlets and is surrounded by rings of vegetation. A mat of grasses may grow on top. As the grasses die and build up, the bog water is replaced by a spongy mass of peat.

branch One of the two main streams that join to form a larger river.

butte A flat-topped hill formed when hard rock on the surface protects softer soil underneath it from being eroded. A butte is often steep sided.

canyon A valley with very steep sides and a flat bottom, usually cut into the rock by a river. A canyon is larger than a gorge.

cape A point of land that extends into a sea or an ocean.

chinook A warm, dry wind that blows down the slopes of the Rocky Mountains in winter and in early spring, and melts the snow at the base of the mountains.

city A place where a large number of people live close together; an urban area.

cliff A high, steep rock face.

climate The usual weather in a particular place over a period of time.

coast The land beside a sea or ocean.

commercial area A part of a city where business or industry is located.

continent A large mass of land surrounded by oceans.

continental climate A type of climate with hot summers and cold winters, common in the center of continents.

continental divide A highland or ridge of mountains that causes rivers and streams to flow in different directions across continents, eventually reaching different oceans.

continental drift The movement of the continents on the earth's surface.

continental shelf The part of the continents that extends below sea level toward the deeper ocean.

core The center part of the earth, consisting of a molten outer core and a solid inner core.

course, river The part of a river between its source and its mouth.

crater The cup-shaped indentation at the top of a volcano.

crevasse A deep crack in a glacier.

crust The outer layer of the earth.

cuisine A particular style of preparing food.

culture The behavior—language, beliefs, traditions, arts and crafts, political systems, and technologies—of a group of people.

current Cold and warm "rivers" of seawater that flow in the oceans. Also, streams of cold or warm air that flow through the atmosphere.

customs The traditions of a group of people.

cyclone A name for various air movements involving spiral motion, including typhoon, hurricane, and tornado. Also the common name for a hurricane-type storm in the Pacific.

delta An area of land shaped like a triangle where a river deposits mud, sand, or pebbles as it enters the sea.

desert A dry region, with fewer than 10 inches of precipitation annually.

developed country A developed country has a lot of industry and a high standard of living.

developing country A developing country has little industry and a low standard of living.

divide High land—either a hill or a mountain—that causes rivers to flow in different directions.

downstream The direction of a river's flow.

downtown The main business area of a city.

drainage The running off of rainwater from land.

drift Soil, silt, and rock deposited by a glacier.

drought An extra-long period without precipitation.

drumlin A long, narrow hill formed by glacial deposits.

dune A hill of sand formed by blowing winds.

eclipse, lunar Event that occurs when light from the sun is blocked by the earth passing between the sun and moon, so that the earth casts a shadow on the moon (see p. 14).

eclipse, solar Event that occurs when sunlight is blocked by the moon as it passes between the sun and earth, casting a shadow on the earth (see p. 14).

economy The system used by a state, region, or country to manage its industry, trade, and finance.

equator A line on a map or globe halfway between the north and south poles. The equator is almost 25,000 miles around.

escarpment A cliff or steep bank located inland rather than at the shore.

esker A long, narrow ridge of coarse gravel deposited by a stream flowing under or through a glacier.

estuary The part of a river affected by the tides of the sea it's about to flow into.

exurb A sparsely populated residential area just outside the suburbs of a city.

fall line The region where elevation drops and rivers descend over a waterfall or rapids to lower elevations.

fault A huge crack in the earth's surface, usually caused by earth's movements.

fishery The business of fishing; also, a fish farm.

floodplain The low, flat area on either side of a river, which the river will flood in times of high water.

forest A large, dense growth of trees, plants, and underbrush.

forestry The process of growing, maintaining, and harvesting forests.

fork A separation into two or more branches, as of a stream.

geographic grid The intersecting pattern formed by the lines of longitude and latitude.

geographic north pole Also true north pole. The point on the earth located at 90 degrees (90°) north latitude, where the lines of longitude meet.

geography The study of the world, how it works, and how people use and change the world as they live in it.

geopolitical A geopolitical map shows both political and physical features.

geyser A spout of water heated by molten rock underground.

glacier A thick bed of ice that covers a continent or a river of thick ice that moves slowly down a slope or valley.

globe A sphere-shaped model of the earth.

gorge A steep-sided, V-shaped canyon, usually caused by swiftly flowing water.

gross domestic product The total output of a country or region, including all its products and the labor of its people.

groundwater Water found beneath the earth's surface.

gulf A large area of sea that is partly surrounded by land.

headwater The source of a river or river system.

hemispheres Halves of the earth. The equator divides the earth into northern and southern hemispheres. The prime meridian and 180 degrees (180°) longitude divide the earth into eastern and western hemispheres.

hill A part of the earth's surface that rises gently above the level of the surrounding land.

humid When air is humid, it contains a lot of moisture.

humus Soil made up of decomposed animals and plants.

hurricane A violent, usually late-summer storm in the Atlantic Ocean.

iceberg A mass of floating ice broken off from a glacier. Only a small patch of an iceberg shows above water.

ice-cap climate An area with an ice-cap climate is constantly covered by snow and ice.

ice floe A sheet of floating, frozen seawater.

industry The making and selling of products.

international date line A line on a map or globe drawn from the north pole to the south pole, roughly following 180 degrees (180°) longitude, but turning and twisting to miss islands and other bodies of land. It is where the days of the week change. It is one day earlier east of the date line than it is west.

island A body of land completely surrounded by water.

isthmus A narrow strip of land that connects two larger bodies of land.

jungle A very dense tangle of tropical vegetation.

lagoon A shallow body of calm water separated from the sea by a narrow strip of land.

lake A body of water surrounded by land. The water in lakes is usually fresh, but may be salty.

landform Any of a number of natural features on the earth's surface, including mountains, plains, plateaus, hills, canyons, cliffs, etc.

language The use of voice sounds, gestures, and written symbols to communicate thoughts and feelings.

leeward Facing the direction toward which the wind is blowing.

loam Soil that contains sand and clay as well as silt and humus.

loess Fine soil particles and dust that are carried by the wind and water and pile up to form a rich, thick soil.

magnetic north pole The point on the earth to which a magnetized compass needle points.

mantle The part of earth that lies between the core and the crust.

manufacturing The creation of products from raw and recycled materials.

map A picture of a place drawn on a flat surface.

marine climate A mild and wet climate usually found near the sea.

marsh A body of moving water, fresh or salty, with reeds growing in it. A marsh is usually near a river or sea coast.

megalopolis A group of cities whose boundaries have extended to meet each other.

mental maps Pictures in your mind of familiar places or regions.

mesa A hill or mountain feature with a flat top and steep sides. A mesa is larger than a butte.

metropolis A large city.

migration, human The movement of people from one place to another, usually for economic or political reasons.

mining Taking minerals out of the earth.

mistral A strong, cold, dry northerly wind that sometimes brings very cold air down the Rhone River valley in France.

monsoon Seasonal reversal in wind direction that brings heavy rainfall in parts of southern Asia.

moraine A mound of soil and pebbles were carried by a glacier and then dropped when the glacier receded.

mountain A part of the land that rises abruptly to at least 1,000 feet above the surrounding land.

mouth, river The place where a river flows into a larger body of water.

neighborhood Area within a city or town that has a unique cultural makeup.

north pole See geographic north pole and magnetic north pole.

oasis A place in a desert where there is a source of water that can support some plant life.

ocean A large body of salt water that separates continents.

oxbow A u-shaped bend in a river.

peak The highest point of a mountain.

peninsula A piece of land that juts into a body of water and is surrounded by water on three sides.

permafrost Permanently frozen subsoil.

plain Nearly flat region of land.

plate One of the hard sections of the earth's crust on which the continents lie.

plateau A large, mostly level area of land that stands higher than the surrounding area. A plateau is larger than a butte.

political system A method of government.

pond A small body of fresh water.

population The total number of people who live in a particular place.

population data Facts about populations, including history, migration patterns, and current information.

population profile A graph that shows different age groups within a population.

population pyramid A bar graph that shows total population in terms of age and gender.

postindustrial economy An economy that was once based on industry but is now based on services such as banking, computers, and health care.

prairie Treeless plain, usually covered by tall grass.

precipitation Any of the forms in which water falls on the earth's surface (rain, snow, hail, etc.).

pre-industrial economy An economy with very little industry.

prevailing wind The direction the wind usually blows across a particular place or region.

prime meridian The line of longitude drawn from the north pole to the south pole at zero degrees (0°).

projections, map Representations of the geographic grid used to make world maps.

rain forest Forest in tropical climates with dense canopies, vines, and understories of growth.

range A large area of open land. Animals usually graze on the grass on range lands.

range, mountain A group or chain of mountains.

ravine A deep, narrow canyon.

reef A ridge of sand, coral, or bedrock under water but near the surface.

rift valley A valley formed by the folding and the faulting of the earth's crust along parallel lines.

river A large stream that flows from a source to a larger body of water, for example, a larger river, lake, sea, or ocean.

rural A rural area is made up of farmland or countryside.

savanna Tropical grassland with few trees.

sea A large body of salt water surrounded partly by or next to land.

seamount Underwater mountain with steep sides that rises from the ocean floor.

shore The land beside a body of water.

silt Fine grains of soil carried by water.

soil Particles of bedrock, decomposed animal and plant matter, water, and air pockets that cover the earth's surface and that plants grow in.

source, river The beginning of a river.

south pole The point on the earth located at 90 degrees (90°) south latitude where the lines of longitude meet.

standard of living A measurement of the availability of jobs, housing, food, and education to average citizens in a specific area or country. A high standard of living means greater availability, a low standard, lesser availability.

steppe Any of the vast, treeless plains found in southeastern Europe and Asia.

steppe climate Dry climate, but with greater precipitation than in a desert climate.

strait A narrow body of water that connects two larger bodies of water.

stream A small river.

suburb Residential area lying just outside a city or town.

swamp A wetland similar to a marsh but usually larger in area. It supports a wider variety of plant life, including trees and shrubs.

tableland A plateau.

taiga Cool, high-latitude land with low trees.

technology The use of scientific knowledge, usually to improve industry or commerce.

tectonic plates The pieces of the earth's crust that float on the mantel.

temperate climate A climate without extremes of either heat or cold.

temperature A measurement of heat.

thunderstorm A storm accompanied by lightning, thunder, heavy rain, and sometimes hail.

tide A change in the level of an ocean or a sea, both daily and over a year, due to the pull of gravity between the earth and the moon.

till Soil and rock deposits spread out by a glacier as it moves on or melts.

tornado Violent and destructive cyclone that occurs inland.

trade wind The prevailing wind of the tropics.

tributary A stream or river that flows into a larger stream or river.

Tropic of Cancer A line of latitude that runs parallel to the equator. It is located at 23 degrees 30 minutes (23° 30′) north of the equator. During the summer solstice (June 21), the sun is directly overhead at the Tropic of Cancer.

Tropic of Capricorn A line of latitude that runs parallel to the equator. It is located at 23 degrees 30 minutes (23° 30′) south of the equator. During the winter solstice (December 21), the sun is directly overhead at the Tropic of Capricorn.

tsunami A huge wave that may sometimes move through the water faster than 400 miles an hour and reach a height of more than 100 feet.

tundra A plain in the arctic where mosses and low-growing plants grow, but not trees.

typhoon A violent late-summer storm in the northwest Pacific.

urban An urban area is a city or town.

valley A U-shaped lowland between hills or mountains.

volcano An opening in the earth's crust from which molten rocks erupt. The rocks usually form a mountain around the opening.

watershed Area whose rainfall runs, on the surface and as groundwater, to feed a particular river.

weather The conditions in the earth's atmosphere at a certain place and time.

weathering The breakdown of rock on the earth's surface due to wind, water, and chemical actions.

wind Air moving across the earth's surface.

windward Facing the direction from which the wind is blowing.

2. Atlas

North America 101

South America 102

Africa 103

Europe 104–105

Asia 106–107

Middle East 108

Oceania 109

United States of America 110–111

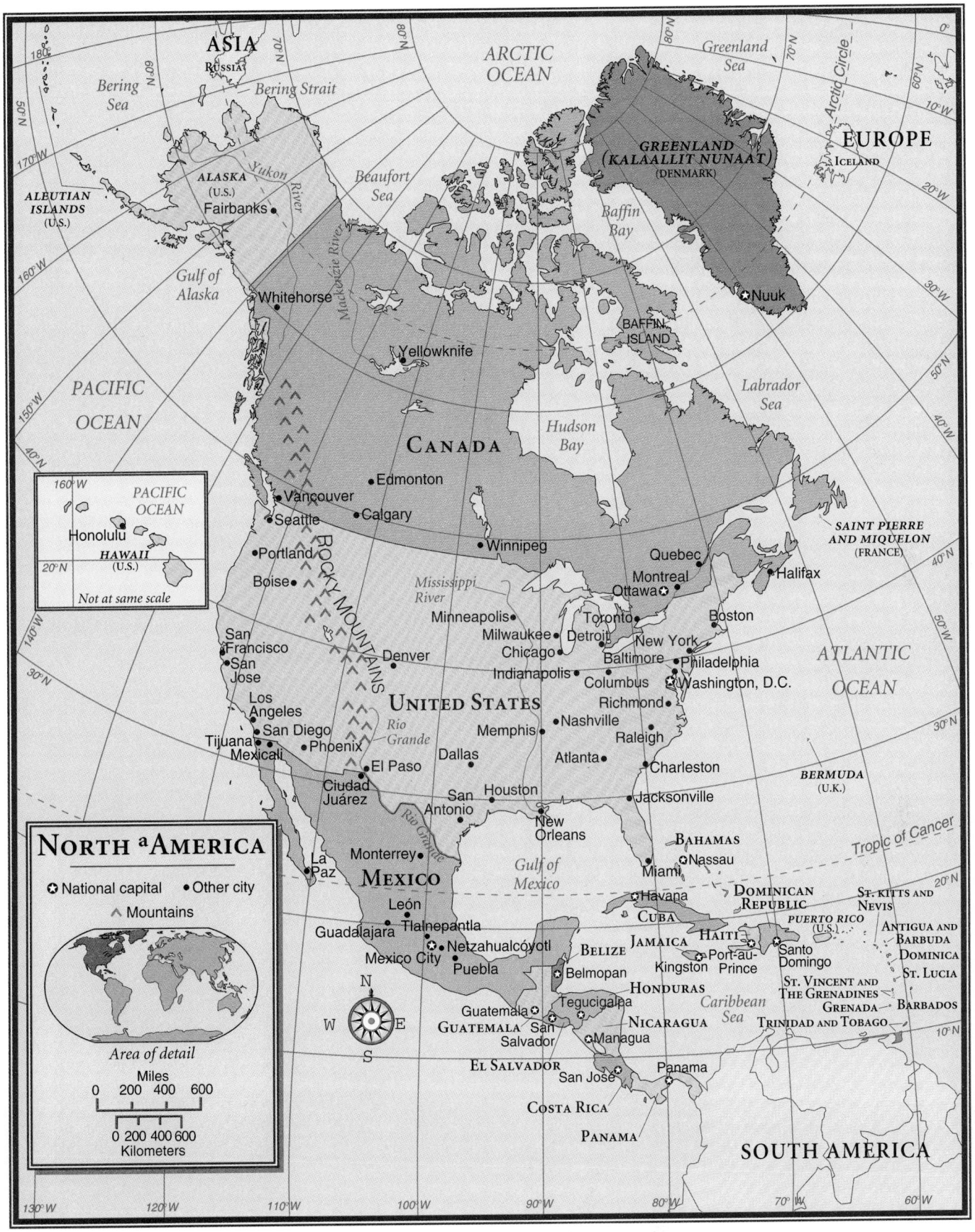
NORTH AMERICA
National capital
Other city
Mountains
Area of detail
Miles
0 200 400 600
0 200 400 600
Kilometers
ASIA
RUSSIA
Bering Sea
Bering Strait
ARCTIC OCEAN
Greenland Sea
Arctic Circle
EUROPE
ICELAND
GREENLAND (KALAALLIT NUNAAT)
(DENMARK)
ALASKA
(U.S.)
Fairbanks
ALEUTIAN ISLANDS
(U.S.)
Yukon River
Beaufort Sea
Baffin Bay
Gulf of Alaska
Mackenzie River
Whitehorse
Nuuk
BAFFIN ISLAND
Yellowknife
PACIFIC OCEAN
Labrador Sea
Hudson Bay
CANADA
Edmonton
Vancouver
Calgary
Seattle
Winnipeg
Portland
Boise
Quebec
Montreal
Halifax
SAINT PIERRE AND MIQUELON
(FRANCE)
Ottawa
Mississippi River
Minneapolis
Toronto
Boston
Milwaukee
Detroit
New York
Chicago
Baltimore
Philadelphia
San Francisco
San Jose
Denver
Indianapolis
Columbus
Washington, D.C.
ATLANTIC OCEAN
ROCKY MOUNTAINS
Los Angeles
UNITED STATES
Richmond
San Diego
Rio Grande
Nashville
Memphis
Raleigh
Tijuana
Mexicali
Phoenix
Dallas
Atlanta
El Paso
Charleston
Ciudad Juárez
San Antonio
Houston
Jacksonville
BERMUDA
(U.K.)
New Orleans
Rio Grande
BAHAMAS
Nassau
Tropic of Cancer
La Paz
Monterrey
MEXICO
Gulf of Mexico
Miami
Havana
DOMINICAN REPUBLIC
ST. KITTS AND NEVIS
CUBA
PUERTO RICO
(U.S.)
ANTIGUA AND BARBUDA
León
Guadalajara
Tlalnepantla
HAITI
JAMAICA
DOMINICA
Netzahualcóyotl
BELIZE
Port-au-Prince
Santo Domingo
Mexico City
Puebla
Kingston
ST. LUCIA
Belmopan
HONDURAS
ST. VINCENT AND THE GRENADINES
Tegucigalpa
Caribbean Sea
GRENADA
BARBADOS
Guatemala
NICARAGUA
TRINIDAD AND TOBAGO
GUATEMALA
San Salvador
Managua
EL SALVADOR
Panama
San José
COSTA RICA
PANAMA
SOUTH AMERICA
N
W
E
S
180°
170°W
160°W
150°W
140°W
130°W
120°W
110°W
100°W
90°W
80°W
70°W
60°W
50°W
40°W
30°W
20°W
10°W
0°
80°N
70°N
60°N
50°N
40°N
30°N
20°N
10°N
160°W
PACIFIC OCEAN
Honolulu
HAWAII
(U.S.)
20°N
Not at same scale

Caribbean Sea
ATLANTIC OCEAN
NORTH AMERICA
Maracaibo
Barranquilla
Caracas
Valencia
Cartagena
VENEZUELA
GUYANA
Georgetown
Paramaribo
Orinoco River
Medellín
Bogotá
Cali
COLOMBIA
FRENCH GUIANA (FRANCE)
SURINAME
Quito
ECUADOR
GALAPAGOS ISLANDS (ECUADOR)
Guayaquil
Manaus
Belém
Fortaleza
PERU
BRAZIL
Recife
Lima
Salvador
Bolivia
ANDES MOUNTAINS
La Paz
Brasília
Sucre
Belo Horizonte
Paraná River
Paraguay
São Paulo
Rio de Janeiro
Asunción
Curitiba
Pôrto Alegre
Córdoba
Valparaíso
Rosario
Uruguay
Santiago
Montevideo
Buenos Aires
PACIFIC OCEAN
Concepción
Argentina
Chile
Puerto Montt
Strait of Magellan
FALKLAND ISLANDS (ISLAS MALVINAS) (U.K.)
SOUTH GEORGIA ISLAND (U.K.)
Cape Horn
20° N
10° N
10° S
20° S
30° S
40° S
50° S
110° W
100° W
90° W
80° W
70° W
60° W
50° W
40° W
30° W
20° W
10° W
N
W
E
S
SOUTH AMERICA
National capital
Other city
Mountains
Area of detail
Miles
0 200 400 600
0 200 400 600
Kilometers

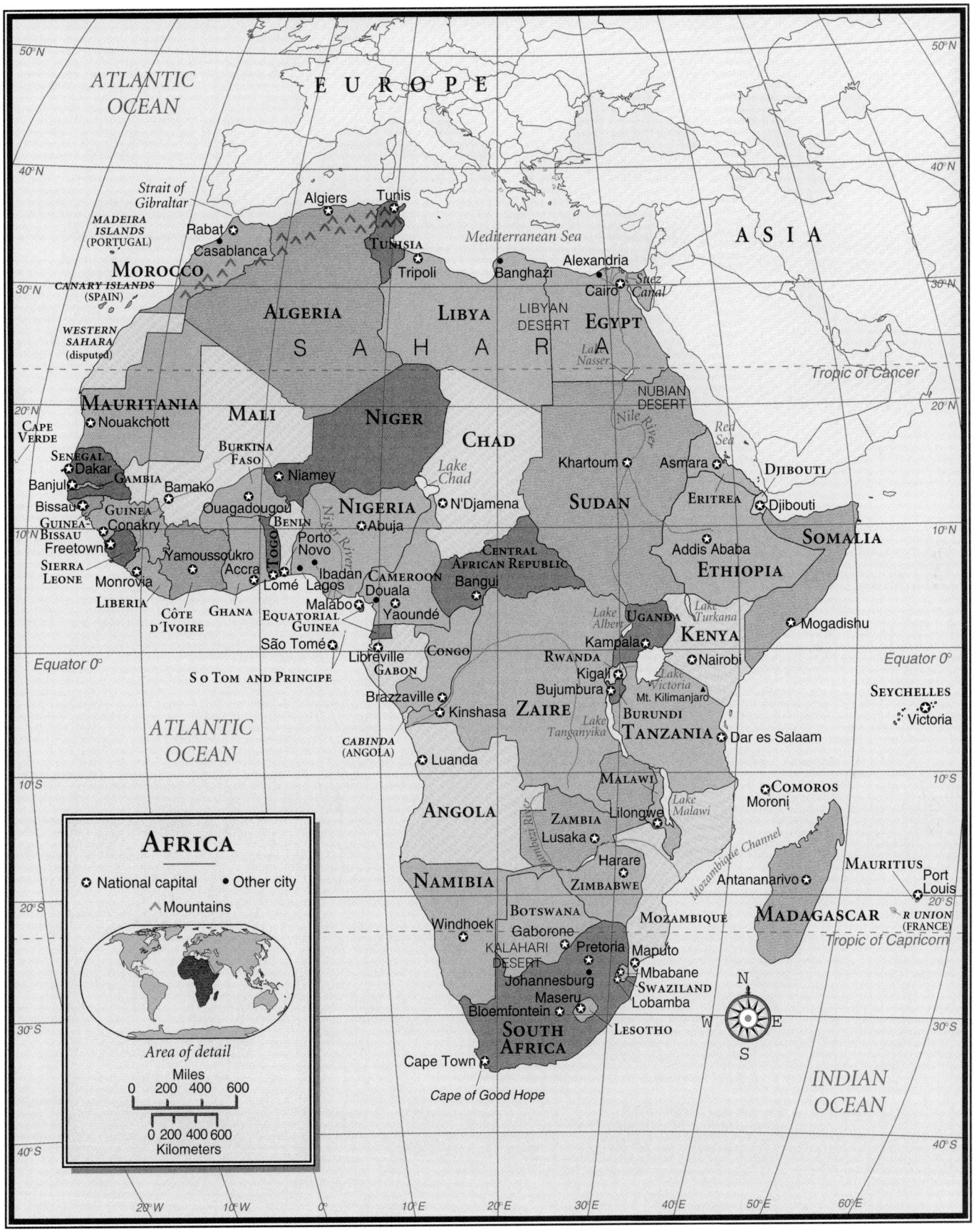
AFRICA
National capital
Other city
Mountains
Area of detail
Miles
0 200 400 600
0 200 400 600
Kilometers
ATLANTIC OCEAN
EUROPE
ASIA
Mediterranean Sea
Strait of Gibraltar
MADEIRA ISLANDS (PORTUGAL)
CANARY ISLANDS (SPAIN)
WESTERN SAHARA (disputed)
MOROCCO
Rabat
Casablanca
Algiers
Tunis
TUNISIA
Tripoli
Banghazi
Alexandria
Cairo
Suez Canal
ALGERIA
LIBYA
LIBYAN DESERT
EGYPT
SAHARA
Lake Nasser
Tropic of Cancer
NUBIAN DESERT
Nile River
Red Sea
MAURITANIA
Nouakchott
CAPE VERDE
MALI
NIGER
CHAD
Lake Chad
SENEGAL
Dakar
GAMBIA
Banjul
Bamako
BURKINA FASO
Niamey
Bissau
GUINEA
Conakry
GUINEA-BISSAU
Freetown
SIERRA LEONE
Monrovia
LIBERIA
Yamoussoukro
CÔTE D'IVOIRE
Accra
GHANA
Ouagadougou
TOGO
Lomé
BENIN
Porto Novo
Niger River
NIGERIA
Abuja
Ibadan
Lagos
N'Djamena
SUDAN
Khartoum
Asmara
ERITREA
Djibouti
DJIBOUTI
SOMALIA
Mogadishu
Addis Ababa
ETHIOPIA
CENTRAL AFRICAN REPUBLIC
Bangui
CAMEROON
Douala
Yaoundé
Malabo
EQUATORIAL GUINEA
São Tomé
Libreville
GABON
CONGO
Brazzaville
Kinshasa
ZAIRE
Lake Albert
UGANDA
Kampala
Lake Turkana
KENYA
Nairobi
RWANDA
Kigali
Bujumbura
BURUNDI
Lake Victoria
Mt. Kilimanjaro
Lake Tanganyika
TANZANIA
Dar es Salaam
Equator 0°
SO TOM AND PRINCIPE
SEYCHELLES
Victoria
CABINDA (ANGOLA)
Luanda
ANGOLA
MALAWI
Lilongwe
Lake Malawi
COMOROS
Moroni
ZAMBIA
Lusaka
Zambezi River
Harare
ZIMBABWE
Mozambique Channel
Antananarivo
MADAGASCAR
MAURITIUS
Port Louis
RÉUNION (FRANCE)
NAMIBIA
Windhoek
BOTSWANA
Gaborone
KALAHARI DESERT
Pretoria
Johannesburg
MOZAMBIQUE
Maputo
Mbabane
SWAZILAND
Lobamba
Maseru
LESOTHO
Bloemfontein
SOUTH AFRICA
Cape Town
Cape of Good Hope
Tropic of Capricorn
INDIAN OCEAN
N
W
E
S
50° N
40° N
30° N
20° N
10° N
10° S
20° S
30° S
40° S
20° W
10° W
0°
10° E
20° E
30° E
40° E
50° E
60° E

ARCTIC OCEAN
70°N
Arctic Circle
Reykjavík
ICELAND
30°W
60°N
Norwegian Sea
FAEROE ISLANDS (DENMARK)
SHETLAND ISLANDS (U.K.)
SWEDEN
Gulf of Bothnia
FINLAN
NORWAY
Bergen
Oslo
Helsinki
Stockholm
Baltic Sea
ESTON
Goteborg
Riga
LAT
NORTHERN IRELAND (U.K.)
SCOTLAND
Edinburgh
Glasgow
North Sea
ATLANTIC OCEAN
20°W
Belfast
IRELAND
UNITED KINGDOM
DENMARK
Copenhagen
LITHUANI
Vilni
Dublin
Cork
Manchester
50°N
RUSSIA
NETHERLANDS
Birmingham
WALES
ENGLAND
London
Thames
Hamburg
Elbe River
Amsterdam
The Hague
Rhine River
Berlin
Warsaw
Vistula River
POLAND
Lodz
Wrocław
English Channel
BELGIUM
Brussels
Cologne
GERMANY
Krakow
Luxembourg
LUXEMBOURG
Prague
CZECH REPUBLIC
N
W
E
S
Paris
LIECHTENSTEIN
Danube River
SLOVAKIA
Bratislava
Vienna
Loire River
Seine River
Nantes
Vaduz
Munich
AUSTRIA
Budapest
Bay of Biscay
FRANCE
Bern
SWITZERLAND
HUNGARY
Bordeaux
Lyon
ALPS
SLOVENIA
Ljubljana
Zagreb
Milan
CROATIA
Po River
Turin
Toulouse
Rhône River
SAN MARINO
BOSNIA AND HERZEGOVINA
Belgrade
Oporto
Monaco
San Marino
Sarajevo
40°N
ANDORRA
Andorra la Vella
Marseilles
MONACO
SERBIA AND MONTENEGRO (YUGOSLAVIA)
PORTUGAL
VATICAN CITY
Adriatic Sea
Madrid
Barcelona
CORSICA (FRANCE)
Skopje
MACED
Lisbon
Tagus River
Rome
Tiranë
SPAIN
Naples
ITALY
ALBANIA
Valencia
Seville
BALEARIC ISLANDS (SPAIN)
SARDINIA (ITALY)
Tyrrhenian Sea
GREEC
Strait of Gibraltar
GIBRALTAR (U.K.)
Mediterranean Sea
Palermo
SICILY (ITALY)
Ionian Sea
10°W
AFRICA
Valletta
MALTA
0°
10°E
20°E

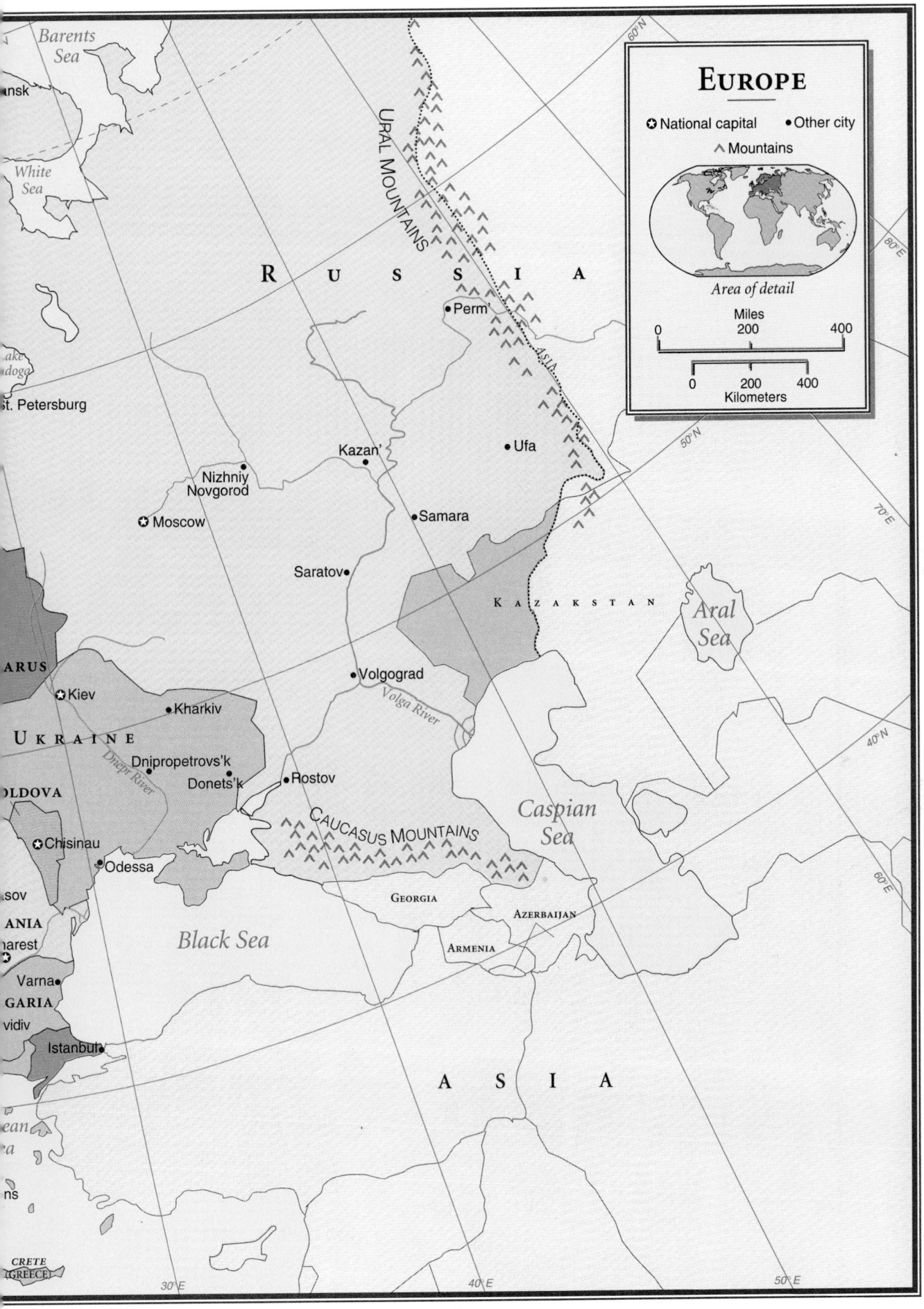
EUROPE
National capital
Other city
Mountains
Area of detail
Miles
0
200
400
0
200
400
Kilometers
Barents Sea
White Sea
URAL MOUNTAINS
RUSSIA
Perm'
ASIA
St. Petersburg
Kazan'
Ufa
Nizhniy Novgorod
Moscow
Samara
Saratov
KAZAKSTAN
Aral Sea
Volgograd
Volga River
Kiev
Kharkiv
UKRAINE
Dnipropetrovs'k
Dnepr River
Donets'k
Rostov
Caspian Sea
CAUCASUS MOUNTAINS
Chisinau
Odessa
GEORGIA
AZERBAIJAN
ARMENIA
Black Sea
Varna
Istanbul
ASIA
CRETE (GREECE)
60°N
50°N
40°N
30°E
40°E
50°E
60°E
70°E
80°E

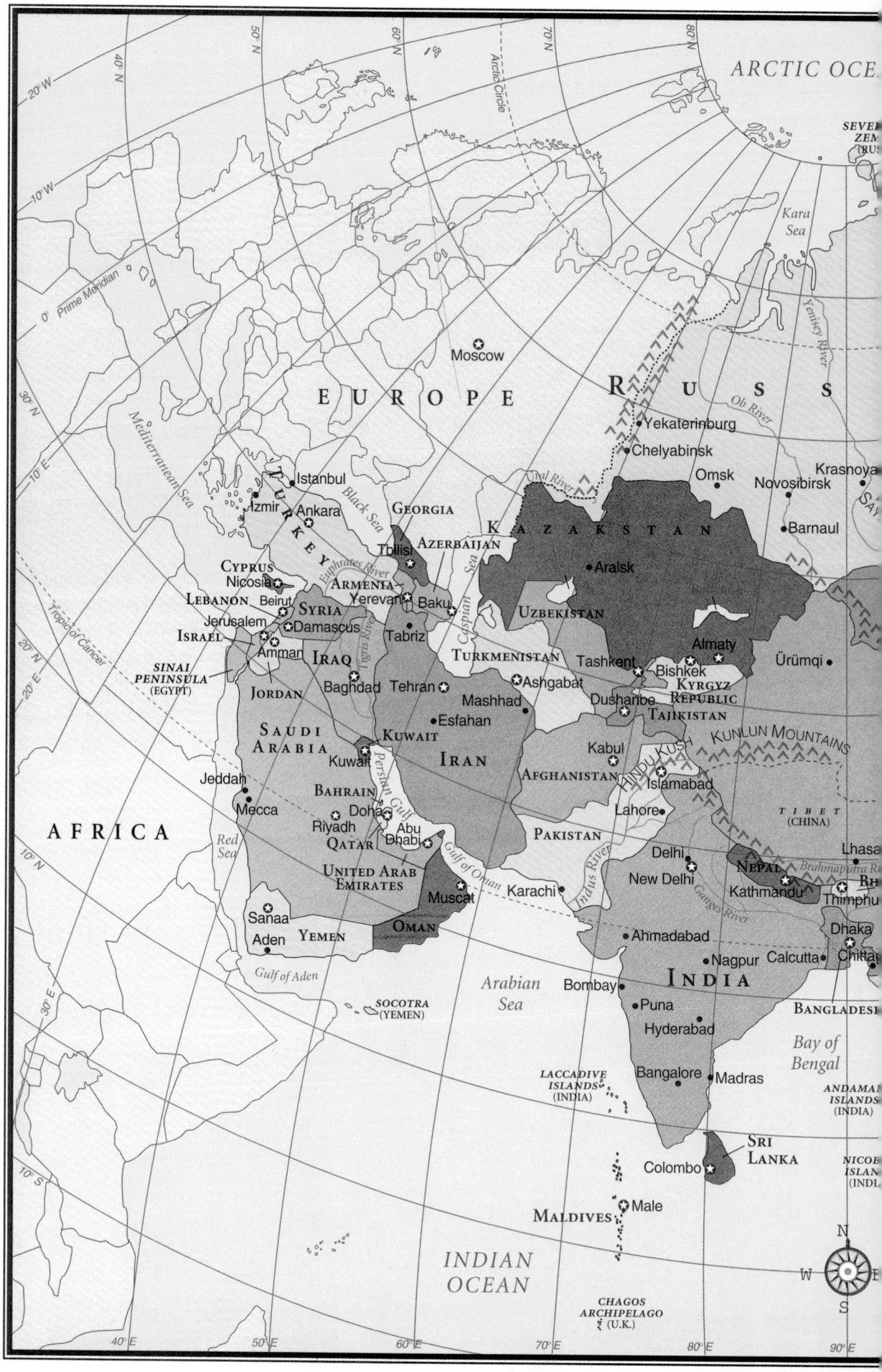
ARCTIC OCE
Arctic Circle
Kara Sea
Yenisey River
Ob River
Moscow
EUROPE
RUSS
Yekaterinburg
Chelyabinsk
Omsk
Novosibirsk
Krasnoya
Barnaul
Ural River
KAZAKSTAN
Aralsk
Aral Sea
UZBEKISTAN
Almaty
Ürümqi
Tashkent
Bishkek
KYRGYZ REPUBLIC
Dushanbe
TAJIKISTAN
KUNLUN MOUNTAINS
HINDU KUSH
Islamabad
Lahore
TIBET (CHINA)
Lhasa
Brahmaputra R
NEPAL
Kathmandu
Thimphu
Dhaka
Chitta
Delhi
New Delhi
Ganges River
Ahmadabad
Nagpur
Calcutta
INDIA
Bombay
Puna
Hyderabad
Bangalore
Madras
BANGLADESH
Bay of Bengal
ANDAMAN ISLANDS (INDIA)
LACCADIVE ISLANDS (INDIA)
SRI LANKA
Colombo
NICOB ISLAN (INDI
MALDIVES
Male
INDIAN OCEAN
CHAGOS ARCHIPELAGO (U.K.)
Arabian Sea
Indus River
Karachi
PAKISTAN
AFGHANISTAN
Kabul
IRAN
Mashhad
Esfahan
Tehran
Tabriz
Ashgabat
TURKMENISTAN
Caspian Sea
Baku
AZERBAIJAN
Tbilisi
GEORGIA
Black Sea
Istanbul
Izmir
Ankara
TURKEY
Mediterranean Sea
Euphrates River
Tigris River
ARMENIA
Yerevan
SYRIA
Damascus
IRAQ
Baghdad
Nicosia
CYPRUS
LEBANON
Beirut
Jerusalem
ISRAEL
Amman
JORDAN
SINAI PENINSULA (EGYPT)
Tropic of Cancer
Prime Meridian
AFRICA
Red Sea
Jeddah
Mecca
SAUDI ARABIA
Riyadh
KUWAIT
Kuwait
Persian Gulf
BAHRAIN
Doha
QATAR
Abu Dhabi
UNITED ARAB EMIRATES
Gulf of Oman
Muscat
OMAN
Sanaa
Aden
YEMEN
Gulf of Aden
SOCOTRA (YEMEN)
EUROPE
AFRICA
ASIA
INDIA
10° W
20° W
40° N
50° N
60° N
70° N
80° N
90° N
10° E
20° E
30° E
40° E
50° E
60° E
70° E
80° E
90° E
10° N
20° N
10° S
30° S
N
S
W
E

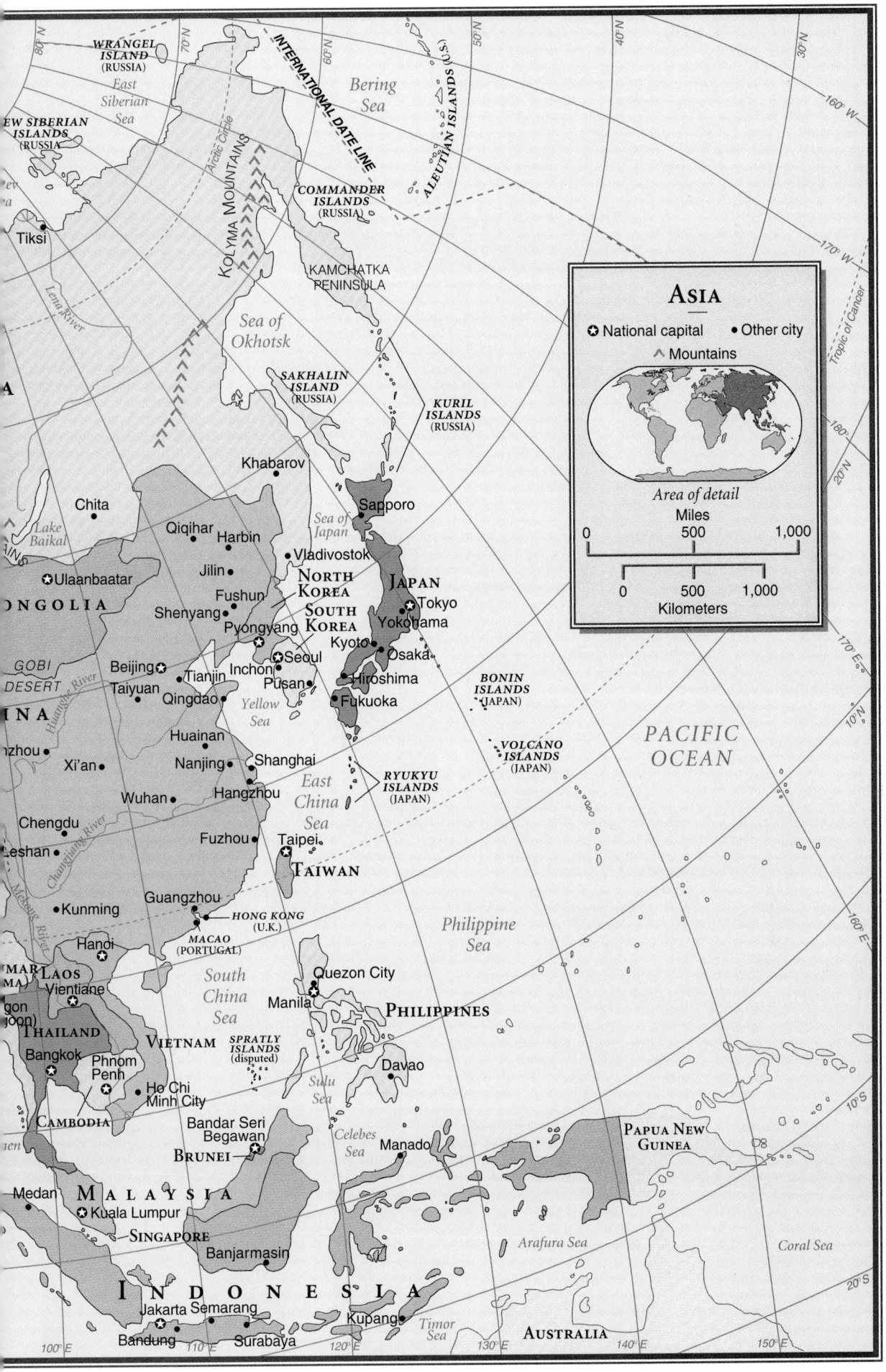
ASIA
National capital
Other city
Mountains
Area of detail
Miles
0
500
1,000
0
500
1,000
Kilometers
WRANGEL ISLAND (RUSSIA)
East Siberian Sea
NEW SIBERIAN ISLANDS (RUSSIA)
Arctic Circle
KOLYMA MOUNTAINS
INTERNATIONAL DATE LINE
Bering Sea
ALEUTIAN ISLANDS (U.S.)
COMMANDER ISLANDS (RUSSIA)
KAMCHATKA PENINSULA
Tiksi
Lena River
Sea of Okhotsk
SAKHALIN ISLAND (RUSSIA)
KURIL ISLANDS (RUSSIA)
Khabarov
Sapporo
Sea of Japan
Chita
Lake Baikal
Qiqihar
Harbin
Vladivostok
Jilin
Ulaanbaatar
MONGOLIA
NORTH KOREA
JAPAN
Tokyo
Fushun
Shenyang
SOUTH KOREA
Pyongyang
Yokohama
Kyoto
Osaka
Seoul
GOBI DESERT
Beijing
Tianjin
Inchon
Pusan
Hiroshima
Taiyuan
Qingdao
Yellow Sea
Fukuoka
BONIN ISLANDS (JAPAN)
CHINA
Huanghe River
Huainan
VOLCANO ISLANDS (JAPAN)
PACIFIC OCEAN
Xi'an
Nanjing
Shanghai
RYUKYU ISLANDS (JAPAN)
Wuhan
Hangzhou
East China Sea
Chengdu
Fuzhou
Taipei
Leshan
Changjiang River
TAIWAN
Mekong River
Guangzhou
Kunming
HONG KONG (U.K.)
MACAO (PORTUGAL)
Philippine Sea
Hanoi
LAOS
Vientiane
South China Sea
Quezon City
Manila
PHILIPPINES
THAILAND
VIETNAM
SPRATLY ISLANDS (disputed)
Bangkok
Phnom Penh
Davao
Sulu Sea
Ho Chi Minh City
CAMBODIA
Bandar Seri Begawan
Celebes Sea
Manado
PAPUA NEW GUINEA
BRUNEI
Medan
MALAYSIA
Kuala Lumpur
SINGAPORE
Banjarmasin
Arafura Sea
Coral Sea
INDONESIA
Jakarta
Semarang
Kupang
Timor Sea
Bandung
Surabaya
AUSTRALIA
80° N
70° N
60° N
50° N
40° N
30° N
160° W
170° W
180°
170° E
160° E
150° E
140° E
130° E
120° E
110° E
100° E
Tropic of Cancer
20° N
10° N
10° S
20° S

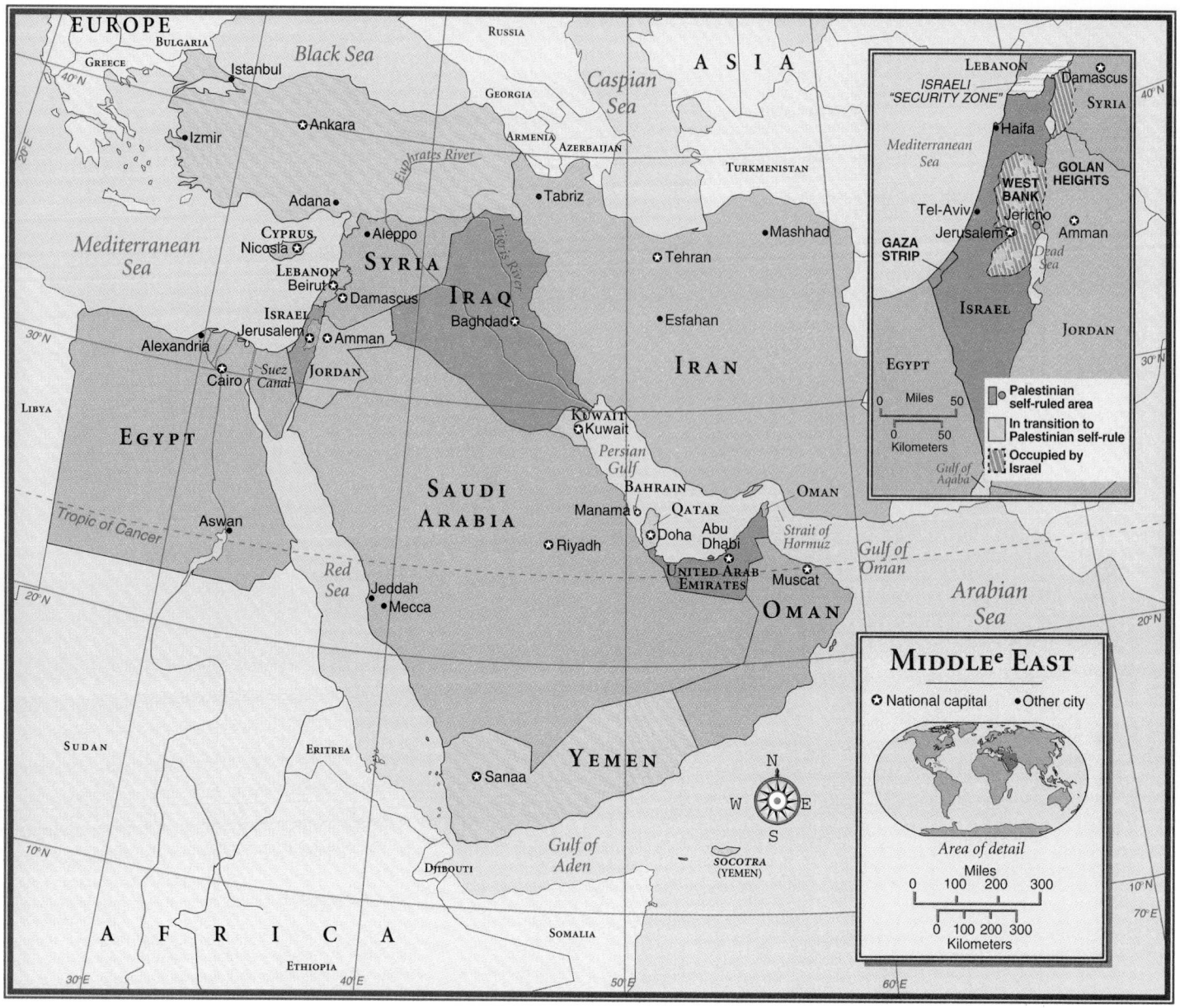
EUROPE
BULGARIA
GREECE
Istanbul
Black Sea
RUSSIA
GEORGIA
Caspian Sea
ASIA
Ankara
Izmir
ARMENIA
AZERBAIJAN
TURKMENISTAN
Euphrates River
Adana
Tabriz
Mashhad
Mediterranean Sea
CYPRUS
Nicosia
Aleppo
SYRIA
Tigris River
Tehran
LEBANON
Beirut
Damascus
IRAQ
Baghdad
ISRAEL
Jerusalem
Amman
Esfahan
Alexandria
Cairo
Suez Canal
JORDAN
IRAN
LIBYA
EGYPT
KUWAIT
Kuwait
Persian Gulf
SAUDI ARABIA
BAHRAIN
Manama
QATAR
Doha
Abu Dhabi
OMAN
Strait of Hormuz
Gulf of Oman
Tropic of Cancer
Aswan
Riyadh
UNITED ARAB EMIRATES
Muscat
Red Sea
Jeddah
Mecca
Arabian Sea
SUDAN
ERITREA
YEMEN
Sanaa
Gulf of Aden
SOCOTRA (YEMEN)
DJIBOUTI
AFRICA
SOMALIA
ETHIOPIA
40°N
30°N
20°N
10°N
20°E
30°E
40°E
50°E
60°E
70°E
LEBANON
ISRAELI "SECURITY ZONE"
Damascus
SYRIA
Haifa
Mediterranean Sea
GOLAN HEIGHTS
WEST BANK
Tel-Aviv
Jericho
Amman
Jerusalem
GAZA STRIP
Dead Sea
ISRAEL
JORDAN
EGYPT
0 Miles 50
0 50 Kilometers
Gulf of Aqaba
Palestinian self-ruled area
In transition to Palestinian self-rule
Occupied by Israel
MIDDLE EAST
National capital
Other city
Area of detail
Miles
0 100 200 300
0 100 200 300 Kilometers
N
W
E
S

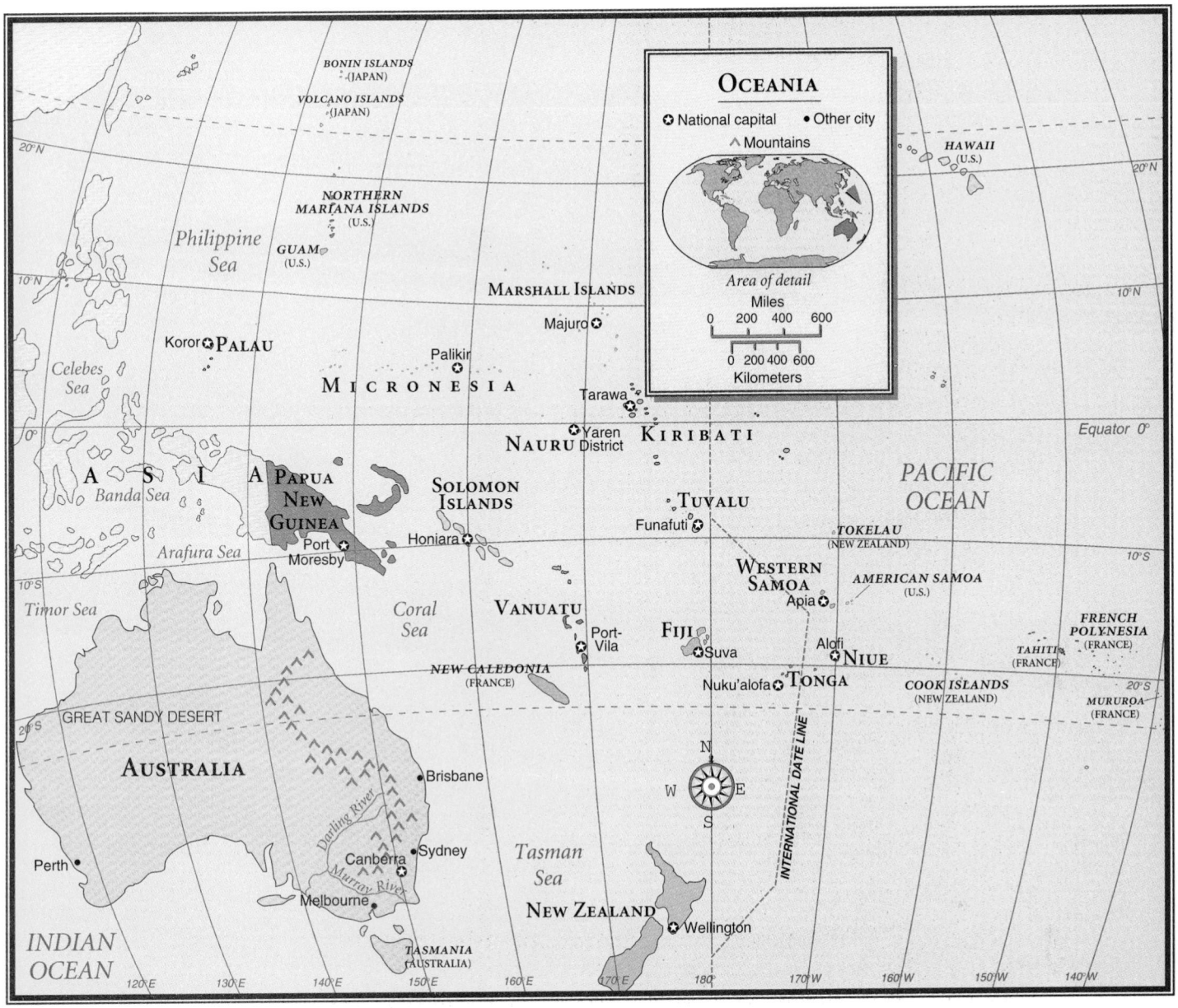
OCEANIA
National capital
Other city
Mountains
Area of detail
Miles
0 200 400 600
0 200 400 600
Kilometers
BONIN ISLANDS (JAPAN)
VOLCANO ISLANDS (JAPAN)
HAWAII (U.S.)
NORTHERN MARIANA ISLANDS (U.S.)
GUAM (U.S.)
Philippine Sea
MARSHALL ISLANDS
Majuro
Koror
PALAU
Palikir
MICRONESIA
Celebes Sea
Tarawa
Yaren District
NAURU
KIRIBATI
Equator 0°
ASIA
Banda Sea
PAPUA NEW GUINEA
SOLOMON ISLANDS
TUVALU
Funafuti
PACIFIC OCEAN
TOKELAU (NEW ZEALAND)
Port Moresby
Honiara
Arafura Sea
WESTERN SAMOA
Apia
AMERICAN SAMOA (U.S.)
Timor Sea
Coral Sea
VANUATU
Port-Vila
FIJI
Suva
Alofi
NIUE
FRENCH POLYNESIA (FRANCE)
TAHITI (FRANCE)
NEW CALEDONIA (FRANCE)
Nuku'alofa
TONGA
COOK ISLANDS (NEW ZEALAND)
MURUROA (FRANCE)
GREAT SANDY DESERT
AUSTRALIA
Brisbane
Darling River
Sydney
Canberra
Murray River
Perth
Melbourne
Tasman Sea
INTERNATIONAL DATE LINE
NEW ZEALAND
Wellington
TASMANIA (AUSTRALIA)
INDIAN OCEAN
N
W
E
S
20° N
10° N
0°
10° S
20° S
120° E
130° E
140° E
150° E
160° E
170° E
180°
170° W
160° W
150° W
140° W

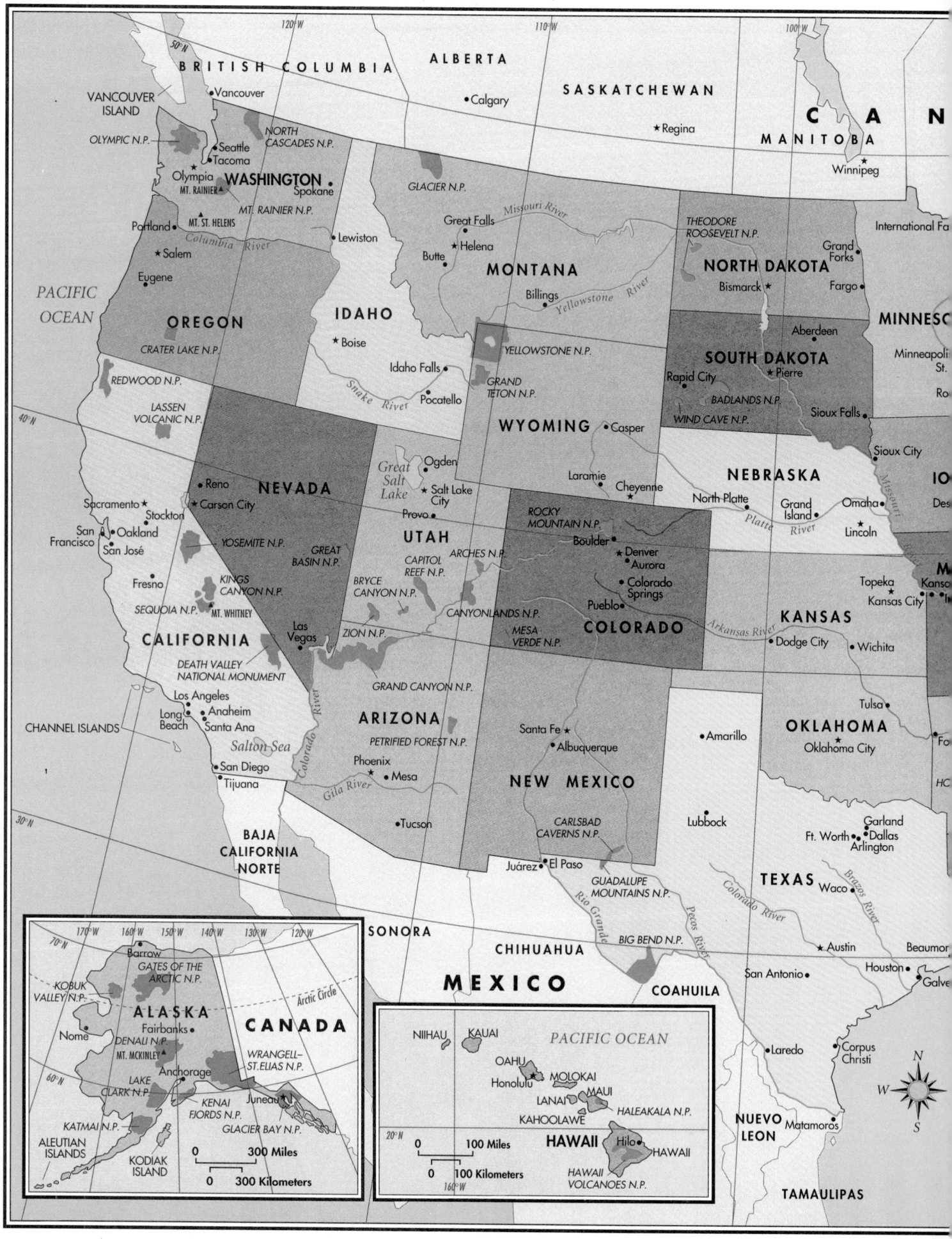
BRITISH COLUMBIA
ALBERTA
SASKATCHEWAN
MANITOBA
VANCOUVER ISLAND
Vancouver
Calgary
Regina
Winnipeg
OLYMPIC N.P.
NORTH CASCADES N.P.
Seattle
Tacoma
Olympia
WASHINGTON
Spokane
MT. RAINIER
MT. RAINIER N.P.
MT. ST. HELENS
Portland
Columbia River
Salem
Eugene
Lewiston
GLACIER N.P.
Great Falls
Missouri River
Helena
Butte
MONTANA
Billings
Yellowstone River
THEODORE ROOSEVELT N.P.
NORTH DAKOTA
Bismarck
Grand Forks
Fargo
International Fa
PACIFIC OCEAN
OREGON
CRATER LAKE N.P.
IDAHO
Boise
Idaho Falls
Pocatello
Snake River
YELLOWSTONE N.P.
GRAND TETON N.P.
WYOMING
Casper
Laramie
Cheyenne
SOUTH DAKOTA
Pierre
Rapid City
BADLANDS N.P.
WIND CAVE N.P.
Aberdeen
Sioux Falls
MINNESC
Minneapoli St.
REDWOOD N.P.
LASSEN VOLCANIC N.P.
40°N
Reno
NEVADA
Carson City
Great Salt Lake
Ogden
Salt Lake City
Provo
UTAH
NEBRASKA
North Platte
Grand Island
Omaha
Lincoln
Sioux City
Missouri River
Platte River
Sacramento
Stockton
San Francisco
Oakland
San José
YOSEMITE N.P.
GREAT BASIN N.P.
CAPITOL REEF N.P.
ARCHES N.P.
BRYCE CANYON N.P.
ROCKY MOUNTAIN N.P.
Boulder
Denver
Aurora
Colorado Springs
Pueblo
COLORADO
Fresno
KINGS CANYON N.P.
SEQUOIA N.P.
MT. WHITNEY
CALIFORNIA
Las Vegas
ZION N.P.
CANYONLANDS N.P.
MESA VERDE N.P.
KANSAS
Topeka
Kansas City
Arkansas River
Dodge City
Wichita
DEATH VALLEY NATIONAL MONUMENT
GRAND CANYON N.P.
Los Angeles
Long Beach
Anaheim
Santa Ana
CHANNEL ISLANDS
Salton Sea
Colorado River
ARIZONA
PETRIFIED FOREST N.P.
Phoenix
Mesa
San Diego
Tijuana
Gila River
Tucson
Santa Fe
Albuquerque
NEW MEXICO
CARLSBAD CAVERNS N.P.
Amarillo
OKLAHOMA
Oklahoma City
Tulsa
Lubbock
Garland
Ft. Worth
Dallas
Arlington
30°N
BAJA CALIFORNIA NORTE
Juárez
El Paso
GUADALUPE MOUNTAINS N.P.
TEXAS
Waco
Brazos River
Colorado River
Pecos River
Rio Grande
BIG BEND N.P.
SONORA
CHIHUAHUA
MEXICO
COAHUILA
Austin
Beaumor
San Antonio
Houston
Galve
Laredo
Corpus Christi
NUEVO LEON
Matamoros
TAMAULIPAS
N
W
S
120°W
110°W
100°W
50°N
170°W
160°W
150°W
140°W
130°W
120°W
70°N
Barrow
GATES OF THE ARCTIC N.P.
KOBUK VALLEY N.P.
Arctic Circle
ALASKA
CANADA
Fairbanks
Nome
DENALI N.P.
MT. MCKINLEY
WRANGELL–ST. ELIAS N.P.
60°N
Anchorage
LAKE CLARK N.P.
KENAI FJORDS N.P.
Juneau
GLACIER BAY N.P.
KATMAI N.P.
ALEUTIAN ISLANDS
KODIAK ISLAND
0 300 Miles
0 300 Kilometers
NIIHAU
KAUAI
PACIFIC OCEAN
OAHU
Honolulu
MOLOKAI
MAUI
LANAI
KAHOOLAWE
HALEAKALA N.P.
20°N
HAWAII
Hilo
0 100 Miles
0 100 Kilometers
160°W
HAWAII VOLCANOES N.P.

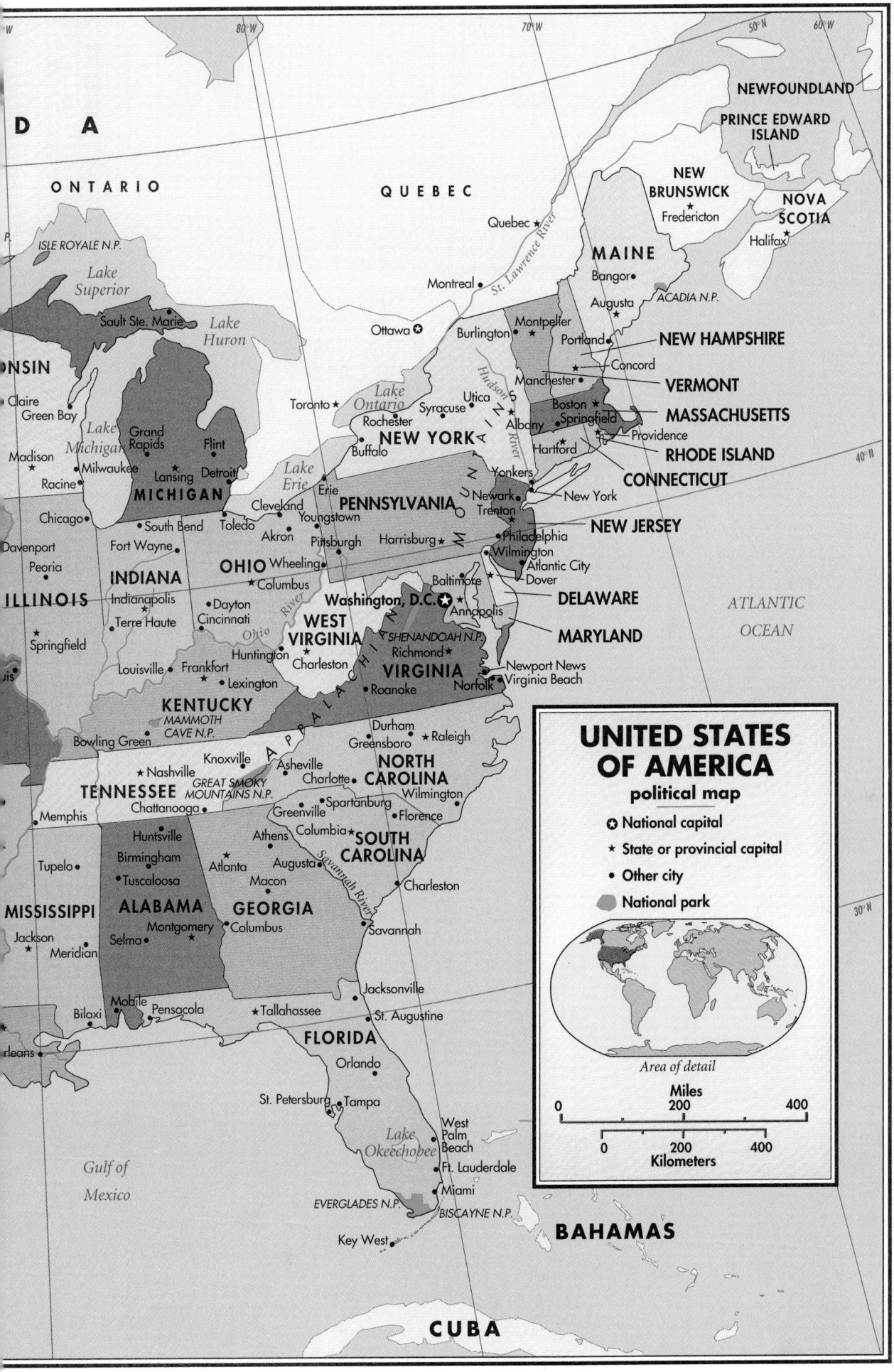
UNITED STATES OF AMERICA
political map
National capital
State or provincial capital
Other city
National park
Area of detail
Miles
0
200
400
0
200
400
Kilometers
NEWFOUNDLAND
PRINCE EDWARD ISLAND
NEW BRUNSWICK
Fredericton
NOVA SCOTIA
Halifax
ONTARIO
QUEBEC
Quebec
Montreal
St. Lawrence River
MAINE
Bangor
Augusta
ACADIA N.P.
ISLE ROYALE N.P.
Lake Superior
Sault Ste. Marie
Lake Huron
Ottawa
Burlington
Montpelier
Portland
NEW HAMPSHIRE
Concord
Manchester
VERMONT
Toronto
Lake Ontario
Rochester
Syracuse
Utica
Hudson River
Boston
Springfield
MASSACHUSETTS
Albany
Providence
Hartford
RHODE ISLAND
CONNECTICUT
Buffalo
NEW YORK
Yonkers
Newark
New York
Trenton
NEW JERSEY
Lake Erie
Erie
PENNSYLVANIA
Philadelphia
Wilmington
Atlantic City
Dover
Harrisburg
Pittsburgh
Cleveland
Youngstown
Toledo
Akron
Wheeling
Columbus
OHIO
Baltimore
DELAWARE
Washington, D.C.
Annapolis
MARYLAND
ATLANTIC OCEAN
Claire
Green Bay
Lake Michigan
Grand Rapids
Flint
Madison
Milwaukee
Racine
Lansing
Detroit
MICHIGAN
Chicago
South Bend
Fort Wayne
Davenport
Peoria
INDIANA
Indianapolis
Terre Haute
ILLINOIS
Springfield
Dayton
Cincinnati
Ohio River
WEST VIRGINIA
Huntington
Charleston
SHENANDOAH N.P.
Richmond
VIRGINIA
Newport News
Virginia Beach
Norfolk
Roanoke
Louisville
Frankfort
Lexington
KENTUCKY
MAMMOTH CAVE N.P.
Bowling Green
Durham
Greensboro
Raleigh
Knoxville
Asheville
Nashville
TENNESSEE
GREAT SMOKY MOUNTAINS N.P.
Charlotte
NORTH CAROLINA
Wilmington
Chattanooga
Memphis
Greenville
Spartanburg
Florence
Huntsville
Athens
Columbia
SOUTH CAROLINA
Birmingham
Atlanta
Augusta
Savannah River
Tupelo
Tuscaloosa
Macon
Charleston
MISSISSIPPI
ALABAMA
GEORGIA
Montgomery
Columbus
Savannah
Jackson
Selma
Meridian
Jacksonville
Mobile
Biloxi
Pensacola
Tallahassee
St. Augustine
FLORIDA
Orlando
St. Petersburg
Tampa
Lake Okeechobee
West Palm Beach
Ft. Lauderdale
Miami
Gulf of Mexico
EVERGLADES N.P.
BISCAYNE N.P.
Key West
BAHAMAS
CUBA

THE WORLD IN FOCUS

If you wanted to go where the people speak Trukese, what country would you visit? Where will you find no head of government, just rival warlords battling for control? Can you name the country that has been independent since the year 301? How many countries have more than one capital city?

These tables make it easy for you to find the answers to those questions and many others about the world. Before you dive into the tables, check out the example at right. It explains the kinds of data you will find here.

Area and population: The size of a country and the number of its people. Divide population by area to get the **population density** (number of people per square mile).

Urban population: This number is the percentage of a country's total population living in urban areas. (To get the rural population, subtract this figure from 100.)

Mexico	736,950	71	Mexico City
	94,800,000	2.2	

Population annual rise: This number shows the percentage of the increase in a country's population in one year. Countries with high figures may face many problems.

Major languages spoken: Noting the languages spoken by a country's people may give you insights into how it was settled and where its people come from.

COUNTRY	AREA (SQ MI) / POPULATION	URBAN POP. (%) / POP. ANNUAL RISE (%)	CAPITAL	MAJOR LANGUAGES	FORM OF GOVERNMENT[1] AND HEAD	DATE OF INDEP.[2] / % OF POP. UNDER 15 YEARS	LITERACY RATE (%)[3] / LIFE EXPECTANCY	PER-CAPITA GDP[4] / HDI[5]
A-D								
Afghanistan	251,770	18	Kabul	Pashtu, Afghan Persian, Turkic languages, others	Rival warlords; President Burhanuddin Rabbani	1919	44/14	NA
	21,500,000	2.8				41	43/44	0.23
Albania	10,580	37	Tiranë	Albanian, Greek	Presidential-parliamentary democracy; Prime Minister Alexander Meksi	1912	80/63	$1,110
	3,300,000	1.7				33	70/76	0.63
Algeria	919,590	50	Algiers	Arabic, French, Berber dialects	Military; President Liamine Zeroual	1962	70/46	$3,480
	29,000,000	2.4				40	67/68	0.75
Andorra	175	65	Andorra la Vella	Catalan, French, Castilian	Parliamentary democracy; Executive Council President Marc Forne	1278	99	$14,000
	63,930	3.0				NA	76/82	NA
Angola	481,350	32	Luanda	Portuguese, Bantu, others	Transitional; President José Eduardo dos Santos	1975	56/28	$620
	11,500,000	2.7				45	44/48	0.28
Antigua and Barbuda	170	31	St. John's	English, local dialects	Dominant party; Prime Minister Lester Bird	1981	90/88	$6,000
	100,000	1.2				25	71/75	0.87
Argentina	1,056,640	87	Buenos Aires	Spanish, English, Italian, German, French	Presidential-legislative democracy; President Carlos Saúl Menem	1816	96/95	$7,990
	34,700,000	1.2				31	69/76	0.89
Armenia	10,890	69	Yerevan	Armenian, Russian, others	Dominant party; President Levon Ter-Petrosyan	1991	99/98	$2,290
	3,800,000	0.7				31	68/74	0.68
Australia	2,941,290	85	Canberra	English, Aboriginal languages	Parliamentary democracy; Prime Minister John Howard	1901	100	$20,720
	18,300,000	0.8				21	75/81	0.93
Austria	31,940	65	Vienna	German	Parliamentary democracy; Chancellor Franz Vranitzky	1918	99	$17,500
	8,100,000	0.1				18	73/80	0.93
Azerbaijan	33,400	53	Baku	Azeri, Russian, Armenian, others	Dominant party; President Gaidar Aliyev	1991	100	$1,790
	7,600,000	1.4				33	66/75	0.67
Bahamas	3,860	84	Nassau	English, Creole	Parliamentary democracy; Prime Minister Hubert Ingraham	1973	90/89	$15,900
	300,000	1.3				29	68/75	0.90

Data compiled and edited by Bryan Brown, Kathy Wilmore, and Karen Peart

FAST FACTS ON 193 COUNTRIES

Form of government and head: This describes the type of government and gives the title and name of the person who heads it.

Literacy rate: This is the percentage of people who can read and write. A single number is the percentage for the country as a whole. Two numbers divided by a slash are for male/female.

Per-capita GDP: The value of all goods and services produced within a country in one year (its gross domestic product), divided by its population. (*Per-capita* means *per-person*.)

Spanish, Indian languages	Dominant party; President Ernesto Zedillo Ponce de Léon	1810	90/85	$7,900
		36	70/76	0.85

Percent of population under age 15: Developing countries with a high percentage of young people may have trouble providing a job for everyone who wants one.

Life expectancy: This is the number of years of life expected at birth. The first number is the life expectancy for males; the second, for females.

HDI (Human Development Index): Use this number—which is calculated using life expectancy, adult literacy rate, and purchasing power—to help you compare one country's quality of life with others'.

COUNTRY	AREA (SQ MI) / POPULATION	URBAN POP. (%) / POP. ANNUAL RISE (%)	CAPITAL	MAJOR LANGUAGES	FORM OF GOVERNMENT[1] AND HEAD	DATE OF INDEP.[2] / % OF POP. UNDER 15 YEARS	LITERACY RATE (%)[3] / LIFE EXPECTANCY	PER-CAPITA GDP[4] / HDI[5]
Bahrain	260	88	Manama	Arabic, English, Farsi, Urdu	Monarchy; Amir Isa ibn Salman Al Khalifa	1971	89/77	$12,100
	600,000	2.6				32	71/76	0.87
Bangladesh	50,260	16	Dhaka	Bangla, English	Parliamentary democracy; Sheikh Hasina Wajed	1971	47/22	$1,040
	119,800,000	2.0				40	57/57	0.37
Barbados	170	38	Bridgetown	English	Parliamentary democracy; Prime Minister Owen Arthur	1966	99/99	$9,200
	300,000	0.5				24	73/78	0.91
Belarus	80,200	69	Minsk	Byelorussian, Russian, others	Presidential dictatorship; President Aleksandr Lukashenko	1991	99/96	$5,130
	10,300,000	-0.3				22	64/74	0.79
Belgium	11,750	97	Brussels	Dutch, French, German, Italian	Parliamentary democracy; Premier Jean-Luc Dehaene	1830	99	$18,040
	10,200,000	0.1				18	73/80	0.93
Belize	8,800	48	Belmopan	English, Spanish, Maya, Garifuna	Parliamentary democracy; Prime Minister Manuel Esquivel	1981	91/91	$2,750
	200,000	3.3				44	70/74	0.75
Benin	42,710	36	Porto-Novo	French, Fon, Yoruba, others	Presidential-parliamentary democracy; President Mathieu Kérékou	1960	32/16	$1,260
	5,600,000	3.1				47	46/49	0.33
Bhutan	18,150	17	Thimphu	Dzongkha; Tibetan and Nepalese dialects	Monarchy; King Jigme Singye Wangchuck	1949	NA	$700
	800,000	2.3				39	51/50	0.31
Bolivia	418,680	58	La Paz and Sucre	Spanish, Quechua, Aymara	Presidential-legislative democracy; President Gonzalo Sánchez de Lozada	1825	88/72	$2,370
	7,600,000	2.6				41	59/62	0.58
Bosnia and Herzevogina	19,740	NA	Sarajevo	Serbo-Croatian	Presidential-parliamentary democracy; Chairman of the Presidency Alija Izetbegovic[6]	1992	NA	NA
	3,600,000	0.6				23	70/75	NA
Botswana	218,810	46	Gaborone	English, Setswana	Parliamentary democracy; President Sir Ketumile Masire	1966	32/16	$3,130
	1,500,000	2.7				43	64/71	0.74
Brazil	3,265,060	76	Brasília	Portuguese, Spanish, English, French	Presidential-legislative democracy; President Fernando Henrique Cardoso	1822	80/80	$5,580
	160,500,000	1.7				34	64/69	0.80
Brunei	2,030	67	Bandar Seri Begawan	Malay, English, Chinese	Monarchy; Sultan and Prime Minister Hassanal Bolkiah Mu'izzadin Waddaulah	1984	92/82	$16,000
	300,000	2.4				35	73/76	0.87

COUNTRY	AREA (SQ MI) / POPULATION	URBAN POP. (%) / POP. ANNUAL RISE (%)	CAPITAL	MAJOR LANGUAGES	FORM OF GOVERNMENT[1] AND HEAD	DATE OF INDEP.[2] / % OF POP. UNDER 15 YEARS	LITERACY RATE (%)[3] / LIFE EXPEC-TANCY	PER-CAPITA GDP[4] / HDI[5]
Bulgaria	42,680	68	Sofia	Bulgarian, others	Parliamentary democracy; Prime Minister Zhan Videnov	1908	99/97	$3,830
	8,400,000	-0.4				19	68/75	0.77
Burkino Faso	105,710	15	Ouagadougou	French, Sudanic languages	Dominant party; President Captain Blaise Compaoré	1960	28/9	$660
	10,600,000	2.8				48	44/46	0.23
Burundi	9,900	6	Bujumbura	Kirundi, French, Swahili	Civilian-military; President Sylvestre Ntibantunganya	1962	61/40	$600
	5,900,000	3.0				46	48/52	0.28
Cambodia	68,150	13	Phnom Penh	Khmer, French	Constitutional monarchy; Prime Ministers Norodom Ranariddh (1st) & Hun Sen (2nd)	1949	48/22	$630
	10,900,000	2.9				46	48/51	0.33
Cameroon	179,690	41	Yaoundé	English, French, African languages	Dominant party; President Paul Biya	1960	66/45	$1,200
	13,600,000	2.9				44	55/58	0.48
Canada	3,560,220	77	Ottawa	English, French	Parliamentary democracy; Prime Minister Jean Chrétien	1867	97	$22,760
	30,000,000	0.6				21	74/81	0.95
Cape Verde	1,560	44	Praia	Portuguese, Crioulo	Presidential-parliamentary democracy; Prime Minister Carlos Veiga	1975	75/53	$1,070
	400,000	1.9				45	64/66	0.54
Central African Republic	240,530	39	Bangui	French, Sangho, Arabic, Hunsa, Swahili	Presidential-parliamentary democracy; President Ange-Felix Patasse	1960	52/25	$700
	3,600,000	2.5				43	47/52	0.36
Chad	486,180	22	N'Djamena	French, Arabic, Sara, others	Transitional; President Lieutenant General Idriss Deby	1960	42/18	$530
	6,500,000	2.6				41	46/49	0.29
Chile	289,110	85	Santiago	Spanish	Presidential-legislative democracy; President Eduardo Frei	1810	95/94	$7,010
	14,500,000	1.6				30	69/76	0.88
China	3,600,930	29	Beijing	Mandarin, other Chinese languages	Communist; President Jiang Zemin	1949	87/68	$2,500
	1,217,600,000	1.1				27	68/72	0.61
Colombia	401,040	67	Bogotá	Spanish	Presidential-legislative democracy; President Ernesto Samper	1810	88/88	$4,850
	38,000,000	2.1				33	66/72	0.84
Comoros	860	29	Moroni	Arabic, French, Comoran	Dominant party; Prime Minister Tadjidine Ben Said Massounei	1975	56/40	$700
	600,000	3.6				48	56/60	0.40
Congo	131,850	58	Brazzaville	French, Lingala, Kikongo, others	Presidential-parliamentary democracy; President Pascal Lissouba	1960	71/49	$2,820
	2,500,000	2.3				44	44/48	0.52
Costa Rica	19,710	44	San José	Spanish, English	Presidential-legislative democracy; President José Maria Figueres	1821	93/93	$5,050
	3,600,000	2.2				34	74/79	0.88
Côte d'Ivoire	122,780	46	Yamous-soukro	French, Dioula, others	Dominant party; President Henri Konan Bédié	1960	44/23	$1,430
	14,700,000	3.5				47	50/52	0.36
Croatia	21,830	54	Zagreb	Serbo-Croatian, others	Presidential-parliamentary democracy; President Franjo Tudjman	1991	99/95	$2,640
	4,400,000	-0.0				20	66/75	NA
Cuba	42,400	74	Havana	Spanish	Communist; President Fidel Castro Ruz	1902	98	$1,260
	11,000,000	0.7				22	73/77	0.73
Cyprus	3,570	53	Nicosia	Greek, Turkish, English	Presidential-legislative democracy; President Glafcos Clerides	1960	98/91	NA
	700,000	0.9				25	75/79	0.91
Czech Republc	30,590	75	Prague	Czech, Slovak	Parliamentary democracy; Prime Minister Vaclav Klaus	1993	99	$7,350
	10,300,000	-0.1				19	70/77	0.87
Denmark	16,360	85	Copenhagen	Danish, Faroese, Greenlandic	Parliamentary democracy; Prime Minister Poul Nyrup Rasmussen	1849	99	$19,860
	5,200,000	0.2				17	73/78	0.92
Djibouti	8,950	77	Djibouti	French, Arabic, Somali, Afar	Dominant party; President Hassan Gouled Aptidon	1977	63/34	$1,200
	600,000	2.2				41	47/50	0.29

COUNTRY	AREA (SQ MI) / POPULATION	URBAN POP. (%) / POP. ANNUAL RISE (%)	CAPITAL	MAJOR LANGUAGES	FORM OF GOVERNMENT[1] AND HEAD	DATE OF INDEP.[2] / % OF POP. UNDER 15 YEARS	LITERACY RATE (%)[3] / LIFE EXPECTANCY	PER-CAPITA GDP[4] / HDI[5]
Dominica	290 / 100,000	61 / 1.3	Roseau	English, French patois	Parliamentary democracy; Prime Minister Edison James	1978 / 32	94/94 / 74/80	$2,260 / 0.76
Dominican Republic	18,680 / 8,100,000	61 / 2.3	Santo Domingo	Spanish	Presidential-legislative democracy; President Joaquín Balaguer Ricardo	1844 / 37	85/82 / 66/71	$3,070 / 0.70
				E-L				
Ecuador	106,890 / 11,700,000	59 / 2.3	Quito	Spanish, Quechua, others	Presidential-legislative democracy; President Sixto Duran Ballen Cordovez	1822 / 36	90/84 / 66/71	$3,840 / 0.76
Egypt	384,340 / 63,700,000	44 / 2.2	Cairo	Arabic, English, French	Dominant party; President Hosni Mubarak	1922 / 40	63/34 / 62/65	$2,490 / 0.61
El Salvador	8,000 / 5,900,000	45 / 2.6	San Salvador	Spanish, Nahua	Presidential-legislative democracy; President Armando Calderón Sol	1821 / 40	76/70 / 65/70	$1,710 / 0.58
Equatorial Guinea	10,830 / 400,000	37 / 2.6	Malabo	Spanish, pidgin English, Fang, Bubi, Ibo	Dominant party; President Brigadier General Teodoro Obiang Nguema Mbasogo	1968 / 43	77/48 / 50/54	$700 / 0.46
Eritrea	48,260 / 3,600,000	17 / 2.8	Asmara	Tigre, Kunama, Cushitic dialects	One-party (transitional); President Issaias Afeworke	1993 / 44	NA / 49/52	$500 / NA
Estonia	17,410 / 1,500,000	70 / -0.5	Tallinn	Estonian, Latvian, Lithuanian, Russian, others	Presidential-parliamentary democracy; Prime Minister Tiit Vahi	1991 / 20	100 / 64/75	$6,460 / 0.75
Ethiopia	376,830 / 57,200,000	15 / 3.1	Addis Ababa	Amharic, Tigrinya, Orominga, others	Dominant party; Prime Minister Meles Zenawi	200 / 49	33/16 / 48/52	$380 / 0.24
Fiji	7,050 / 800,000	39 / 2.0	Suva	English, Fijian, Hindustani	Parliamentary democracy; Prime Minister Sitiveni Rabuka	1970 / 38	90/84 / 61/65	$5,650 / 0.85
Finland	117,610 / 5,100,000	64 / 0.3	Helsinki	Finnish, Swedish, Lapp, Russian	Presidential-parliamentary democracy; President Martti Ahtisaari	1917 / 19	100 / 73/80	$16,140 / 0.94
France	212,390 / 58,400,000	74 / 0.3	Paris	French, regional dialects	Presidential-parliamentary democracy; President Jacques Chirac	1792 / 20	99 / 74/82	$18,670 / 0.94
Gabon	99,490 / 1,200,000	73 / 1.5	Libreville	French, Fang, Myene, others	Dominant party; President Omar Bongo	1960 / 34	74/48 / 52/58	$4,900 / 0.56
Gambia	3,860 / 1,200,000	26 / 2.7	Banjul	English, Mandinka, Wolof, Fula, others	Military; Captain Yahya Jammeh	1965 / 45	39/16 / 48/52	$1,050 / 0.30
Georgia	26,910 / 5,400,000	56 / 0.2	Tbilisi	Georgian, Russian, Armenian, Azeri	Presidential-parliamentary democracy; Chairman of Parliament Eduard A. Shevardnadze	1991 / 24	100/98 / 69/76	$1,060 / 0.65
Germany	134,930 / 81,700,000	85 / -0.1	Berlin	German	Parliamentary democracy; Chancellor Helmut Kohl	1990 / 16	99 / 72/79	$16,580 / 0.92
Ghana	88,810 / 18,000,000	36 / 3.0	Accra	English, Akan, others	Dominant party; President Jerry John Rawlings	1957 / 45	70/51 / 54/58	$1,310 / 0.47
Greece	50,520 / 10,500,000	72 / 0.1	Athens	Greek, English, French	Parliamentary democracy; Prime Minister Konstandinos Simitif	1829 / 18	98/93 / 75/80	$8,870 / 0.90
Grenada	130 / 100,000	NA / 2.4	St. George's	English, French patois	Parliamentary democracy; Prime Minister Keith Mitchell	1974 / 43	98/98 / 68/73	$2,750 / 0.73
Guatemala	41,860 / 9,900,000	39 / 2.9	Guatemala	Spanish, Indian languages	Presidential-legislative democracy with strong military influence; President Alvaro Arzú	1821 / 45	63/47 / 62/67	$3,080 / 0.58
Guinea	94,930 / 7,400,000	29 / 2.4	Conakry	French, various African languages	Dominant party; President General Lansana Conté	1958 / 44	35/13 / 42/46	$980 / 0.31

COUNTRY	AREA (SQ MI) / POPULATION	URBAN POP. (%) / POP. ANNUAL RISE (%)	CAPITAL	MAJOR LANGUAGES	FORM OF GOVERNMENT[1] AND HEAD	DATE OF INDEP.[2] / % OF POP. UNDER 15 YEARS	LITERACY RATE (%)[3] / LIFE EXPEC-TANCY	PER-CAPITA GDP[4] / HDI[5]
Guinea-Bissau	**10,860**	22	**Bissau**	Portuguese, Criolo, others	Presidential-parliamentary democracy; President General João Bernardo Vieira	1974	50/24	$840
	1,100,000	2.1				43	42/45	0.30
Guyana	**76,000**	33	**Georgetown**	English, Amerindian languages	Parliamentary democracy; President Cheddi Jagan	1966	98/95	$1,950
	700,000	1.8				38	62/68	0.63
Haiti	**10,640**	32	**Port-au-Prince**	Creole, French	Presidential-parliamentary democracy; President Rene Préval	1804	37/32	$870
	7,300,000	2.3				40	55/58	0.36
Honduras	**43,200**	47	**Tegucigalpa**	Spanish, Indian languages	Presidential-legislative democracy; President Carlos Roberto Reina	1821	76/71	$1,820
	5,600,000	2.8				45	66/71	0.58
Hungary	**35,650**	64	**Budapest**	Hungarian, others	Parliamentary democracy; Prime Minister Gyula Horn	1001	99/98	$5,700
	10,200,000	-0.3				18	65/74	0.86
Iceland	**38,710**	91	**Reykjavík**	Icelandic	Parliamentary democracy; Prime Minister David Oddsson	1944	100	$17,250
	300,000	1.0				25	77/81	0.93
India	**1,147,950**	26	**New Delhi**	Hindi, English, many others	Parliamentary democracy; Prime Minister H. D. Deve Gowda	1947	64/39	$1,360
	949,600,000	1.9				36	58/59	0.44
Indonesia	**705,190**	31	**Jakarta**	Bahasa Indo-nesian, others	Dominant party; President General Suharto	1945	88/75	$3,090
	201,400,000	1.6				35	61/65	0.64
Iran	**631,660**	58	**Tehran**	Persian, Turkic, Kurdish, Luri, others	Presidential-parliamentary under religious control; President Hashemi Rafsanjani	1979	74/56	$4,720
	63,100,000	2.9				44	65/68	0.75
Iraq	**168,870**	70	**Baghdad**	Arabic, Kurdish, Assyrian, Armenian	One-party; President Saddam Hussein	1932	90/88	NA
	21,400,000	3.7				47	65/67	0.60
Ireland	**26,600**	57	**Dublin**	English, Gaelic	Parliamentary democracy; Prime Minister John Bruton	1921	98	$14,060
	3,600,000	0.5				25	74/79	0.92
Israel[7]	**7,850**	90	**Jerusalem**	Hebrew, Arabic, English	Parliamentary democracy; Prime Minister Benjamin Netanyahu	1948	97/93	$13,880
	5,800,000	1.5				30	75/79	0.91
Italy	**113,540**	68	**Rome**	Italian, others	Parliamentary democracy; Prime Minister Oscar Luigi Scalfaro	1861	98/96	$17,180
	57,300,000	-0.0				15	74/80	0.91
Jamaica	**4,180**	53	**Kingston**	English, Creole	Parliamentary democracy; Prime Minister P. J. Patterson	1962	77/86	$3,050
	2,600,000	1.8				34	71/76	0.70
Japan	**145,370**	78	**Tokyo**	Japanese	Parliamentary democracy; Prime Minister Ryutaro Hashimoto	660 B.C.	99	$20,200
	125,800,000	0.2				16	77/83	0.94
Jordan	**34,340**	78	**Amman**	Arabic, English	Constitutional monarchy; King Hussein I	1946	91/75	$4,280
	4,200,000	2.6				42	66/70	0.74
Kazakstan	**1,049,150**	56	**Almaty**	Kazak, Russian	Dominant party; President Nursultan Nazarbayev	1991	99/96	$3,200
	16,500,000	0.9				31	64/73	0.74
Kenya	**219,960**	27	**Nairobi**	English, Swahili, others	Dominant party; President Daniel arap Moi	1963	81/62	$1,170
	28,200,000	2.7				48	49/52	0.47
Kiribati	**280**	NA	**Tarawa**	English, Gilbertese	Parliamentary democracy; President Teburoro Tito	1979	NA	$800
	77,853	2.0				NA	53/56	NA
Korea, North	**46,490**	61	**Pyongyang**	Korean	Communist; President Kim Jong Il	1948	99/99	$920
	23,900,000	1.8				29	67/73	0.71
Korea, South	**38,120**	74	**Seoul**	Korean, English	Presidential-parliamentary democracy; President Kim Young Sam	1948	99/94	$11,270
	45,300,000	0.9				23	68/76	0.87
Kuwait	**6,880**	96	**Kuwait**	Arabic, English	Constitutional monarchy; Crown Prince Saad al-Abdullah al-Salim al-Sabah	1961	78/69	$16,900
	1,800,000	2.3				29	73/77	0.84

COUNTRY	AREA (SQ MI) / POPULATION	URBAN POP. (%) / POP. ANNUAL RISE (%)	CAPITAL	MAJOR LANGUAGES	FORM OF GOVERNMENT[1] AND HEAD	DATE OF INDEP.[2] / % OF POP. UNDER 15 YEARS	LITERACY RATE (%)[3] / LIFE EXPEC-TANCY	PER-CAPITA GDP[4] / HDI[5]
Kyrgyz Republic	76,640 / 4,600,000	35 / 1.6	Bishkek	Kirghiz, Russian	Presidential-parliamentary democracy; President Askar Akayev	1991 / 38	99/96 / 64/72	$1,790 / 0.66
Laos	89,110 / 5,000,000	19 / 2.9	Vientiane	Lao, French, English	Communist; President Nouhak Phoumsavan	1949 / 45	65/35 / 50/53	$850 / 0.40
Latvia	24,900 / 2,500,000	69 / -0.7	Riga	Lettish, Lithuanian, Russian, others	Presidential-parliamentary democracy; President Andris Skele	1991 / 21	100/99 / 61/73	$4,480 / 0.82
Lebanon	3,950 / 3,800,000	86 / 2.0	Beirut	Arabic, French, Armenian, English	Presidential-parliamentary with military influence President Ilyas Harawi	1943 / 33	88/73 / 73/78	$4,360 / 0.66
Lesotho	11,720 / 2,100,000	16 / 2.6	Maseru	Sesotho, English, Zulu, Xhosa	Parliamentary democracy; Prime Minister Ntsu Mokhehele	1966 / 41	44/68 / 54/57	$1,340 / 0.46
Liberia	37,190 / 2,100,000	44 / 3.1	Monrovia	English, Niger-Congo languages	Transitional; Council of State Chairperson Ruth Perry	1847 / 44	50/29 / 55/60	$770 / 0.31
Libya	679,360 / 5,400,000	85 / 3.7	Tripoli	Arabic, Italian, English	Military; Colonel Muammar al-Qaddafi	1951 / 45	77/42 / 62/66	$6,510 / 0.79
Liechtenstein	60 / 30,000	NA / 0.5	Vaduz	German, Alemannic dialect	Constitutional monarchy; Prince Hans Adam II	1719 / 19	100 / 68/75	$22,300 / NA
Lithuania	25,210 / 3,700,000	69 / -0.1	Vilnius	Lithuanian, Polish, Russian	Presidential-parliamentary democracy; Prime Minister Mindaugas Stankevicius	1991 / 22	99/98 / 63/75	$3,500 / 0.72
Luxembourg	990 / 400,000	86 / 0.4	Luxembourg	Luxembourgisch, German, French	Parliamentary democracy; Prime Minister Jean-Claude Juncker	1839 / 18	100 / 73/79	$22,830 / 0.90
M-Q								
Macedonia	9,930 / 2,100,000	58 / 0.8	Skopje	Macedonian, Albanian, others	Presidential-parliamentary democracy; President Kiro Gligorov	1991 / 24	NA / 70/74	$900 / NA
Madagascar	224,530 / 15,200,000	26 / 3.2	Antananarivo	French, Malagasy	Presidential-parliamentary democracy; President Albert Zafy	1960 / 46	88/73 / 55/58	$790 / 0.35
Malawi	36,320 / 9,500,000	17 / 3.0	Lilongwe	English, Chichewa, others	Presidential-parliamentary democracy; President Bakili Muluzi	1964 / 48	65/34 / 45/46	$750 / 0.32
Malaysia	126,850 / 20,600,000	51 / 2.4	Kuala Lumpur	Malay, English, others	Dominant party; Prime Minister Mahathir bin Mohamad	1957 / 36	86/70 / 70/75	$8,650 / 0.83
Maldives	120 / 300,000	26 / 3.6	Male	Divehi, English	President and legislature controlled by elite families; President Maumoon Abdul Gayoom	1965 / 47	91/92 / 63/66	$1,500 / 0.61
Mali	471,120 / 9,700,000	26 / 3.1	Bamako	French, Bambara, many others	Presidential-parliamentary democracy; President Alpha Oumar Konaré	1960 / 48	27/12 / 44/48	$600 / 0.22
Malta	120 / 400,000	89 / 0.6	Valletta	Maltese, English	Parliamentary democracy; Prime Minister Edward Fenech Adami	1964 / 22	86/82 / 75/79	$10,760 / 0.89
Marshall Islands	70 / 100,000	65 / 2.2	Majuro	English, Japanese, others	Parliamentary democracy; President Amata Kabua	1986 / 51	100/88 / 60/63	$1,500 / NA
Mauritania	395,840 / 2,300,000	39 / 2.5	Nouakchott	Hasaniya Arabic, Wolof, Pular, Soninke	Dominant party; President Maaouya Ould Sid'Ahmed Taya	1960 / 45	46/25 / 50/53	$1,110 / 0.35
Mauritius	710 / 1,100,000	44 / 1.3	Port Louis	English, Creole, French, others	Parliamentary democracy; Prime Minister Navin Ramgoolam	1968 / 29	85/75 / 65/73	$8,600 / 0.83
Mexico	736,950 / 94,800,000	71 / 2.2	Mexico City	Spanish, Indian languages	Dominant party; President Ernesto Zedillo Ponce de Léon	1810 / 36	90/85 / 70/76	$7,900 / 0.85

COUNTRY	AREA (SQ MI) / POPULATION	URBAN POP. (%) / POP. ANNUAL RISE (%)	CAPITAL	MAJOR LANGUAGES	FORM OF GOVERNMENT[1] AND HEAD	DATE OF INDEP.[2] / % OF POP. UNDER 15 YEARS	LITERACY RATE (%)[3] / LIFE EXPECTANCY	PER-CAPITA GDP[4] / HDI[5]
Micronesia	**270** / **100,000**	26 / 3.0	**Palikir**	English, Trukese, others	Parliamentary democracy; President Bailey Olter	1986 / 43	91/88 / 62/66	$1,500 / NA
Moldova	**14,170** / **4,300,000**	47 / 0.3	**Chisinau (Kishinev)**	Moldovan, Russian, Gagauz	Presidential-parliamentary democracy; President Mircea Snegur	1991 / 27	99/94 / 64/71	$2,670 / 0.66
Monaco	**0.75** / **31,280**	NA / 0.8	**Monaco**	French, English, Italian, Monegasque	Constitutional monarchy; Prince Rainier III	1419 / NA	NA / 74/82	$18,000 / NA
Mongolia	**604,830** / **2,300,000**	55 / 1.4	**Ulaanbaatar (Ulan Bator)**	Khalkha Mongol, Turkic, Russian, Chinese	Presidential-parliamentary democracy; Prime Minister Puntsagiyn Jasray	1921 / 40	NA / 62/65	$1,800 / 0.58
Morocco	**172,320** / **27,600,000**	47 / 2.2	**Rabat**	Arabic, Berber dialects, French	Constitutional monarchy; King Hassan II	1956 / 38	61/38 / 66/70	$3,060 / 0.53
Mozambique	**302,740** / **16,500,000**	33 / 2.7	**Maputo**	Portuguese, African languages	Presidential-legislative demoracy; President Joaquím Alberto Chissano	1975 / 46	45/21 / 45/48	$610 / 0.26
Myanmar (Burma)	**253,880** / **46,000,000**	25 / 1.9	**Yangon (Rangoon)**	Burmese, others	Military; General Than Shwe	1948 / 36	89/72 / 60/62	$930 / 0.45
Namibia	**317,870** / **1,600,000**	32 / 2.7	**Windhoek**	Afrikaans, German, English, others	Presidential-legislative democracy; President Sam Nujoma	1990 / 42	45/31 / 58/60	$3,600 / 0.57
Nauru	**8** / **10,000**	NA / 1.3	**no official capital**	Nauruan, English	Parliamentary democracy; President Lagumot Harris	1968 / NA	NA / 64/69	$10,000 / NA
Nepal	**52,820** / **23,200,000**	10 / 2.6	**Kathmandu**	Nepali, others	Parliamentary democracy; Prime Minister Sher Bahadur Deuba	1768 / 42	38/13 / 56/53	$1,060 / 0.33
Netherlands	**13,100** / **15,500,000**	61 / 0.4	**Amsterdam**	Dutch	Parliamentary democracy; Prime Minister Willem Kok	1579 / 18	99 / 74/80	$17,940 / 0.94
New Zealand	**103,470** / **3,600,000**	85 / 0.9	**Wellington**	English, Maori	Parliamentary democracy; Prime Minister James Bolger	1907 / 23	99 / 73/79	$16,640 / 0.93
Nicaragua	**45,850** / **4,600,000**	63 / 2.7	**Managua**	Spanish, English, Indian languages	Presidential-legislative democracy; President Violeta Chamorro	1821 / 44	57/57 / 62/68	$1,570 / 0.57
Niger	**489,070** / **9,500,000**	15 / 3.4	**Niamey**	French, Hausa, Djerma	Military; National Council President Bare Mainassara	1960 / 49	17/5 / 45/48	$550 / 0.21
Nigeria	**351,650** / **103,900,000**	16 / 3.1	**Abuja**	English, Hausa, Yoruba, Ibo, Fulani	Military; General Sani Abacha	1960 / 45	62/40 / 55/58	$1,250 / 0.40
Niue	**100** / **1,900**	NA / 3.7	**Alofi**	Polynesian (related to Tongan and Samoan), English	Parliamentary democracy; Premier Frank Lui	1974 / NA	NA / NA	$1,200 / NA
Norway	**118,470** / **4,400,000**	73 / 0.4	**Oslo**	Norwegian, Lapp, Finnish	Parliamentary democracy; Prime Minister Gro Harlem Brundtland	1905 / 19	99 / 75/81	$22,170 / 0.94
Oman	**82,030** / **2,300,000**	12 / 4.9	**Muscat**	Arabic, English, Baluchi, others	Monarchy; Prime Minister Sultan Qabus ibn Sa'id al Sa'id	1650 / 36	NA / 70/72	$10,020 / 0.72
Pakistan	**297,640** / **133,500,000**	28 / 2.9	**Islamabad**	Urdu, English, Punjabi, others	Presidential-parliamentary democracy; Prime Minister Benazir Bhutto	1947 / 41	47/21 / 61/61	$1,930 / 0.44
Palau	**190** / **20,000**	69 / 1.4	**Koror**	English, Angaur, Sonsorolese, Japanese, others	Presidential-legislative democracy; President Kuniwo Nakamura	1994 / 30	93/90 / NA	$5,000 / NA
Panama	**29,340** / **2,700,000**	55 / 1.8	**Panama**	Spanish, English	Presidential-legislative democracy; President Ernesto Pérez Balladares	1903 / 33	89/88 / 71/75	$4,670 / 0.86
Papua New Guinea	**174,850** / **4,300,000**	15 / 2.3	**Port Moresby**	English, pidgin English, Motu, many others	Parliamentary democracy; Prime Minister Julius Chan	1975 / 42	65/38 / 56/57	$2,200 / 0.50

COUNTRY	AREA (SQ MI) / POPULATION	URBAN POP. (%) / POP. ANNUAL RISE (%)	CAPITAL	MAJOR LANGUAGES	FORM OF GOVERNMENT[1] AND HEAD	DATE OF INDEP.[2] / % OF POP. UNDER 15 YEARS	LITERACY RATE (%)[3] / LIFE EXPEC-TANCY	PER-CAPITA GDP[4] / HDI[5]
Paraguay	153,400 / 5,000,000	50 / 2.8	Asunción	Spanish, Guarani	Presidential-legislative democracy; President Juan Carlos Wasmosy	1811 / 42	92/88 / 66/71	$2,950 / 0.70
Peru	494,210 / 24,000,000	70 / 2.1	Lima	Spanish, Quechua, Aymara	Presidential dictatorship; President Alberto Kenyo Fujimori	1821 / 36	92/74 / 64/68	$3,110 / 0.70
Philippines	115,120 / 72,000,000	49 / 2.1	Manila	Pilipino, English	Presidential-legislative democracy; President Fidel Ramos	1946 / 38	94/93 / 63/66	$2,310 / 0.67
Poland	117,550 / 38,600,000	62 / 0.2	Warsaw	Polish	Presidential-parliamentary democracy; President Aleksander Kwasniewski	1918 / 23	99/98 / 68/76	$4,920 / 0.82
Portugal	35,500 / 9,900,000	48 / 0.1	Lisbon	Portuguese	Presidential-parliamentary democracy; Prime Minister Antonio Guterres	1910 / 18	89/82 / 71/78	$10,190 / 0.88
Qatar	4,250 / 700,000	91 / 1.6	Doha	Arabic, English	Monarchy; Amir and Prime Minister Khalifa ibn Hamad Al Thani	1971 / 30	77/72 / 70/75	$20,820 / 0.84
R-S								
Romania	88,930 / 22,600,000	55 / -0.2	Bucharest	Romanian, Hungarian, German	Presidential-parliamentary democracy; President Nicolae Vacaroiu	1947 / 21	98/95 / 66/73	$2,790 / 0.74
Russia	6,592,800 / 147,700,000	73 / -0.5	Moscow	Russian, other languages	Presidential-parliamentary democracy; President Boris Yeltsin	1991 / 21	100/97 / 57/71	$4,820 / 0.80
Rwanda	9,530 / 6,900,000	5 / 2.7	Kigali	Kinyarwanda, French, Kiswahili	Dominant party; President Pasteur Bizimungu	1962 / 48	64/37 / 46/49	$950 / 0.33
Saint Kitts and Nevis	140 / 40,000	42 / 1.3	Basseterre	English	Parliamentary democracy; Prime Minister Denzil Douglas	1983 / 32	97/98 / 66/71	$5,300 / 0.86
Saint Lucia	240 / 100,000	48 / 2.0	Castries	English, French patois	Parliamentary democracy; Prime Minister John Compton	1979 / 37	65/69 / 69/75	$4,200 / 0.73
Saint Vincent and the Grenadines	150 / 100,000	25 / 1.8	Kingstown	English, French patois	Parliamentary democracy; Prime Minister James F. Mitchell	1979 / 37	96/96 / 71/74	$2,000 / 0.74
San Marino	20 / 30,000	91 / 0.3	San Marino	Italian	Parliamentary democracy; Secretary of State Gabriele Gatti	301 / 15	97/95 / 73/79	$15,800 / NA
São Tomé and Principe	370 / 100,000	46 / 2.6	São Tomé	Portuguese	Presidential-parliamentary democracy; President Miguel Trovoada	1975 / 47	85/62 / 62/65	$1,000 / 0.46
Saudi Arabia	830,000 / 19,400,000	79 / 3.2	Riyadh	Arabic	Monarchy; King and Prime Minister Fahd ibn Abd al-Aziz Al Sa'ud	1932 / 43	73/48 / 69/72	$9,510 / 0.77
Senegal	74,340 / 8,500,000	43 / 2.7	Dakar	French, Wolof, others	Dominant party; President Abdou Diouf	1960 / 45	37/18 / 48/50	$1,450 / 0.33
Serbia and Montenegro (Yugoslavia)	26,940 / 10,200,000	57 / 0.3	Belgrade	Serbo-Croatian, Albanian	Dominant party; Prime Minister Radoje Kontic[8]	1992 / 22	NA / 69/74	$1,000 / NA
Seychelles	100 / 100,000	50 / 1.5	Victoria	English, French, Creole	Presidential-legislative democracy; President France Albert René	1976 / 31	56/60 / 68/73	$6,000 / 0.79
Sierra Leone	27,650 / 4,600,000	35 / 2.7	Freetown	English, Krio, Mende, Temne	Military; President Ahmad Tejan Kabbah	1961 / 44	31/11 / 44/47	$1,000 / 0.22
Singapore	240 / 3,000,000	100 / 1.1	Singapore	Chinese, Malay, Tamil, English	Dominant party; Prime Minister Goh Chok Tong	1965 / 23	95/83 / 74/79	$19,940 / 0.88
Slovakia	18,790 / 5,400,000	57 / 0.3	Bratislava	Slovak, Hungarian	Parliamentary democracy; Prime Minister Vladimir Meciar	1993 / 23	NA / 68/77	$6,070 / 0.86

COUNTRY	AREA (SQ MI) / POPULATION	URBAN POP. (%) / POP. ANNUAL RISE (%)	CAPITAL	MAJOR LANGUAGES	FORM OF GOVERNMENT[1] AND HEAD	DATE OF INDEP.[2] / % OF POP. UNDER 15 YEARS	LITERACY RATE (%)[3] / LIFE EXPEC-TANCY	PER-CAPITA GDP[4] / HDI[5]
Slovenia	7,820 / 2,000,000	50 / 0.0	Ljubljana	Slovenian, Serbo-Croatian, others	Presidential-parliamentary democracy; Prime Minister Janez Drnovsek	1991 / 19	NA / 69/77	$8,110 / NA
Solomon Islands	10,810 / 400,000	13 / 3.4	Honiara	Melanesian pidgin, English, others	Parliamentary democracy; Prime Minister Solomon Mamaloni	1978 / 47	NA / 68/73	$2,590 / 0.56
Somalia	242,220 / 9,500,000	24 / 3.2	Mogadishu	Somali, Arabic, Italian, English	Rival warlords; no leader	1960 / 48	36/14 / 45/49	$500 / 0.22
South Africa	471,440 / 44,500,000	57 / 2.3	Cape Town, Pretoria, and Bloemfontein	English, Afrikaans, Zulu, Xhosa, Sotho, others	Presidential-legislative democracy; President Nelson Mandela	1910 / 37	78/75 / 63/68	$4,420 / 0.65
Spain	192,830 / 39,300,000	64 / 0.1	Madrid	Spanish, Catalan, Galician, Basque	Parliamentary democracy; Prime Minister José Maria Aznar	1492 / 17	98/94 / 73/81	$13,120 / 0.93
Sri Lanka	24,950 / 18,400,000	22 / 1.5	Colombo	Sinhala, Tamil, English	Presidential-parliamentary democracy; President Chandrika Bandaranike Kumaratunga	1948 / 35	93/84 / 70/75	$3,190 / 0.70
Sudan	917,370 / 28,900,000	27 / 3.0	Khartoum	Arabic, regional languages, English	Military; Lieutenant General Omar Hassan Ahmad al-'Bashir	1956 / 43	44/21 / 53/55	$870 / 0.36
Suriname	60,230 / 400,000	49 / 1.6	Paramaribo	Dutch, English, Sranan Tongo	Presidential-parliamentary democracy; President Ronald R. Venetiaan	1975 / 35	95/95 / 68/73	$2,800 / 0.74
Swaziland	6,640 / 1,000,000	30 / 3.2	Mbabane and Lobamba	English, siSwati	Monarchy; King Mswati III	1968 / 46	70/65 / 52/61	$3,490 / 0.59
Sweden	158,930 / 8,800,000	83 / 0.1	Stockholm	Swedish, Lapp, Finnish	Parliamentary democracy; Prime Minister Goran Persson	1809 / 19	99 / 76/81	$18,580 / 0.93
Switzerland	15,360 / 7,100,000	68 / 0.3	Bern	German, French, Italian, Romansch	Parliamentary democracy; President of Federal Council Jean-Pascal Delamuraz	1291 / 18	99 / 75/82	$22,080 / 0.93
Syria	71,070 / 15,600,000	51 / 3.7	Damascus	Arabic, Kurdish, Armenian, others	Dominant party; President Hafez al-Assad	1946 / 49	78/51 / 65/67	$5,000 / 0.69
T-Z								
Taiwan	13,900 / 21,400,000	75 / 1.0	Taipei	Mandarin Chinese, Taiwanese, others	Presidential-legislative government moving toward democracy; President Lee Teng-hui	1947 / 24	93/79 / 72/77	$12,070 / NA
Tajikistan	54,290 / 5,900,000	28 / 2.1	Dushanbe	Tajik, Russian	Dominant party; President Emomili Rakhmanov	1991 / 43	99/97 / 65/71	$1,415 / 0.62
Tanzania	342,100 / 29,100,000	21 / 3.0	Dar es Salaam	Swahili, English	Dominant party; Prime Minister Benjamin Mkapa	1964 / 47	71/48 / 47/50	$750 / 0.36
Thailand	197,250 / 60,700,000	19 / 1.4	Bangkok	Thai, English, others	Parliamentary democracy; Prime Minister Chuan Leekpai	1238 / 30	96/91 / 68/72	$5,970 / 0.83
Togo	21,000 / 4,600,000	30 / 3.6	Lomé	French, Ewe, Mina, Dagomba, Kabye	Military; President General Gnassingbé Eyadéma	1960 / 49	56/31 / 55/59	$800 / 0.39
Tonga	301 / 104,780	NA / 0.8	Nuku'alofa	Tongan, English	Constitutional monarchy; King Taufa'ahau Tupou IV	1970 / NA	100 / 65/70	$2,050 / NA
Trinidad and Tobago	1,980 / 1,300,000	65 / 1.2	Port-of-Spain	English, Hindi, French, Spanish	Parliamentary democracy; Prime Minister Patrick Manning	1962 / 31	98/96 / 68/73	$11,280 / 0.87
Tunisia	59,980 / 9,200,000	60 / 1.7	Tunis	Arabic, French	Dominant party; President Zine el-Abidine Ben Ali	1956 / 37	69/45 / 67/69	$4,250 / 0.73
Turkey	297,150 / 63,900,000	63 / 1.6	Ankara	Turkish, Kurdish, Arabic	Presidential-parliamentary democracy; Prime Minister Necmettin Erbakan	1923 / 33	90/68 / 65/70	$4,910 / 0.71

COUNTRY	AREA (SQ MI) / POPULATION	URBAN POP. (%) / POP. ANNUAL RISE (%)	CAPITAL	MAJOR LANGUAGES	FORM OF GOVERNMENT[1] AND HEAD	DATE OF INDEP.[2] / % OF POP. UNDER 15 YEARS	LITERACY RATE (%)[3] / LIFE EXPECTANCY	PER-CAPITA GDP[4] / HDI[5]
Turkmenistan	**188,500** / **4,600,000**	45 / 2.4	**Ashgabat**	Turkmen, Russian, Uzbek, others	Dominant party; President Saparmurad Niyazov	1991 / 41	99/97 / 62/69	$3,280 / 0.70
Tuvalu	**9.4** / **9,830**	NA / 1.7	**Funafuti**	Tuvaluan, English	Parliamentary democracy; Prime Minister Kamuta Latasi	1978 / NA	NA / 62/64	$800 / NA
Uganda	**77,050** / **22,000,000**	11 / 3.3	**Kampala**	English, Luganda, Swahili, others	Dominant party; President Yoweri Kaguta Museveni	1962 / 47	68/45 / 44/46	$850 / 0.33
Ukraine	**233,100** / **51,100,000**	68 / -0.5	**Kiev**	Ukrainian, Russian, Romanian, Polish	Presidential-parliamentary democracy; President Leonid Kuchma	1991 / 20	100/97 / 63/73	$3,650 / 0.72
United Arab Emirates	**32,280** / **1,900,000**	82 / 1.9	**Abu Dhabi**	Arabic, Persian, English, others	Federation of traditional monarchies; President Zayid ibn Sultan al-Nahayan	1971 / 32	72/69 / 70/74	$22,480 / 0.86
United Kingdom (Great Britain)	**93,280** / **58,800,000**	90 / 0.2	**London**	English, Welsh, Scottish Gaelic	Parliamentary democracy; Prime Minister John Major	1801 / 19	99 / 74/79	$17,980 / 0.92
United States	**3,539,230** / **265,200,000**	75 / 0.6	**Washington, D.C.**	English, Spanish, others	Presidential-legislative democracy; President Bill Clinton	1776 / 22	97/97 / 72/79	$25,850 / 0.94
Uruguay	**67,490** / **3,200,000**	90 / 0.8	**Montevideo**	Spanish, Brazilero	Presidential-legislative democracy; President Julio Maria Sanguinetti	1828 / 26	97/96 / 69/76	$7,200 / 0.88
Uzbekistan	**172,740** / **23,200,000**	39 / 2.3	**Tashkent**	Uzbek, Russian, Tajik, others	Dominant party; President Islam Karimov	1991 / 41	98/96 / 66/72	$2,400 / 0.68
Vanuatu	**4,710** / **200,000**	18 / 2.9	**Port-Vila**	English, French, Bislama	Parliamentary democracy; Prime Minister Maxime Carlot Korman	1980 / 44	57/48 / NA	$1,200 / 0.56
Vatican City	**109 acres** / **821**	NA / 1.2	**Vatican City**	Italian, Latin, others	No political parties; papal state; Pope John Paul II	1929 / —	100 / NA	NA / NA
Venezuela	**340,560** / **22,300,000**	84 / 2.1	**Caracas**	Spanish, Indian languages	Presidential-legislative democracy; President Rafael Caldera Rodriguez	1811 / 38	91/89 / 69/75	$8,670 / 0.86
Vietnam	**125,670** / **76,600,000**	19 / 2.3	**Hanoi**	Vietnamese, French, Chinese, others	Communist; Prime Minister Vo Van Kiet	1976 / 40	93/83 / 63/67	$1,140 / 0.52
Western Samoa	**1,090** / **200,000**	21 / 2.3	**Apia**	Samoan, English	Parliamentary democracy; Chief of State Malietoa Tanumafili II	1962 / 41	97/97 / NA	$2,000 / 0.70
Yemen	**203,850** / **14,700,000**	23 / 3.2	**Sanaa**	Arabic	Two-party coalition; President Lieutenant General Ali Abdullah Salih	1990 / 52	53/26 / 51/53	$1,955 / 0.37
Zaire	**875,520** / **46,500,000**	29 / 3.2	**Kinshasa**	French, Lingala, Swahili, others	Presidential-military; President Mobutu Sese Seko	1960 / 48	84/61 / 46/50	$440 / 0.37
Zambia	**287,020** / **9,200,000**	42 / 3.0	**Lusaka**	English, many African languages	Presidential-parliamentary democracy; President Frederick Chiluba	1964 / 47	81/65 / 48/50	$860 / 0.41
Zimbabwe	**149,290** / **11,500,000**	31 / 2.5	**Harare**	English, Shona, Sindebele	Dominant party; President Robert Mugabe	1980 / 45	84/72 / 61/62	$1,580 / 0.53

NOTES

NA: Means figure(s) not available. [1]**Form of government and head:** Some countries have two heads: a head of state and a head of government. These tables list only the latter. (For instance, Queen Elizabeth is Britain's head of state, but John Major runs the government.) [2]**Date of independence:** The most recent year in which a country won control of its internal and external affairs, or when smaller areas joined to form a larger nation. [3]**Literacy rate:** Experts doubt some estimates. [4]**Per-capita gross domestic product:** Given in U.S. dollars. [5]**Human Development Index:** A number from zero to one, based on how a country's people fare in terms of life expectancy, adult literacy, and purchasing power (a person's ability to buy food, clothing, and other necessities). The higher the number, the better the rating. [6]After its September 1996 elections, Bosnia switched to a three-member collective presidency (one Croat, one Muslim, one Serb), with one president—winner of the most votes—serving as chairman. [7]Figures do not include the Gaza Strip or the West Bank, which are in transition to Palestinian control. [8]Serbia has its own president (Slobodan Milosevic), as does Montenegro (Momir Bulatovic). Together, under the name Yugoslavia, they have a government headed by Prime Minister Radoje Kontic. The state of Yugoslavia has not been formally recognized as a country.

SOURCES

For area, population, urban population, population annual rise, percent of population under 15 years, and life expectancy: *1996 World Population Data Sheet* (Population Reference Bureau, Inc.) • **For capital, major languages, date of independence, literacy rate, and per-capita GDP:** *The World Factbook 1995* (Central Intelligence Agency) • **For form of government:** *Freedom in the World: 1995-1996* (Freedom House) and information from the U.S. Department of State. • **For head of government:** *The Statesman's Yearbook, 1996-97* (St. Martin's Press), *The World Factbook 1995*, and information from the U.S. Department of State. • **For HDI:** *Human Development Report 1996* (United Nations Development Program)

The form of government and head information is up-to-date as of September 20, 1996.

4. The U.S. in Focus

You live in the U.S., but how much do you know about it? Who are the movers and shakers who head the federal government's three branches? Which of the 50 states has a name that means *sky-tinted waters*? What territory did the U.S. buy from Denmark for $25 million?

If you don't know the answers off the top of your head, no problem. They are all in this table—Part 1 of the U.S. in Focus section. These three pages provide a wealth of information about the 50 states, the District of Columbia, and U.S. territories and commonwealths. Happy exploring!

Area: 3,536,338 square miles; ranks fourth[1] in the world.
Population: 260,341,000; ranks third[2] in the world.
Capital: Washington, D.C.
Form of Government: Presidential-legislative democracy. The U.S. Constitution divides **federal** (national) powers among three independent branches of government: the legislative, the executive, and the judicial. Powers not given to the federal government by the Constitution are held by the states.
Chief Justice of the U.S.: William H. Rehnquist.

State Name / Nickname	Origin of Name	Entered Union	Land Area (sq mi) / Population	Capital
ALABAMA / **The Heart of Dixie**	Named for Alibamu Indian tribes	1819	50,750 / 4,219,000	**Montgomery**
ALASKA / **The Last Frontier (unofficial)**	Russian version of an Aleut word	1959	570,374 / 606,000	
ARIZONA / **The Grand Canyon State**	Indian word *arizonac*, means *small spring*	1912	113,642 / 4,075,000	**Phoenix**
ARKANSAS / **The Land of Opportunity**	From an Indian word meaning *land of downstream people*	1836	52,075 / 2,453,000	**Little Rock**
CALIFORNIA / **The Golden State**	After a treasure island in a popular Spanish tale	1850	155,973 / 31,431,000	**Sacramento**
COLORADO / **The Centennial State**	Spanish for *colored red*	1876	103,729 / 3,656,000	**Denver**
CONNECTICUT / **The Constitution State**	Algonquian Indian word; means *on the long tidal river*	1788	4,845 / 3,275,000	**Hartford**
DELAWARE / **The First State**	Honors Lord De La Warre, first governor, Virginia Colony	1787	1,955 / 706,000	**Dover**
FLORIDA / **The Sunshine State**	Spanish word for *flowery*	1845	53,997 / 13,953,000	**Tallahassee**
GEORGIA / **The Empire State of the South**	Honors King George II of Great Britain	1788	57,919 / 7,055,000	**Atlanta**
HAWAII / **The Aloha State**	Native word for *homeland*	1959	6,423 / 1,179,000	**Honolulu**
IDAHO / **The Gem State**	Word invented to mean *gem of the mountains*	1890	82,751 / 1,133,000	**Boise**
ILLINOIS / **The Prairie State**	For Iliniwek Indians; name means *superior men*	1818	55,593 / 11,752,000	**Springfield**
INDIANA / **The Hoosier State**	Word *indian* plus suffix *a*	1816	35,870 / 5,752,000	**Indianapolis**
IOWA / **The Hawkeye State**	Indian word for *beautiful land*	1846	55,875 / 2,829,000	**Des Moines**

Data compiled by Kathy Wilmore and Bryan Brown

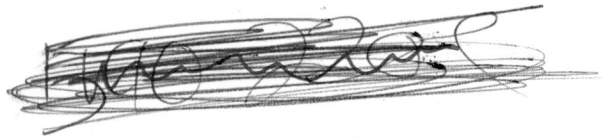

State Name / Nickname	Origin of Name	Entered Union	Land Area (sq mi) / Population	Capital
KANSAS / **The Sunflower State**	For Kansa Indians; name means *people of the south wind*	1861	81,823 / 2,554,000	Topeka
KENTUCKY / **The Bluegrass State**	Cherokee word for *meadowland*	1792	39,732 / 3,827,000	Frankfort
LOUISIANA / **The Pelican State**	Honors Louis XIV, king of France	1812	43,566 / 4,315,000	Baton Rouge
MAINE / **The Pine Tree State**	Honors ancient French province of Maine	1820	30,865 / 1,240,000	Augusta
MARYLAND / **The Old Line State; The Free State**	Honors Queen Henrietta Maria of England	1788	9,775 / 5,006,000	Annapolis
MASSACHUSETTS / **The Bay State**	For Massachusett Indians; name means *near the great hill*	1788	7,838 / 6,041,000	Boston
MICHIGAN / **The Wolverine State**	Chippewa word *Michigama*; means *great water*	1837	56,809 / 9,496,000	Lansing
MINNESOTA / **The North Star State**	Sioux Indian word for *sky-tinted waters*	1858	79,617 / 4,567,000	St. Paul
MISSISSIPPI / **The Magnolia State**	Indian word meaning *father of waters*	1817	46,914 / 2,669,000	Jackson
MISSOURI / **The Show Me State**	Indian word meaning *town of the large canoes*	1821	68,898 / 5,278,000	Jefferson City
MONTANA / **The Treasure State**	Spanish word for *mountainous*	1889	145,556 / 856,000	Helena
NEBRASKA / **The Cornhusker State**	Oto Indian word *nebrathka*; means *flat water*	1867	76,878 / 1,623,000	Lincoln
NEVADA / **The Silver State**	Spanish word for *snow-clad*	1864	109,806 / 1,457,000	Carson City
NEW HAMPSHIRE / **The Granite State**	Named for Hampshire, a county in England	1788	8,969 / 1,137,000	Concord
NEW JERSEY / **The Garden State**	Named for Jersey, an island in England	1787	7,419 / 7,904,000	Trenton
NEW MEXICO / **The Land of Enchantment**	For Aztec Indian war god Mexitil	1912	121,364 / 1,654,000	Santa Fe
NEW YORK / **The Empire State**	Honors England's Duke of York	1788	47,224 / 18,169,000	Albany
NORTH CAROLINA / **The Tar Heel State**	Honors King Charles I of Great Britain	1789	48,718 / 7,070,000	Raleigh
NORTH DAKOTA / **The Peace Garden State**	Named for Dakota Sioux Indians of the region	1889	68,994 / 638,000	Bismarck
OHIO / **The Buckeye State**	Iroquois Indian word; means *something great*	1803	40,953 / 11,102,000	Columbus
OKLAHOMA / **The Sooner State**	Choctaw Indian words *okla*, meaning *people*, and *homma*, meaning *red*	1907	68,679 / 3,258,000	Oklahoma City
OREGON / **The Beaver State**	French word *ouragan*; means *hurricane*	1859	96,002 / 3,086,000	Salem
PENNSYLVANIA / **The Keystone State**	Honors Sir William Penn (father of the founder of the colony), plus the Latin word for *woods*	1787	44,820 / 12,052,000	Harrisburg
RHODE ISLAND / **Little Rhody; The Ocean State**	After the Greek isle of Rhodes (for its red clay)	1790	1,045 / 997,000	Providence

State Name / Nickname	Origin of Name	Entered Union	Land Area (sq mi) / Population	Capital
SOUTH CAROLINA / The Palmetto State	Honors King Charles I of Great Britain	1788	30,111 / 3,664,000	Columbia
SOUTH DAKOTA / The Coyote State	Named for Dakota Sioux Indians of the region	1889	75,896 / 721,000	Pierre
TENNESSEE / The Volunteer State	From *Tanasie*, name of a Cherokee village	1796	41,219 / 5,175,000	Nashville
TEXAS / The Lone Star State	From Caddo Indian word; means *friends*	1845	261,914 / 18,378,000	Austin
UTAH / The Beehive State	Named for Ute Indians of the region	1896	82,168 / 1,908,000	Salt Lake City
VERMONT / The Green Mountain State	French words *vert mont*; mean *green mountain*	1791	9,249 / 580,000	Montpelier
VIRGINIA / The Old Dominion	Honors "the Virgin Queen," Great Britain's Elizabeth I	1788	39,598 / 6,552,000	Richmond
WASHINGTON / The Evergreen State	Named after George Washington	1889	66,581 / 5,343,000	Olympia
WEST VIRGINIA / The Mountain State	Honors "the Virgin Queen," Great Britain's Elizabeth I	1863	24,087 / 1,822,000	Charleston
WISCONSIN / The Badger State	Chippewa word *ouisconsin*; means *grassy place*	1848	54,314 / 5,082,000	Madison
WYOMING / The Equality State; The Cowboy State	From Delaware Indian word meaning *upon the great plain*	1890	97,105 / 476,000	Cheyenne

Capital District, Territories, and Commonwealths

Name	Origin of Name	Status / Date Acquired	Area (sq mi) / Population	Capital
DISTRICT OF COLUMBIA (D.C.)	Honors Christopher Columbus	Capital district[5] / 1800[6]	61 / 570,000	Washington
AMERICAN SAMOA	Ancient Pacific deity	U.S. territory / 1900[7]	77 / 46,700	Pago Pago
GUAM	From Guajan; in local dialect, means *We have*	U.S. territory / 1898[8]	210 / 133,000	Agana
NORTHERN MARIANA ISLANDS	Honors Mariana of Austria, Regent of Spain	Self-governing commonwealth / 1947[9]	179 / 43,000	Saipan
PUERTO RICO	Spanish for *rich port*	Self-governing commonwealth / 1898[10]	3,427 / 3,522,000	San Juan
U.S. VIRGIN ISLANDS	Virgins of St. Ursula, early religious order; patron saint of Spanish sailors	U.S. territory / 1917[12]	134 / 102,000	Charlotte Amalie

FOOTNOTES

[1]After Russia, China, and Canada. [2]After China and India. [3]A Jan. 30 election in Oregon will fill one Senate seat; a special election in California will fill one House seat. [4]I is for Independent (no political party). [5]Seat of the U.S. government. [6]Date when the federal government moved from Philadelphia to Washington. [7]Date gained by treaty with the U.K. and Germany. [8]Date ceded to the U.S. by Spain after the Spanish-American War; became a U.S. territory in 1950. [9]Date administration by the U.S. began (in a trusteeship for the United Nations); became a self-governing commonwealth in 1978. [10]Date became a U.S. territory; became a self-governing commonwealth in 1952. [11]NPP stands for New Progressive Party. [12]Purchased from Denmark for $25 million.

SOURCES

For nickname, date entered union/date acquired, and capital: *The Book of the States*, 1994-95 edition (Lexington, KY: The Council of State Governments, 1994) • **For origin of name:** *The World Book Encyclopedia*, 1992 edition • **For land area (1990) and population (1994):** *Statistical Abstract of the United States, 1995* (Washington, D.C.: U.S. Department of Commerce, Bureau of the Census, 1995) • **For governor/head of government:** National Governors' Association, the U.S. Department of the Interior, and the Puerto Rico Federal Affairs Administration • **For U.S. senators and representatives:** *The Congressional Quarterly*

The quality of life where you live is affected by many things. Is employment rising or falling? How much do people earn? How many of the tax dollars that they pay are put to work in your state? These are just a few of the factors to consider. Another factor: How do conditions in your state compare with those in the rest of the country?

This table—Part 2 of the U.S. in Focus section—can help you answer those questions and many others. (What others? Use your imagination, and you are sure to think of some!)

As you explore the data on these two pages, remember: Although **statistics** (a collection of measurable data) can be useful, they cannot tell the whole story. For instance, this table can tell you *which* state had the highest job-growth rate in the U.S. for 1989-1994, but it cannot tell you *why*.

Put on your thinking cap and poke around. How much can you find out about the 50 states, D.C., and the U.S. as a whole? Then ask yourself: What does this table *not* tell me? Where can I find the answers?

	Population change, 1990-94	Population in metropolitan areas, 1992[1]	Population under 18 years of age, 1994[2]	Population age 65 and over, 1994	Personal income per capita, 1994[3]	Population living in poverty, 1994[4]	Job growth, 1989-94[5]	Federal taxes paid per capita, 1994	U.S. federal spending per capita, 1994[6]	Public-school spending per student, 1994-95	Students who dropped out of high school, 1990[7]	Violent crimes per 100,000 people, 1994[8]
THE U.S.	4.7%	**79.7%**	26.1%	**12.7%**	$21,809	**14.5%**	5.7%	**$4,728**	$4,935	**$5,442**	11.2%	**716.0**
ALABAMA	4.4%	**67.4%**	25.6%	**13.1%**	$18,010	**16.4%**	9.4%	**$3,691**	$5,273	**$4,194**	12.6%	**683.7**
ALASKA	10.2%	**41.8%**	31.7%	**4.6%**	$23,788	**10.2%**	14.6%	**$5,585**	$7,703	**$8,120**	9.6%	**766.3**
ARIZONA	11.2%	**84.7%**	28.0%	**13.4%**	$19,001	**15.9%**	15.9%	**$3,832**	$4,693	**$3,982**	14.3%	**703.1**
ARKANSAS	4.3%	**44.7%**	26.1%	**14.8%**	$16,898	**15.3%**	15.9%	**$3,525**	$4,627	**$3,795**	10.9%	**595.1**
CALIFORNIA	5.6%	**96.7%**	27.6%	**10.6%**	$22,493	**17.9%**	-0.8%	**$4,905**	$4,960	**$4,606**	14.3%	**1,013.0**
COLORADO	11.0%	**81.8%**	26.5%	**10.1%**	$22,333	**9.0%**	18.0%	**$4,931**	$5,205	**$5,101**	9.6%	**509.6**
CONNECTICUT	-0.4%	**95.7%**	24.1%	**14.2%**	$29,402	**10.8%**	-7.4%	**$7,300**	$5,055	**$8,147**	9.2%	**455.5**
DELAWARE	6.0%	**82.7%**	24.8%	**12.7%**	$22,828	**8.3%**	3.0%	**$5,665**	$4,181	**$6,591**	11.2%	**561.0**
D.C.	-6.1%	**100.0%**	20.9%	**13.5%**	$31,136	**21.2%**	-3.4%	**$6,896**	$37,962	**$7,520**	19.1%	**2,662.6**
FLORIDA	7.8%	**93.0%**	23.4%	**18.4%**	$21,677	**14.9%**	10.2%	**$4,771**	$5,120	**$5,185**	14.2%	**1,146.8**
GEORGIA	8.9%	**67.7%**	26.8%	**10.1%**	$20,251	**14.0%**	11.0%	**$4,203**	$4,557	**$4,595**	14.1%	**667.7**
HAWAII	6.3%	**74.7%**	25.8%	**12.1%**	$24,057	**8.7%**	6.1%	**$5,104**	$6,457	**$5,740**	7.0%	**262.2**
IDAHO	12.5%	**30.0%**	29.9%	**11.6%**	$18,231	**12.0%**	26.6%	**$3,782**	$4,386	**$3,976**	9.6%	**285.8**
ILLINOIS	2.8%	**84.0%**	26.2%	**12.6%**	$23,784	**12.4%**	4.8%	**$5,390**	$4,238	**$4,752**	10.4%	**960.9**
INDIANA	3.8%	**71.6%**	25.6%	**12.8%**	$20,378	**13.7%**	9.4%	**$4,240**	$3,834	**$5,158**	11.4%	**525.1**
IOWA	1.9%	**43.8%**	25.8%	**15.4%**	$20,265	**10.7%**	9.9%	**$4,008**	$4,570	**$5,139**	6.5%	**315.1**
KANSAS	3.1%	**54.6%**	27.0%	**13.9%**	$20,896	**14.9%**	9.6%	**$4,495**	$4,889	**$5,318**	8.4%	**478.7**
KENTUCKY	3.8%	**48.5%**	25.3%	**12.8%**	$17,807	**18.5%**	11.6%	**$3,603**	$4,563	**$5,007**	13.0%	**605.3**
LOUISIANA	2.2%	**75.0%**	28.6%	**11.4%**	$17,651	**25.7%**	12.3%	**$3,597**	$5,002	**$4,525**	11.9%	**981.9**
MAINE	1.0%	**35.7%**	24.7%	**13.9%**	$19,663	**9.4%**	-2.0%	**$3,864**	$5,404	**$6,048**	8.4%	**129.9**
MARYLAND	4.7%	**92.8%**	25.2%	**11.2%**	$24,933	**10.7%**	-0.5%	**$5,478**	$7,311	**$6,212**	11.0%	**948.0**
MASSACHUSETTS	0.4%	**96.2%**	23.6%	**14.1%**	$25,616	**9.7%**	-6.5%	**$5,754**	$5,843	**$6,383**	9.5%	**707.6**

Data compiled by Kathy Wilmore

	Population change, 1990-94	Population in metropolitan areas, 1992[1]	Population under 18 years of age, 1994[2]	Population age 65 and over, 1994	Personal income per capita, 1994[3]	Population living in poverty 1994[4]	Job growth, 1989-94[5]	Federal taxes paid per capita, 1994	U.S. federal spending per capita, 1994[6]	Public-school spending per student, 1994-95	Students who dropped out of high school, 1990[7]	Violent crimes per 100,000 people, 1994[8]
MICHIGAN	2.2%	**82.7%**	26.6%	**12.4%**	$22,333	**14.1%**	5.6%	**$4,765**	$4,093	**$6,240**	9.9%	**766.1**
MINNESOTA	4.4%	**69.3%**	27.2%	**12.5%**	$22,453	**11.7%**	10.8%	**$4,930**	$4,113	**$5,413**	6.1%	**359.0**
MISSISSIPPI	3.6%	**34.6%**	28.3%	**12.5%**	$15,838	**19.9%**	14.6%	**$2,980**	$5,262	**$3,469**	11.7%	**493.7**
MISSOURI	3.1%	**68.3%**	26.1%	**14.1%**	$20,717	**15.6%**	6.8%	**$4,314**	$6,008	**$4,502**	11.2%	**743.5**
MONTANA	7.1%	**24.0%**	27.8%	**13.3%**	$17,865	**11.5%**	17.0%	**$3,823**	$5,411	**$5,091**	7.1%	**177.1**
NEBRASKA	2.8%	**50.6%**	27.2%	**14.1%**	$20,488	**8.8%**	12.4%	**$4,302**	$4,572	**$5,018**	6.6%	**389.5**
NEVADA	21.2%	**84.8%**	25.8%	**11.3%**	$24,023	**11.1%**	26.8%	**$5,262**	$4,233	**$4,677**	14.9%	**1,001.9**
NEW HAMPSHIRE	2.5%	**59.4%**	25.7%	**11.9%**	$23,434	**7.7%**	-1.3%	**$5,169**	$4,084	**$5,845**	9.9%	**116.8**
NEW JERSEY	2.2%	**100.0%**	24.4%	**13.6%**	$28,038	**9.2%**	-3.8%	**$6,482**	$4,715	**$9,206**	9.3%	**614.2**
NEW MEXICO	9.1%	**56.0%**	30.1%	**11.0%**	$17,106	**21.1%**	17.1%	**$3,477**	$6,831	**$4,870**	10.8%	**889.2**
NEW YORK	1.0%	**91.7%**	24.8%	**13.2%**	$25,999	**17.0%**	-5.4%	**$5,817**	$4,960	**$8,217**	10.1%	**965.6**
NORTH CAROLINA	6.6%	**66.3%**	24.8%	**12.5%**	$19,669	**14.2%**	9.3%	**$4,001**	$4,085	**$4,739**	13.2%	**655.0**
NORTH DAKOTA	-0.1%	**41.6%**	27.0%	**14.7%**	$18,546	**10.4%**	13.2%	**$3,762**	$6,103	**$4,459**	4.3%	**81.8**
OHIO	2.4%	**81.3%**	25.7%	**13.4%**	$20,928	**14.1%**	5.4%	**$4,543**	$4,314	**$5,452**	8.8%	**485.8**
OKLAHOMA	3.6%	**60.1%**	27.0%	**13.6%**	$17,744	**16.7%**	9.9%	**$3,677**	$4,817	**$4,042**	9.9%	**651.5**
OREGON	8.6%	**70.0%**	25.4%	**13.7%**	$20,419	**11.8%**	13.1%	**$4,345**	$4,232	**$5,710**	11.0%	**520.6**
PENNSYLVANIA	1.4%	**84.8%**	24.0%	**15.9%**	$22,324	**12.5%**	1.0%	**$4,859**	$5,049	**$6,909**	9.4%	**426.7**
RHODE ISLAND	-0.7%	**93.6%**	24.1%	**15.6%**	$22,251	**10.3%**	-6.0%	**$4,977**	$5,478	**$6,729**	12.9%	**375.5**
SOUTH CAROLINA	5.1%	**69.8%**	26.0%	**11.9%**	$17,695	**13.8%**	7.2%	**$3,587**	$4,668	**$4,401**	11.9%	**1,030.5**
SOUTH DAKOTA	3.6%	**32.6%**	28.8%	**14.7%**	$19,577	**14.5%**	20.6%	**$3,926**	$5,279	**$4,693**	7.1%	**227.6**
TENNESSEE	6.1%	**67.7%**	25.1%	**12.7%**	$19,482	**14.6%**	11.7%	**$4,144**	$4,839	**$4,208**	13.6%	**747.9**
TEXAS	8.2%	**83.9%**	28.8%	**10.2%**	$19,857	**19.1%**	13.2%	**$4,287**	$4,326	**$4,894**	12.5%	**706.5**
UTAH	10.7%	**77.5%**	35.2%	**8.8%**	$17,043	**8.0%**	24.6%	**$3,408**	$3,991	**$3,431**	7.9%	**304.5**
VERMONT	3.1%	**27.0%**	25.2%	**12.1%**	$20,224	**7.6%**	0.8%	**$4,246**	$4,155	**$6,879**	8.7%	**96.9**
VIRGINIA	5.9%	**77.5%**	24.5%	**11.1%**	$22,594	**10.7%**	5.0%	**$4,830**	$7,013	**$5,303**	10.4%	**357.7**
WASHINGTON	9.8%	**83.0%**	26.4%	**11.6%**	$22,610	**11.7%**	12.8%	**$5,123**	$4,999	**$5,563**	10.2%	**511.3**
WEST VIRGINIA	1.6%	**41.8%**	23.5%	**15.4%**	$17,208	**18.6%**	9.8%	**$3,309**	$5,216	**$5,565**	10.6%	**215.8**
WISCONSIN	3.9%	**68.1%**	26.5%	**13.4%**	$21,019	**9.0%**	11.0%	**$4,505**	$3,864	**$6,358**	6.9%	**270.5**
WYOMING	4.9%	**29.7%**	28.8%	**11.1%**	$20,436	**9.3%**	12.5%	**$4,524**	$4,909	**$5,582**	6.3%	**272.5**

FOOTNOTES

[1]Percentage of a state's people living in a metropolitan area. (A *metropolitan area* is a heavily populated city and surrounding communities that have close economic and social ties with the city.) [2]Figures are estimates. [3]Income received from all sources during the year, divided by the population. (*Per capita* means *per person*.) [4]The percentage of persons whose income falls below the poverty line of each state. (The poverty line varies, depending on the size of families and other factors. In 1994, the national poverty line for a family of four was $15,141.) [5]Farm payroll employment not included. [6]The amount that the U.S. government spent in a state, divided by the number of people in that state. [7]Ages 16-19. [8]Violent crimes are offenses of murder, forcible rape, robbery, and aggravated assault.

SOURCES

For poverty rate: U.S. Department of Commerce, Bureau of the Census • **For job growth:** Bureau of Labor Statistics, U.S. Department of Labor • **For federal taxes paid per capita and U.S. federal spending per capita:** Tax Foundation • **For public school spending per student:** National Education Association • **For dropout rate:** U.S. Department of Education • **For violent crimes per 100,000 people:** Federal Bureau of Investigation (FBI) • **For all other categories:** *Statistical Abstract of the United States: 1995* (Washington, D.C.: U.S. Bureau of the Census, 1994)

INDEX

a

Aborigines, 70
abyssal plain, 38
acid rain, 88
active volcano, 32
Africa, 31
  first humans, 85
  major rivers, 40, 41
  maps of, 28, 29
Afro-Asian language family, 67
Age of Exploration, 86
agricultural geography, 5
agriculture. *See* farming
air, 43–49
  water in, 48
air pressure, 44
  wind formation, 46
almanac, 25
Amazon River, 40
Amur River, 40
anarchy, 74
Anchorage, Alaska, 12
animals
  Antarctic, 55
  arboreal, 51
  Arctic, 55
  biogeography, 5
  biomes, 18, 50–56
  cool forest, 53
  cool grassland, 54
  desert, 54
  farm, 76, 77
  Mediterranean, 52
  nocturnal, 54
  temperate forest, 53
  tropical grassland, 52
  tropical rain forest, 51
  tundra, 55
Antarctica, 31
  cold desert, 54
  polar region, 55
Antarctic Circle, 88
apatite, 78
aquifer, 88
arboreal animals, 51
archipelago, 88
architecture, 72
Arctic Circle, 88
Arctic Ocean
  size and depth, 37
  trenches, 37
Arctic regions, 51, 55
area, 16
arid, definition of, 88
arroyo, 88
artificial lake, 42
arts, 68, 71
Asia
  architecture, 72
  continent, 31
  cuisine, 73
  major rivers, 40
  migration, 85
assembly line, 81
Atlantic Ocean
  hurricanes, 47
  size and depth, 37
  trenches, 37
atmosphere, 18, 43
  heat in, 44
atoll, 88
Australia, 31
  major rivers, 40
automobile
  invention, 86
  production, 81
azimuthal projection, 17

b

Babylon, 19
Bangkok, Thailand, 12
basin, 88
bay, 42, 88
bayou, 89
Bedouins, 72
bedrock, 89
beliefs, 68
belief system, 68
biogeography, 5
biomes, 18, 50–56
  mountain impact, 56
birthrate, 59, 89
  world, 64
Black African language family, 67
blizzard, 89
block mountain, 32
blubber, 55
bluff, 34
bog, 34, 89
Bombay, India, 12
boreal forest, 53
Brahmaputra River, 40
branch (river), 89
Brisbane, Australia, 12
Buddhism, 69
bulge (ocean), 39
businesses, 63
butte, 34, 89

c

Cairo, Egypt, 12
calcite, 78
Cambodia, 84
Canada, 24
canopy, 51
canyon, 89
cape (land formation), 89
Capetown, South Africa, 12
cartogram, 24
cartographer, 18
cartography
  defined, 5, 18
  early, 19
  projection maps, 16, 18
  word origin, 18
Cayman Trench, 37
central business district (CBD), 63
Chad, 84
chaparral, 52
charts (waterway maps), 19, 21
Chiang Jiang River, 40
China, 70
  population cartogram, 24
  time zones, 94
chinook, 89
Christianity, 69
cities
  model, 63
  population map, 65
  urban geography, 5
city, 89
clay tablet maps, 19
cliff, 89
climate, 18, 44–49
  Antarctic, 55
  Arctic, 55
  cool forest, 53
  cool grassland, 54
  defined, 89
  desert, 54
  and food, 73
  and home construction, 72
  maps, 23
  Mediterranean, 52
  study of, 5
  and sun's rays, 45
  temperate forest, 53
  tropical grassland, 52
  tropical rain forest, 51
  tundra, 55
climatology, 5
clouds
  condensation in, 48
  formation of, 45
  as insulation, 49
coast, 89
cold front, 45
commercial area, 63, 89
commercial farm, 77
compass, 11
compass rose, 26
confederacy, 74
conglomerates (rock), 78
Congo River, 40, 41
conic projection, 17
conifers, 53
conservation, 5
continent, 31, 90
continental climate, 89
continental divide, 89
continental drift, 31
continental shelf, 38, 89
contour map, 23
contours, 23, 26
cool forest region, 50, 51
cool grassland region, 50, 54
cooperative farm, 77
coordinates, map, 27
Copenhagen, Denmark, 12
copper, 79
core, earth, 30, 89
corn, 80
corporate farm, 77
corundum, 78
cottage industries, 81
countryside, 63
course, river, 42, 89
crafts, 68, 71
crater, 90
crater lake, 42
crevasse, 90
crop farm, 77
crust, of earth, 30, 90
cuisine, 73, 90
cultural geography, 5
cultural maps, 21
cultural mosaic, 66
culture, 65–74
  basics of, 67–75
  definition of, 65, 90
  study of, 5
currents, ocean, 38, 49, 90
customs, 68, 70
cyclone, 47, 90
cylindrical projection, 17

d

dairy farm, 77
Dalol, Ethiopia, 44
Danube River, 40, 41
Darling River, 40
dates, on maps, 27, 29
day, 13
death rate, 59
degrees, on maps, 10
delta, 90
democracy, 74
demographer, 58
demographics, 58
desert region, 50–51, 54
  defined, 90
developing country, 90
developing countries, 84, 90
dialect, 67
Diamantina Trench, 37
diamond, 78
dictatorship, 74
dictionary, geographical, 25
direction, 16
directional arrow, 26
distance, 16
distribution map, 22
divide (high land), 90
dome mountain, 32
dormant volcano, 32
doubling time, 59
downstream, 90
downtown (commercial
  area), 6, 90
drainage, 90
Dravidian language family, 67
drift (glacier deposit), 90
drift mine, 79
drought, 90
drumlin, 34, 90
dune, 90

e

earth
  axis rotation, 13
  circumference, 12
  features of, 18
  formation, 30
  from outer space, 9
  light on, 13
  locating places on, 12
  natural regions, 50–56
  representations, 8–29
  shape and size calculations, 7, 10
earthquake, 33
  Pacific Ocean, 33
  under water, 39
eastern hemisphere, 10
eclipse, 14
  lunar, 90
  solar, 90
economics
  and migration, 87
  systems, 84
economy,90
Egypt, ancient, 19
elevation, 26
emigration, 86
empire, 74
English language, 67
environmental interaction, 3
equator, 90
Eratosthenes of Cyrene, 12
erosion, 35
  under water, 39
escarpment, 90
esker, 34, 90
estuary, 40, 90
Euphrates River, 40
Eurasia, 31
  major rivers, 40, 41
Eurasia Basin, 37
Europe, 31
  Age of Exploration, 86
  Industrial Revolution, 81
  major rivers, 40, 41
  migration to, 85
evaporation, 48
exosphere, 43
explorers
  European, 86
  as first geographers, 7
extinct volcano, 32
exurb, 63, 90

f

factory, 57
fall line, 90
family farm, 77
family size, 59
farming, 75, 76–78
  agricultural geography, 5
  cool grasslands, 54
  location, 57
  subsistence, 75, 77
  world map, 78
fault, 90
fault line, 31, 90
feldspar, 78
fine arts, 71
fishery, 90
fishing and fisheries, 75, 80
floodplain, 91
fluorite, 78
foehn, 91
fold mountain, 32
food, 73
forest, 91, 94
forest canopy, 51
forestry, 75, 79, 91
fork (water branch), 91
fossil fuels, 78
front (weather), 45
frozen desert, 54, 56

g

galactic address, 6
Ganges River, 40, 41
gazetteer, 25
GDP (gross domestic product), 84, 91
gemstones, 78
geographer, 2
  ancient, 7, 10
Geographia (Ptolemy), 12
Geographia (Strabo), 12
geographical dictionary, 25
geographical thinking, 6
geographic grid, 12, 91
geographic north pole, 11, 91
geography
  defined, 2, 91
  five themes of, 2
  glossary, 88–96
  mental maps, 4
  subfields, 5
  word origin, 2
geomorphology, 5, 35
geyser, 91
glacial lake, 42
glaciers, 36, 91
  and land erosion, 35
globe, 8–15, 91
gold, 78, 79
gorge, 91
graphs
  population profile, 60
  population pyramid, 60
  world birthrates, 64
  world population growth, 59
Greece, ancient
  geographers, 12
  geography study, 7, 10
Greece, modern, and waving gesture, 70
greetings, 70
gross domestic product, 84, 91
groundwater, 91
gulf, 42, 91
Gulf of Mexico hurricanes, 47
gully erosion, 35
gypsum, 78

h

hand gestures, 70
headwater, 91
heat
  from sunlight, 44
  insulation, 49
  weather conditions due to, 48
heavy industries, 75
hemisphere, 9, 91
herding farm, 77
highlands, 34
high mountain region, 51
high pressure, 44
  wind formation, 46
high tide, 39

hill, 34, 91
Hindi language, 67
Hinduism, 69
Hipparchus, 12
historical geography, 5
homes, 72
Huang He River, 40
human interaction, 3
human-made features, 18
human movement. *See* migration
humidity
  causes, 48
  defined, 91
  measurement, 48
humus, 91
hunter-gatherers, 75
hurricane, 47, 91

i

ice, glacial, 35, 36
iceberg
  defined, 91
  formation, 36
ice-cap climate, 92
ice floe, 92
icons (map symbols), 26, 29
immigration, 86
index, map, 26
India
  greeting custom, 70
  population cartogram, 24
Indian Ocean
  cyclones, 47
  size and depth, 37
  trenches, 37
Indo-European language family, 67
Indus River, 40, 41
industrial geography, 5
industrially developed countries, 84
Industrial Revolution, 81
  machine inventions, 81, 86
industry, 63, 75–81, 92
inland waterway, 92
inlet, map of, 21
inner core, 30
insulation, 49
intermittent volcano, 32
international date line, 10, 15
  defined, 92
interrupted projection, 17
Inuit, 72, 73
Ionian Basin, 37
ionosphere, 43
iron ore, 79
Islam, 69
island, 92
isthmus, 92
Italy, 73

j

Japan
  greeting custom, 70
  industrial development, 84
Japanese language family, 67
Japura River, 40, 41
Java Trench, 37
Judaism, 69
jungle, 92

k

Kermadec Trench, 37
key (map legend), 27, 28
Korean language family, 67
Kuwait, 84

l

lagoon, 92
lake, 42, 92
land biomes. *See* biomes
landforms, 34–36
  defined, 92
language, 67–68
  barriers, 68
  defined, 67, 92
  families, 67, 68
latitude, 10, 12
  divisions, 11
  measurement, 10, 12
lava, 32
leeward, 56, 92
legend (map key), 27, 28
life expectancy, 59
light
  cloud shielding effect, 49
  on earth, 13
  heat and, 44
light industries, 75
lines of latitude. *See* latitude
lines of longitude. *See* longitude
livestock farms, 76, 77
loam, 92
location, 3
  place versus, 57
loess, 92
longitude, 10, 12
  divisions, 11
  measurement, 10, 12
lowlands, 35
low pressure, 44
  storm formation, 47
  wind formation, 46
low tide, 39
lunar eclipse, 14

m

Mackenzie River, 40
Madeira River, 40
magma, 32
magnetic north pole, 11, 92
Malayo-Polynesian language family, 67
mammals, Arctic, 55
Mandarin Chinese language, 67
manners, 68, 70
mantle, 30, 92
manufacturing, 75, 80–81, 94
  factory location, 57
  history, 81
map grid, 27
mapmaking. *See* cartography
maps
  of bodies of water, 19, 21
  comparing, 29
  cultural, 65
  defined, 16
  economic world, 82–83
  European explorations, 86
  first, 19
  mental, 4
  parts of, 26–27
  reading, 28

solar system, 8
special uses, 22–24
types, 16, 20–24
Wisconsin population density, 61
world agriculture, 78
world language families, 68
world population growth, 58
world population patterns, 62
See also projection maps
map sketch, 4
Mariana Trench, 37
marine climate, 92
marketing geography, 5
marsh, 34, 92
Masai people, 72
mass production, 81
Mediterranean region, 50, 52
Mediterranean Sea trenches, 37
megalopolis, 92
Mekong River, 40
mental map(s), 4, 6, 92
Mercator projection, 17
meridians, 10
mesa, 34, 92
mesosphere, 43
metals, 78
meteorology, 5
metropolis, 63, 92
Mexico, 84
Mexico City, Mexico, 12
migration, 3, 85–87
defined, 86, 93
overview, 85
reasons for, 87
minerals
consumption, 79
hardness, 78
mining, 78, 79
mining, 75, 78–79, 93
minutes (longitude/latitude), 11
Mississippi River, 40
Missouri River, 40
mistral, 93
mixed farms, 76, 77
Mohs, Friedrich, 78
Mohs scale, 78
monarchy, 74
Mon-Khmer language family, 67
monsoon, 93
moon
impact on tides, 39
lunar eclipse, 14
position in relation to earth, 13
moraine, 36, 93
mountain
biomes, 56
defined, 34, 93
formation, 32
mountain range, 94
on ocean floor, 38
mouth, of river, 40, 93
multinational companies, 81

n

Native Americans
languages, 68
teepees, 72
natural features, 18
natural gas, 78, 79
natural regions. See biomes
natural resources, 5
Nedostupnosti Polyus, Antarctica, 44
neighborhoods, 63, 93
Niger River, 40, 41
night, 12, 13
Nile River, 40, 41
nocturnal animal, 54
North America, 31
major rivers, 40, 41
northern hemisphere, 10
summer in, 14
north pole, 11
Arctic polar region, 55
defined, 93

o

oasis, 93
Ob-Irtysh, 40, 41
Ob' Trench, 37
occluded front, 45
ocean, 37–39, 93
currents, 38, 49
floor, 38
natural events under, 39
sizes and depths, 37
temperatures, 46
trenches, 37, 38
water maps, 21
Ohio-Allegheny River, 40
oil, 78, 79
oil rig, 79
open pit mine, 79
outer core, 30
oval projection, 17
ox-bow, 93
ozone layer, 43

p

Pacific Ocean
size and depth, 37
trenches, 37
typhoons, 47
volcanic activity, 33, 39
palm leaf map, 19
pampa, 93
Pangaea, 31
paper production, 79
parallels. *See* latitude
Parana River, 40, 41
parliamentary government, 74
peak, mountain, 93
penguins, 55
peninsula, 93
permafrost, 55, 93
Philippine Trench, 37
photosynthesis, 44
physical maps, 20
place, 3
location versus, 57
plains, 34, 35, 93
plantation, 77
plantation style house, 72
plants
biogeography, 5
biomes, 18, 50
cool forest, 53
cool grassland, 54
desert, 54
Mediterranean, 52
temperate forest, 53
tropical grassland, 52
tropical rain forest, 51
tundra, 55
plate, 93
plateau, 93
plate tectonics, 31–33

polar ice caps, 55
polar projection, 17
polar regions, 45, 55
political geography, 5
political map, 20
political oppression, 87
political systems, 74, 93
pond, 42, 93
population, 58–64
  cartogram, 24
  defined, 58, 93
  world growth, 58, 59
population data, 59, 93
population density, 61
population distribution, 61
population growth rate, 59
population patterns, 61
  world map, 62
population profile, 60, 93
population pyramid, 60, 93
population structure, 59
postindustrial economy, 84, 93
prairie, 54, 93
precipitation
  causes, 44, 48
  defined, 94
  weather fronts and, 45
  See also rainfall; snow
pre-industrial (economies), 84, 94
prevailing wind, 94
prime meridian, 10, 94
  time zones and, 15
projection maps, 16–18, 94
  making, 18
  types, 17
Ptolemy, Claudius, 12
Puerto Rico Trench, 37
Purus River, 40, 41

q

quartz, 78

r

radio waves, 43
rainfall
  Antarctic, 55
  Arctic, 55
  cool forest, 53
  cool grassland, 54
  desert, 54
  Mediterranean region, 52
  mountain range, 56
  temperate forest, 53
  tropical grassland, 52
  tropical rain forest, 51
  tundra, 55
rain forest, 94
ranch, 77
range (mountain), 94
range (open land), 94
ravine, 94
raw materials, 80
recycled materials, 80
reef, 94
reference works, 25
regions, 3
relative location map, 22
religion, 68, 69
republic, 74
residential area, 63
resource geography, 5
ridges (ocean floor), 38
rift valley, 94
rift valley lake, 42
rill erosion, 35
Ring of Fire, 33
Rio Grande River, 40
rivers, 40, 94
  land erosion, 35
  maps of, 21
  world's major, 40–41
Robinson projection, 17
rocks, mining, 78
Romanche Gap, 37
Royal Naval Observatory
  (Greenwich, England), 10
rural (areas), 62, 94
Russia, 84
Russian language, 67

s

Santiago, Chile, 12
Sao Francisco River, 40, 41
satellites (man-made), 43
savanna, 52, 94
scale, map, 27, 28
seaboard, 94
seamount, 94
seas, 42, 94
seasons
  Antarctic, 55
  Arctic, 55
  change of, 14
  cool forest, 53
  cool grassland, 54
  desert, 54
  Mediterranean region, 52
  temperate forest, 53
  tropical grassland, 52
  tundra, 55
sewing machine, 81
shaft mine, 79
shamba (Masai home), 72
shape, 16
sheet erosion, 35
shore, 94
Siberia, 54
silt, 35, 95
silver, 78, 79
Sino-Tibetan language family, 67
sirocco, 95
slang, 67
snow
  formation, 44, 48
  on glaciers, 36
  polar regions, 55
social traits, 3
soil, 95
solar eclipse, 14
solar system, 4, 8
source, river, 95
South America, 31
  major rivers, 40, 41
southern hemisphere, 10
  winter in, 14
south pole, 95
South Sandwich Trench, 37
Soviet Union, 84
Spanish language, 67
spinning wheel, 81
standard of living, 84, 95
stationary front, 45
steam engine, 81
steppe, 95
steppe climate, 95
Strabo, 12
strait, 95

stratosphere, 43
streams, 95
  land erosion, 35
subsistence farm, 75, 77
suburb(s), 63, 95
  homes in, 72
succulent plant, 54
sun
  cloud shield, 49
  effect on earth, 13, 14
  impact on tides, 39
  rays and climate, 45
  solar eclipse, 14
swamp, 34, 95
symbols, map, 26, 29

t

tableland, 95
taiga, 95
Taiwan, 84
talc, 78
technology, 75, 97
tectonic plates, 31, 95
  movement, 31, 32, 33
  underwater movement, 38
teepees, 72
temperate climate, 95
temperate forest, 50, 53
temperate zones, 10, 45
temperature
  Antarctic, 55
  Arctic polar region, 55
  average annual, 44
  cloud impact on, 49
  cool forest, 53
  cool grassland, 54
  defined, 95
  desert, 54
  humidity and, 48
  land, 46
  Mediterranean region, 52
  ocean, 46
  temperate forest, 53
  tropical grassland, 52
  tropical rain forest, 51
  tundra, 55
Thales, 7
thermosphere, 43
thunderstorm, 95
  formation, 45
tide, 39, 95
Tigris River, 40
till, 95
time zone, 15, 94
  maps, 15, 23
title, map, 26, 28
Tonga Trench, 37
tongue gestures, 70
topaz, 78
topographic maps, 23
tornado, 47, 95
town, 63
trade wind, 95
transportation, 86
tree, 79
trench, 37, 38
tributary, 42, 95
tropical grassland, 50, 52
tropical rain forest, 50, 51, 56
Tropic of Cancer, 10, 96
Tropic of Capricorn, 10, 96
tropic zones, 10, 45
troposphere, 43
truck farm, 77
true north, 11
tsunami, 39, 96
tundra, 51, 55, 56, 96
Turkey, 70
typhoon, 47, 96

u

understory (rain forest), 51
United States
  city neighborhoods, 63
  industrial development, 84
  population cartogram, 24
  tornadoes, 47
  weather map, 23
universe, 4, 6
Uralic Altaic language family, 67
Ural River, 40, 41
uranium, 79
urban (area), 62, 96
urban geography, 5

v

valley, 96
Vema Trench, 37
vents (volcano), 32
volcano, 32, 96
  Pacific Ocean, 33
  under water, 39
Volga River, 40, 41

w

wadi (streambed), 96
warm front, 45
water, 37–42
  heat and, 48
  land erosion, 35
  natural events under, 39
watershed, 96
water vapor, 48
Watt, James, 81
waving (hand gesture), 70
weather, 18, 44–49
  defined, 96
  fronts, 45
weathering, 35, 96
weather map, 23
westerly wind, 96
western hemisphere, 10
wind
  defined, 96
  formation, 44, 46
  land erosion, 35
  at sea, 49
  in stratosphere, 43
windward, 56, 96
Wisconsin, 61

x-y-z

Yangtze River, 40
Yellow River, 40
Yenlsey River, 40, 41
Yukon River, 40
Zambezi River, 40, 41